The Autobiographical Eye

EDITED BY

Daniel Halpern

THE ECCO PRESS

First published by The Ecco Press in 1982
100 West Broad Street
Hopewell, NJ 08525
Published simultaneously in Canada by
Penguin Books Canada Ltd., Ontario
Printed in the United States of America
First Paperback Edition

Library of Congress Cataloging-in-Publication Data

The Autobiographical eye / edited by Daniel Halpern; with
illustrations by John Sokol. —1st paperback ed.
                    p.   cm.
          ISBN 0-88001-329-X: $12.95
1. Authors—Biography. 2. Autobiography. I. Halpern, Daniel,
                    1945-
          PN451.A97   1993
      809'.93592—dc20   92-44646
                              CIP

ISBN 0-88001-329-X

CONTENTS

Preface

It has been ten years since I assembled these two-dozen essays for a special issue of the literary magazine *Antaeus*. I commissioned the pieces from a variety of writers—fiction writers, poets, a playwright, a screenwriter—asking them to pen brief, free-form essays about themselves.

What follows is a wonderfully varied collection of autobiographical sketches by such accomplished writers as Italo Calvino, John Fowles, Nadine Gordimer, Elizabeth Hardwick, Derek Walcott, Tennessee Williams, and James Wright. Calvino tells us about his moviegoing days; Annie Dillard describes a world transformed during a total eclipse ("I turned back to the sun. It was going. The sun was going, and the world was wrong....People on all the hillsides, including, I think, myself, screamed when the black body of the moon detached from the sky and rolled over the sun."); Stanley Elkin begins his essay "Once I spent a year in bed reading"; Gail Godwin writes about her face; and Edouard Roditi relates a story of cruising for sailors with the poet Hart Crane.

The writers included in *The Autobiographical Eye* have each cast back into time to retrieve a chapter of their past, reinventing what already occurred, bringing these events to life once again—this time for us as well.

—DANIEL HALPERN
April, 1993

Russell Banks as Searching for Survivors

John Sokol © *1981*

Russell Banks

auto-biography

1

I've always wanted a chance to say a few kind words about my mother, and now that I'm getting one, what happens—I find myself immediately concerned with fine points, or I should say "fine points," insofar as the foremost question is now not the question of which particular kind words might be said by me about my mother but rather exactly what do we have here, a chance to say a few kind words about my mother? for really, can it be called that, treated as such, when what's probably meant by "chance" is not chance at all, has nothing whatsoever to do with chance, is more likely a compunction that I've previously lacked and have been complaining about, because of its absence, that is, and that therefore what's been denied me all these silent years has not been a "chance" to say a few kind words about my mother but rather the *desire* to do so—and I mean "desire" here as raised to the power of *compunction*, to the *nth* power, as it were—and goddammit, it's true, and even though I'm ashamed to say it, I say it nonetheless, yes, I've never had much of a desire to say anything kind about my mother, not even a bare few words, and God knows I've had opportunities, going way back, essay contests, short stories that could have been autobiographical but weren't, dinner-party conversations in which my mother's failings, her meanness, her manic stupidity, were used to regale the guests, late-night descriptions of my childhood to a woman I was trying to convince to love me, so I told her stories in which I was inevitably cast as the hero-as-victim, that is to say, I told her of my "childhood," casting my mother as Wicked Witch, the cackling old lady with the wen on her nose, I the blond boy standing innocently by the open oven door, asking in my high-pitched voice, "What's in the oven?" bending over, the better to see inside, as she sweetly had advised me to do, when suddenly she shoves me inside, locks me in the oven and turns on the hateful gas, which I hear hissing slowly through the jets into the darkness, smell its cold invisible presence, hear the murmur of the pilot light, when *Wham!* I woke up, groaning, sweating, explaining to my poor wife, the woman I was trying to make love me, that I had this awful dream, all about my mother, she was old, with a wen on her nose, a wicked witch in a little house in the forest, and she had this oven, see, large, dark, scary— "Like a womb?" my wife asked, and I answered, "Yes, yes, exactly, well, not *exactly*, I mean, I've never seen a womb, at least not so's I'd remember, but it was more on the order of an iron vagina, now that you mention it," which caused her suspiciously to ask, "Are you free associating?" and I answered, a little angry and maybe even hurt, "No, of course not, and besides, there's no such thing as a 'free' association, that's a ridiculous idea, who ever heard of *free* associations? I mean, can you think of one *free* association? If I had a million dollars for every free association I've ever had, I'd be broke," I joked, trying to change the mood, the frosty atmosphere, if not the subject itself. "Besides," I asserted, "I *love* my mother, and she loves me, which means that I could never dream her into a threatening-womb dream, and even if I could, she would never use it to hurt me." Then, a few minutes later, I thought, though I did not say: The problem is never one of subject, there's always the subject, even if the subject's my mother and any possible kind words about her; what's often lacking, however, is the occasion that, like sleep, gives way to the subject, lets it bubble to life, like a dream, so that, I realized, what's hardest for anyone wishing to say a few kind words about his mother is the clearing away of subjects, all the subjects, even the subject of "motherhood," getting everything of "interest" out of his head, until nothing remains there and he is a man dreaming freshly of his mother. What a dream *that* is! Who could be that lucid, that purely in front of his subject, and still be of interest to anyone but himself?

2

The plot thickens. Suddenly as many things are significant as are insignificant. Suddenly there are worlds of sheer irrelevance, unmentionables, discards, litter, and one finds himself compelled to get on with it, with the concessions—or should one say, the conceding.

Look here, that fellow who earlier spoke of a dream, of telling the dream to his "poor wife," of the oven, the womb, the iron vagina, all that—here's what kind of man he is: lonely, yet deeply convinced that his loneliness has significance. Reason why this is so: he has confused "loneliness" with "solitude," and everyone knows that "solitude" is something significant. Even I concede it. *Thesis:* fellow is lonely, a state asserted by fellow to be significant, *i.e.*, worth signifying (*vide*, second paragraph of fellow's Part One). *Antithesis:* fellow has confused himself and probably reader too by not making essential distinctions between mere loneliness and solitude, which, if made, would reveal trivial nature of former experience and non-trivial nature of latter (because of latter's extra-personal possibilities, its self-transcendent impulse). *Synthesis:* fellow here gets himself exposed as literary character or some other type of invention, gets lapped up by the mother tongue, swallowed close to whole and shoved down into the belly of felt argument. Thus the meditation is permitted to continue unimpeded. Concessions appear one after the other. We go on entering the world. As in: *What do you think of me?* Am I an improvement over the other fellow, now that I've revealed his callow attitude toward what we in the field like to call "thinking"? I speak more slowly than he does, I know, but necessarily so, because what I am saying is considerably more complex and because I depend more upon a careful dialectical ordering of experience than he did (I'll refer to him in the past tense from now on, for obvious reasons). Also, I'm far less sentimental than he was, and for that reason, if I'm to obtain a sympathetic and continuing reading, must proceed at a slower pace than his. If you yourself in your way through the world tend to depend upon dialectical procedures, you might by now be wondering why I'm taking your time to indulge in what might be construed as special pleading. A reasonable thing to wonder. My response: I see this as a battle, a moral encounter, between the Forces of the Personal, the "lyric sensibility," if you will, sometimes called "subjectivism," "romanticism," or, in my own vocabulary, "sentimentality"—and the forces of the extra-personal, God love 'em, *viz.*, the meditative mind, objectivity, lucidity, self-transcendence. I am one who thinks of an identity crisis as a moral question whose answer can be obtained only from an examination of phenomena that are essentially metaphysical. Thus: You might want to know where I am standing at this moment as I speak, you might wish to know what I look like, how old I am, what turns my sex life takes, what part of the country I hail from, what my hobbies are. You might even want to know what I think of you. But obviously I am not the sort of person who can reveal any of these things to you. On principle. See above. This is *serious business*. This is not a talk show but rather a show-and-tell raised to the highest power I can presently imagine, the *nth* power. If in the course of the telling part I find myself able to imagine it a little higher, that's exactly where it'll go. *As in*: I'll bet you're starting to hate me. Just remember, though: it's not perfect to be perfect. I'll concede that much, confident that it's not dropped into the text merely to obtain your good favor. I'm not interested in pretexts of any kind. Against odds, I'm seeking to make a text. I'm not alone, either. Not like that other fellow.

3

By now I guess you all know about the spy and what we're trying to do about the spy, but nevertheless, I understand your present need for explication and will, in that case, be explicit.

We are not so much attempting to capture the spy — that would be pointless, a waste of time — or even to expose him — that would be fruitless, a mere diversion — as we are simply trying to prove he exists. The old philosopher had it right: "The point is not to listen to a series of propositions, but rather to follow the movement of showing." In that way, the work of the spy will be made evident, in the form of a "story," say, or a "character" or two, or perhaps even as "argument." That done, we can return safely, confidently, to our own ongoing work, which, as you must by now understand, is in the natural interest.

I do not mean to make you nervous or anxious or unduly concerned with routine. I am merely trying to be explicit and in that way to evoke a certain helpful quality of attention. You are, every one of you, hardworking, well-trained, loyal and persistent, and I am extremely grateful. I could not be otherwise. And I am sorry, therefore, to have to place this additional burden on you, the burden of staying alert to the work of the spy without at the same time permitting yourself to capture him and end his work or even to reveal him and thus hinder his work. You must attend only to the work itself.

Please forgive me for not being explicit before now, but, as I am sure you understand, it simply could not be done. Please destroy this memorandum when you have read it. It certainly would not do for it to fall into the "wrong hands." You understand. Try to consider this as "off limits" to the spy. Okay?

Try it again.
Again.

4

And so forth. And so on. There is of course much more that I could reveal about my mother, but most of it would tend to reveal *my* mother and not *a* mother, which, because you and I are strangers, would probably be embarrassing to us both. Earlier this year I wanted badly to write a poem about my mother. I set aside two weeks in June for that express purpose, two weeks at the beach. Every day after breakfast I would walk down to the water's edge, and standing there, chin resting thoughtfully in palm of left hand, fingertips scratching lower right cheek, I would try to think of the first line of the poem I wanted to write about my mother. It should have been a simple matter. "Mom, where are you now that I need you?" No, that's awful. Irony becoming sarcasm — cheap. Try this: "I think of you rocking, sweetly rocking . . ." Worse. Self-irony. "Flinty-eyed old battle-ax, bag of weirdo tics and lies, / Bet you never figured I'd come back to get my licks . . ."

Finally, I made a mother up, made her from most of the wrack and garbage of a tidal pool, from flotsam, shells, weeds, from claw of sandcrab, from old Coke bottle, styrofoam cup with bite the shape of a child's lower jaw taken from the side, a three-foot length of Manila hemp covered with black pitch and dripping oil slime, dozens of my barefoot tracks in the sand, some of which were filling with water as the tide started munching its way back. I was astounded, charged with energy and excitement, running around the beach grabbing at whatever elected that moment to reveal itself to my wild eye. I wrote: "The moon a pale half eye in morning closes, and the tide / Runs swiftly onto the sands . . ." And then, further down: "Your shoulders remain laced to your bony chest / As if you are about to shudder from the cold." And toward the end of the poem, a son appeared, her son, who of course was not me at all, not at all: "Bored in Des Moines, he reads the papers, / Or studies tobacco-stain maps upon his slender fingertips, / And then wonders idly how his mother feels tonight, / Her cough, her back." That son went on to finish law school, would you believe, and now is very big in government. That's how his mom describes him to her friends. "My son is very big in government." He's probably no more than a middle-level bureaucrat in the Veterans Administration, but who cares? Standing there on the beach, the water swarming over my knees, I surely didn't care. She's an old woman, alone, deserted. Let her at least have the envy of her few friends.

You might want to think of this as the end of the story. It's not. It's merely the end of the parable that comes in the middle of the story, the play within the play, so to speak, that precedes the rush of action inevitably to the end. The stage is crowded now, and there's a great deal of confusion and milling around by all the characters—that guy with the "poor wife" and the dream, the grumpy guy with all the dialectics, the iron vagina, the spy, the clerks, the kings, "my" mother, "my" family (the folks who spent those two weeks in June at the beach with me), the law student in Des Moines who later becomes "very big in government"—everyone and everything I have dared to concede.

This, however, is the key question: Will the guy with the dream defer to the grump with the dialectics, thus giving up his adoration of the iron vagina, without at the same time exposing the spy who must not be exposed, converting thereby the clerks to kings and vice versa, and without simultaneously revealing my mother to be what I fear she is, which would of course embarrass both me and you, not to mention what it would do to the law student from Des Moines, nor to mention what it would do to other members of my family, all of whom have been extremely supportive throughout?

5

A monologue: *It seems I've been given this moment to be alone.*

Anything else is everything else. There's not much anyone can do about it. It's in the nature of language and presence. Action, true action—*i.e.*, one event following in sequence and causal relation hard upon another—seems damned near impossible. (So this is how I get through, I thought: ruminating in ways that resemble lucid thought sufficiently to hold both my interest and favor, without at the same time becoming lucid in fact. Have you ever thought what would happen if, because of some freak event, some historical accident, you were placed face to face with a wholly lucid idea? You'd have no choice but to give up all your property, forsake your family, job, friends, and join whatever group of worshipers would have already gathered around the person generally held responsible for articulating the idea. Ambiguity gone, ambivalence vanished—truth is known. What wouldn't you sacrifice for that kind of comfort, eh? You'd sacrifice yourself—and that would be the whole point, wouldn't it?)

Anyhow, alone, I remembered sitting on a park bench in St. Petersburg, Florida, reading Schopenhauer. (I've written of this elsewhere.) Sunlight was streaming down behind me, drifting in heavy, moist clouds through deep-green palm fronds. I recalled the tropical flowers, birds, gravel walkways crunching loudly under the careful, slow, arthritic steps of the old people who seem to gather in that city more than any other I have ever sat in, on a park bench, usually not far from a public library, reading Schopenhauer, while the sun filters down through the trees and splashes across my back, warming me without my becoming conscious of it, until suddenly I find myself uncomfortably warm, and I close the book, marking my page with a match, and get up from the bench and walk slowly away, my feet crunching against the white-gravel walkway as I depart.

That's yet another example of what I mean by "getting through." Strange, it seems so little to ask of a life—until you think about it. About life, I mean. Why should anyone expect to "get through"? Why not "getting by"? Or "getting on"? Or "getting over"? These seem to me much more accessible, much more nearly *normal* things to ask for, once you find yourself in a position to ask for something. The next time someone asks you how you are, try answering that you're getting through.

You can see that I'm not myself tonight. I'm alone. Or it may be simply that I am beginning to sense the end of this story, its closure, and the loneliness that inevitably follows. Or it may be something less personal. For instance, what if I told you that only fifteen minutes ago I was informed that sometime during the next three months I will be one of seventy victims of a mass murderer? You'd quite properly ask, "By whom?" meaning, "Who told you this awful thing?" The only person who could have told me this awful thing, and be believed by me, is of course myself—which is possible only if I were to regard my suicide as the seventieth killing. *After slaying sixty-nine of his bound and gagged fellow passengers, Banks turned the murder weapon on himself. He left a brief note, which was found attached with a safety pin to his shirt pocket. It read:* "Once, not long ago, I was sitting on a park bench in St. Petersburg, Florida, reading Schopenhauer. The sunlight was falling across my back and shoulders, warming me, and for a moment, I felt only the sun, its heat, like a hand gently placed on my shoulder. At the end of that moment, I thought: 'It seems I've been given this moment to be alone.' Since that moment, I have lived in terror, devising ways of getting through to the end, desperately trying to invent ways to slide on through without hurting anyone. I wrote this note during a wholly lucid moment about a week ago, carried it in my pocket for several days, pinned it to my shirt where I wore it for a few more days, when I removed it and added this last sentence."

6

I wanted one of them to demonstrate a clear-cut superiority. Either the one named "the guy with the dream" or the one named "the grump with the dialectics." It would have made everything easier for me, simpler, would have given me feelings of increased personal freedom. It certainly would have given me the illusion of being in a company, of belonging to a team or participating in a movement and thereby of being engaged in an enterprise larger than myself. I swung back and forth in my support—as must be evident from the preceding sections of this narrative. First one point of view; then the other; then an examination of the conditions of observing; then an examination of the tools themselves; and finally an examination of the observer himself. I was like two Cambridge scientists trying to catch and measure a quantum jump—he watches one dial, and he watches another; he yells out how fast it's moving now; and he yells out the time of departure and arrival.

But in the end, they've failed. Or at least I have. I draw my laboratory coat off and glumly hang it in the gray metal closet in the corner by the door. Putting on my raincoat, I pick up my briefcase and umbrella and morosely walk out the door, not forgetting to make sure it's locked behind me.

Downstairs, I exit from the building and nod goodnight to Randolph, the night watchman, who's seated by the door, reading his *National Enquirer*. It's raining, a gray, windless rain falling straight down in strings of water that splash heavily against the streets and sidewalks. Rush-hour traffic, cabs, buses slide greasily past, windshield wipers clattering nervously, horns blatting, pedestrians leaping angrily away from the semi-blinded drivers. I make my way with care to the subway station and descend the concrete stairs from the street to the crowded platform below. I pass through the turnstile and in a few seconds find myself waiting at the edge of the track for my car, thinking as I wait that I'm probably no different from any of the several hundred other people waiting here beside me. We're all tired, slightly depressed, kicking against a feeling of having failed in a basic quest. Each of us, in his own odd way, has spent the day trying to choose sides. I recognize the unity of our feelings, yet can take no real comfort from it. The human heart is large, but it keeps striving after comprehension.

After a few moments, there is a roar, and with a screech and a great scattering of sparks, a car rounds the bend in the tunnel and approaches the platform. It stops before me, where the door opens, and a crowd of workers hurrying home squirts out the door, shoving me to the side, pressing me against a window of the car, where, peering in, I see a face staring back at me, a face that, at first, I assume is a reflection of my own. But a second look reveals the face of the young man with the poor wife, "the guy with the dream." I recognize his wool cap, his blue eyes, his preoccupied stare out the window. Once again I'm shoved and am forced further down the platform from the door, and again, facing a window, I see a familiar face. It's the face of the formalist, my dialectical friend, recognized by his wire-rimmed glasses, his crisply intelligent eyes, the tightly pursed mouth, the red scarf he wears in all seasons. But then, suddenly, I realized that I am in fact looking at my own reflection superimposed over the face and shoulders of a stranger on the other side of the glass. Glancing back to where the other man was seen, I realize that probably the same event took place there, too, and that I had been staring only at the image of my face superimposed over a stranger's face. Which face was the real one? I ask myself. The face seen on the near side of the glass, or the face seen on the far side? Or was the only real face the mingled one? Or none of these? All of them?

At this moment, the doors slide abruptly shut, and I realize that the car is leaving, is moving faster and faster. Windows, opaque sliding rectangles, rush away from me, blurring the faces of the passengers on the other side of the glass, but not disturbing the reflection of my own face at all. I start running, vainly hoping to reach the door before it closes completely, and as soon as I, too, am moving, my reflection shudders and shatters into a blur. Losing sight of it altogether, I turn my attention ahead of me, searching for the door of the car, running frantically now, my briefcase banging awkwardly against my thigh, my umbrella hooking a fat man's arm. It's too late. The car is moving too fast for me, and the door has already closed.

7

"An era, any time of year."

I stood alone at the edge of the platform, whispering these words to myself and wishing there were a man standing next to me, a fine-boned, fragile-looking man in a wool overcoat and beret, with a slightly concerned expression on his face, leaning politely towards me and whispering with sympathy, "An era, any time of year."

An event like that at a time like that would have helped me be less afraid.

I would have turned to the old man (older than I by perhaps three decades), and I would have asked him, "Which face was the *real* one? There *was* a real one, wasn't there?"

He would have smiled up at me (I was several inches taller than he, but only to my disadvantage, for it made me feel physically awkward next to him). "In many ways, young man, you resemble your mother, and in many ways you do not, but at times you remind me oddly of a student I loved." Then he shrugged his shoulders, a peculiar shrug, first one shoulder, then the other, as if remarking on his loss with shy gratitude for the tiny piece of it that I had just returned to him. Or that my face had just returned to him.

He wasn't there. I reminded no one of no one. The opposite was what's true.

I stepped into the car, and the door closed behind me like a curtain, and the car, rocking and rumbling, started to leave the station. Before it plunged into the darkness of the tunnel, I glanced out the window opposite me and saw a face, the face of a man standing at the end of the platform, probably waiting for the next car. A fraction of a second, and in that time I saw my mother's face—sharp, pinkly blond, with an assassin's hysteria cutting against stoical self pity, establishing in the eyes, the tautly drawn mouth, the jutting chin, the tendons in her throat, a static terror—and in that time I also saw the face of the student I will have once loved, when I am older, more of a solitary man than I am now, and less lonely.

The car dropped into the darkness of the tunnel, and with gentle mockery I promised myself that I would never forget anything, whether it really happened or would never happen. It's not clear to me, now, as I sit here writing this, that I forgave myself for my limitations, but I know that I acknowledged them. Goodbye, I said to myself. Goodbye, goodbye.

Marvin Bell as Stars Which See, Stars Which Do Not See   *John Sokol* © 1981

Marvin Bell

The Hours Musicians Keep

My friend Roger called last night, and Dorothy, reading at the kitchen table, gave me a look of bewilderment-going-to-alarm when I held the phone to my ear but said nothing. I knew who it was. I could hear a bass figure in 6/8ths time and knew that it was only a matter of measures until a whistle would begin to the tune of that hoary cornet solo, "The Carnival of Venice." If things went well, the whistler might try the first variation from J. B. Arban's version or Herbert L. Clarke's — the arrangement on which I had soloed at the New York State High School Music Festival in my senior year. But there would be no attempt to whistle the cadenza at the start of Del Staigers' fearful version: lip slurs so rapidly up and down that it was rumored that Del Staigers, the redhead, could only play it drunk, and it could be approached by only one high-school cornetist in my acquaintance — my friend Roger.

In college, however, I would sit second chair to Artie Shaw (not the clarinetist), whose father owned a dairy in Hornell and whose credentials included, not only the ability to play Del Staigers' diabolical cadenza, but also to hit double high C, a note my horn has never known, on a cold cornet. He was the closest I would come to the kind of range which was all the rage then and which reached both its zenith and apex in the joint recordings of Maynard Ferguson and Yma Sumac — he of the freak lip with a high range to rival Cat Anderson's, she of the otherworldly Peruvian voice of five or more octaves which could come up from the tombs or shriek like a bird. Was her name really Amy Camus? There were existential rumors.

Music was my earliest way into the world of nighthawks, bohemians (as we called them before the word "beatnik" arrived) and culture. I played from the fourth grade on, eventually owning a handmade Bach cornet bought used from Ned Mahoney, who played second chair to the Goldman Band cornet soloist, the always rapid, sometimes sloppy, one-armed virtuoso, James F. Burke, and an Olds trumpet model named for the legendary Rafael Mendez, who could play high C on a trumpet suspended by a string and who had once destroyed his embouchure against a swinging door and had taught himself a new position on the lips for the mouthpiece. In Mexico to end a brief marriage which left me with a son, I would spend half a day searching out a beer garden where Mendez was appearing, only to learn that it was his day off. The trumpet named for him had first and third valve triggers with which to flatten notes otherwise sharp because of the normal characteristics of the trumpet, but I preferred to lip them down, and in fact I preferred the more flexible, warmer tone of the cornet to the colder penetration of the trumpet.

Most young cornet players with a normal embouchure used a Vega 2 mouthpiece, but Roger and I used a Bach 10½ C. Its deeper cup produced a deeper tone, though there was a penalty when the player went high. Things could go wrong, and did. In the long run, trumpet players grew barrel-chested and fought their instruments all the way to heart attacks. In the short run, there were sore lips from long gigs (alleviated by the cushion-rim mouthpiece, which resembles an ordinary mouthpiece with a doughnut for a rim), sticky valves (we used trick fingerings to make up for a lack of valve oil, and Roger once soloed on "The Minnehaha Waltz" with a stuck third valve), and a convention that called for the drummers to fire blanks to punctuate the endings of marches — a loud addition said to have been popularized at the University of Michigan.

There were also plumber's helpers to wah-wah the white blues, plastic hand guards to save the silver or gold plating from a sweaty grip, clothespins to keep the music in sight during outdoor concerts, and sometimes a banana to increase salivation in the cottony mouth that afflicts the nervous soloist.

As a soloist, I was always nervous. At my high school graduation, I played Clarke's "Stars in a Velvety Sky," while my cap tassel swung in time. It's the trumpet music of Herbert L. Clarke which one hears, incidentally, behind the action in the movie *Hester Street*, and it was a revelation to me, on first viewing the film, that someone else had noticed the melancholy at the heart of Clarke's lyrical solos for cornet.

Roger and I would drive to New York, two hours west, to take in a Goldman Band concert in Central Park and then go to Birdland or Basin Street or the Metropole. Burke would solo every night that the band played in Central or Prospect Parks, make a token move toward reclaiming his seat, and be summoned forth to play an encore, always something easier—"Dreams of Karen," for example, which was dedicated to Burke by its author, Roy H. Milligan, and which he would play at about one and a quarter times its normal pace. When he was on a run, one could hear the holes in the valves lining up with the openings of the slides with little explosions of spit and breath. Roger and I sometimes unfolded across our laps the score to that night's solo, and, one night when Burke chose to ignore the high, optional counterpoint the soloist may play while the band carries the melody to a Goldman solo called "Scherzo," we looked up at him and we thought he smiled down.

At G. Schirmer's very famous music store, then at 3 East 43rd Street, we could appraise new solos from the Fischer, Fillmore and Mills music houses, and we would ask to see more and more difficult scores before making a choice.

Going to Birdland to hear trombonists J. J. Johnson and Kai Winding, we were likely to see Miles Davis or Don Elliot too. The stadium dates and big record-distribution routes had yet to weaken the club system for jazz, and the artists came to hear one another and sometimes to sit in. Even then, the beer came only in paper cups, to cut down on violence, and the drinks were hustled to tables little bigger than the napkins. Still, to teen-agers it *seemed* spacious and cheerful. We didn't know shit, but we knew something.

Elliot was interesting to us because he tripled on cornet, French horn and vibraphone. The Modern Jazz Quartet and the Australian Jazz Quintet were new sounds, mixing jazz with the classical. Miles' solos were already ethereal and he had begun to use a mute on all standards. Nobody knew Cannonball Adderley's little brother, Nat, yet, but I thought he was terrific. Thad Jones teamed up with bassist Charles Mingus, and, when Stan Kenton made what seemed to be a racist response to *Down Beat*'s jazz awards, Mingus published a long poem in reply. A Connecticut station played records by Shorty Rogers in what came to be known as the "cool" sound and, later, the "West Coast" sound when Rogers went off to work for Hollywood. The hottest trumpeter, to my mind, was Clifford Brown, whose records with drummer Max Roach were electric and who would die young in an automobile accident. The trumpet had a value in those years it would never occupy again in a world of jazz that would never again seem so new, to anyone, nor evolve so rapidly, nor be so richly intertwined with an American lifestyle outside the mainstream.

And what does it mean that so many artists have come to their art by way of another art—writers, in particular, by way of music and painting? I believe I can distinguish between poets who came to poetry from painting and those who came to it by way of music: it goes beyond sound versus image, and is rooted in the difference between the populist spread of bands and group lessons in public schools in small towns and the parallel study of painting which, back then, was more likely to be undertaken seriously only by the urban and privileged. I'm afraid I still hear the difference when the band follows the orchestra, or vice versa, at the local junior high, though I hasten to add that I am talking now about childhood influences and not about professional accomplishment, and that there will never occur again, I believe, such clear lines in American culture. For one thing, we now see an increased participation in second-level artistic activity in our country which seems to derive from a feeling that everyone is important and no one is special. It is harder now, I think, to be an outsider unless one draws the lines on a political basis against most of America. It is possible, therefore, that what I, and others like me, took by way of lifestyle and attitude from the jazz world then must now come from the more greatly splintered sphere of racial, sexual and revolutionary politics—in which it will prove increasingly difficult to align a literary majority to judge poets or to give convincing approval to a handful of the "best." To me, these thoughts follow, as childhood trails middle age, waiting.

I knew I would never be good enough. I was insecure up high, I stayed too close to the chords on solos; worse, I saw notes when I played—the result of the way I had been taught, the only way I could have been taught. I quit the horn by not going to music school, though my trumpet teacher, Chester Osborne—a composer, historian and author of serious books for youth—disagreed with my decision. I quit my musical future when I went to college, though I continued to play for several years: with a dixieland band on the radio, with orchestras, concert bands, marching bands and dance bands. I played the "Trumpet Voluntary" by Jeremiah Clarke, long mis-attributed to Henry Purcell, on Easter Sunday in a black robe at the pulpit. I played duets with Lyle S. in fundamentalist churches in upstate New York. I jammed with friends in the college chapel. I even took lessons for two more years, and worked up additional solos by Haydn and Hindemith. Meanwhile, I taught myself to fake a popular piano. It was fun making it up, finding ways to make it come out well without being able to do it right.

Flutter tongue and double-tongue. Pedal notes and shakes. *Schmaltz*, hand vibrato, and Frank Sinatra playing on just his mouthpiece in "From Here to Eternity." The half-valved neighing of a horse. Straight mutes and cup mutes. I played solos, duets, trios, quintets, sextets, with bands, orchestras and combos. I played for fun and money but never to be better than someone else or even to have someone say so. Because of the hours musicians keep, I saw things differently, listened to different radio programs, and had time to think.

Six months ago, sitting in a Roman *piazza* on the outskirts of a fountain, I heard someone whistling "Carnival of Venice." I couldn't see who. If it was corny to identify so quickly, it would be far cornier to play the unaffected bystander. Was he whistling it well, or even correctly? It would not have occurred to me to care. And that's why poets are poets. And that's the name of that tune. And that's why Roger whistles me up twenty-five years later — old friend, Roger.

Italo Calvino as If on a Winter's Night a Traveler

John Sokol © *1981*

Italo Calvino

Translated from the Italian by William Weaver

Autobiography of a Spectator

There were years when I went to the movies almost every day, sometimes even twice a day; and these were roughly the years between 1936 and the war, the period of my adolescence in other words. Years when for me movies were the world. A different world from the one surrounding me; and for me only what I saw on the screen had the properties of a world — fullness, necessity, coherence — while off the screen heterogeneous elements accumulated, apparently assembled at random, the materials of my life which seemed to me completely lacking in form.

Cinema as escape: this formula, meant as a condemnation, has often been repeated. True, this is what movies were for me, satisfying a need for expatriation, for turning my attention to a different area. I believe this need represents a basic part of our adapting to the world, an indispensable phase in every education. Of course, there are other, more substantial and personal ways of creating a different space for yourself; for me, movies were the easiest, handiest solution, and also the one that carried me farthest. Every day, when I strolled down the main street of my little city, I had eyes for the movie theaters, three first-run houses which changed features every Monday and every Thursday plus a couple of fleabags that ran fairly old or tawdry pictures, three a week. I already knew in advance what film was playing in each house, but my eye sought out the posters displayed beside the entrance, where the next attraction was announced. The surprise, the promise lay there, the expectation that would accompany me through the next few days.

I went to the movies in the afternoon, either slipping out of the house stealthily or saying I was going to a classmate's to study with him: during school months my parents granted me little freedom. The proof of my genuine passion was my yearning to dive straight into a movie theater the minute the doors opened, at two o'clock. There were several advantages in seeing the first show: the half-empty house, which seemed all mine and allowed me to sprawl in the middle of the cheap section, my legs curled over the back of the seat in front of me; the hope of getting back to the house before my flight had been noticed, so that I would have permission to go out again (and maybe see another picture); and a slight daze that lingered on for the rest of the afternoon, harmful for any studying but congenial to daydreaming. And besides these reasons, all unconfessable for different motives, there was a more serious one: if I came in when they were opening up, I could be sure of seeing the movie from the beginning—a rare piece of luck—instead of from any old point in the middle or at the end, as when I reached the theater only in mid-afternoon or towards evening.

Coming into an already-begun movie, for that matter, was the barbarous, widespread habit among Italian moviegoers, and it still obtains. In those days there was already a foreshadowing, I would say, of the most sophisticated narrative techniques of today's cinema, where the story's temporal line is broken up and transformed into a jigsaw puzzle that has to be put together piece by piece or else accepted as a fragmentary corpus. I should add, however, in self-consolation, that seeing the beginning of a film when you already knew the ending afforded some special satisfactions, as you discovered not the denouement of the mysteries and the dramas but rather their genesis, and you felt a vague prescience about the characters. Vague, as the prescience of soothsayers must be, for that matter, because it was not always easy to reconstruct the maimed story, especially if it was a detective plot and the identification of the murderer before the presentation of the crime left an even murkier zone in between them. Moreover, between beginning and end there occasionally remained a missing bit, because on looking at my watch I would suddenly realize it was late and, if I wanted to spare myself the family's wrath, I had to run off before the sequence where I had come in could reappear on the screen. So many films for me still have a hole in the middle, and even today, after more than thirty years—what am I talking about? closer to forty—when I happen to see again, on television perhaps, one of the movies from those days, I recognize the moment when I entered the theater, the scenes I had watched uncomprehendingly, I retrieve the lost footage, I put the puzzle together as if I had left it unfinished only the day before.

(I'm referring to movies I saw between the ages of, say, thirteen and eighteen, when cinema possessed me with a power that cannot be compared to the years before and those afterwards; memories of films seen in my childhood are hazy; films seen as an adult are mingled with many other impressions and experiences. I have the memories of someone who was just discovering movies at that time. I had been brought up on a short leash, and my mother, for as long as possible, tried to shield me from any contact with the world that had not been carefully planned, that did not have a purpose. When I was little she took me to the movies rarely and then only to films she considered "suitable" or "educational." I have few recollections of the silent era and the early days of sound: some Chaplin, a film about Noah's Ark, *Ben Hur* with Ramon Novarro, *Dirigible* (in which a Zeppelin crashed at the Pole), the documentary *Africa Speaks*, a science-fiction movie about the year 2000, the African adventures of *Trader Horn*. Douglas Fairbanks and Buster Keaton occupy places of honor in my mythology only because I inserted them later, retrospectively, into an imaginary childhood of mine to which they could not help but belong; as a child I knew them only from looking at colored posters. Generally I was kept away from any movie with a love story, which I would not understand anyhow because, unfamiliar as I was with movie faces, I confused one actor with another, especially if they had moustaches, and I also got actresses mixed up, especially if they were blonde. In aviation movies, popular during my boyhood, the male characters resembled one another like identical twins, and since the plot was based on the jealousy of two pilots who for me were a single pilot, I was thoroughly bewildered. In short, my apprenticeship as a spectator had been slow and contested; and this is why the passion I speak of then exploded).

If, as it happened, I entered the theater at four o'clock, or five, on coming out I was struck by the sense of time passing, the contrast between two different temporal dimensions, inside and outside the films. I had come in from broad daylight, and now outside I found darkness, the lighted streets that prolonged the black-and-white of the screen. To some extent the darkness diminished the gap between the two worlds and, to some extent, also underlined it, because it marked the passing of those two hours I had not lived, swallowed up in a suspension of time, either in the living of an imaginary life or in a backward leap over centuries. There was a special emotion in discovering, at this moment, how the days had grown shorter or longer: the sense of the changing seasons (always mild in the temperate locality where I lived) came over me as I left the movie house. When it rained in the film, I would prick up my ears, trying to discover if it had started raining outside as well, if a downpour had trapped me, after I had rushed from the house without an umbrella. This was the only moment when, still immersed in that other world, I remembered the world outside; and the effect was anguish. Even today rain in a movie stirs in me that reaction, that feeling of anguish.

If it was not yet supper time, I would join my friends, sauntering up and down the sidewalks of the main street. I would pass again in front of the theater I had just left, and from the projection booth I could hear snatches of dialogue reecho in the street. I picked them up now with a sense of unreality, no longer of identification, because at this point I had moved into the outside world. But there was also a feeling kin to nostalgia, as of someone looking back at a frontier.

I remember especially one theater, the oldest in the city, associated with my earliest memories of the silent era, a building which retained (until a few years ago) an art nouveau sign decorated with medallions and the shape of the auditorium, a big long room that sloped forward, flanked by a corridor with columns. The projection booth had a little window that opened onto the main street and from it the absurd voices of the film resounded, metallically distorted by the apparatus of the period and all the more absurd because of the stilted speech of the Italian dubbing, which bore no relation to any spoken language of past or future. And yet the falsity of those voices must have had its own power of communication, like the sirens' song, for every time I walked beneath that little window I felt the call of that other world which was the world.

The side doors of the hall opened onto an alley; during intermissions the usher in a frogged tunic would pull the red plush curtains and the color of the outside air discreetly appeared at the threshold; passersby and the seated audience looked at one another somewhat uneasily, as if at an improper intrusion on one side or the other. In particular the intermission between the first and second halves of the film (another curious, exclusively Italian custom, which has inexplicably endured to the present day) came to remind me that I was still in that city, on that day, at that hour; and depending on the moment's mood, it increased my contentment at the knowledge that in no time I would again be plunged into the China seas or the San Francisco earthquake, or else it oppressed me with the warning not to forget I was still here and should not lose myself in faraway places.

In what was then the city's major movie house the interruptions were less abrupt, as the air was renewed by opening a metal dome in the center of the ceiling frescoed with centaurs and nymphs. The sight of the sky, halfway through the film, afforded a pause for meditation, with the slow passage of a cloud arriving perhaps from other continents, from other centuries. On summer evenings the dome was left open through the whole show, and the presence of the firmament was the sum of all distances, comprehended in a single universe.

During the long holidays I went to the movies with greater calm and freedom. In the summer most of my schoolmates left our seaside town for the mountains or the country, and I was on my own week after week. For me this meant the annual opening of a hunting season, pursuit of the old films which were then revived, pictures from the years when this omnivorous appetite had not yet possessed me. So during those months I could recapture lost years, gain a seniority as spectator that was not really mine. Films of the regular commercial circuit: these are what I am talking about (the exploration of the retrospective universe by Film Clubs, the hallowed history preserved in archives: these belong to another stage of my life, in a relationship with other cities and worlds; then cinema would become part of a broader argument, a history). In any event I still bear within me the emotion I felt at catching a Greta Garbo film, perhaps only three or four years old, but for me a part of prehistory, co-starring a very young Clark Gable, without moustache. *Susan Lenox* it was called. Or was that the other one? Because there were two Garbo movies added to my list in that summer series of re-runs, whose pearl, however, was *Red Dust* with Jean Harlow.

I have not yet specified, but I presume it has been understood, that for me movies meant American movies, the current Hollywood production. My "period" goes more or less from *The Lives of a Bengal Lancer* with Gary Cooper and *Mutiny on the Bounty* with Charles Laughton and Clark Gable, up to the death of Jean Harlow (which I relived many years later in the death of Marilyn Monroe, in an era more aware of the neurotic power of every symbol), with many comedies in between, the flippant murder stories with Myrna Loy and William Powell and their dog Asta, the musicals of Fred Astaire and Ginger Rogers, the thrillers with the Chinese detective Charlie Chan, and the horror films of Boris Karloff. I was more conscious of actors' names than of directors', except for a few like Frank Capra, Gregory La Cava, and Frank Borzage, who depicted, instead of millionaires, the lives of poor men, usually with Spencer Tracy. These were the well-meaning directors of the Roosevelt years; but I learned this only later; then I devoured everything, making few distinctions. American movies of that time could boast an array of actors' faces unequaled before or since (so it seems to me, at least); and the stories were mere devices to bring together these faces (leading men and women, character actors, bit players) in constantly different combinations. Surrounding those conventional plots there was little that smacked of a society or a period; but for this very reason that context reached me, though I could not have defined its substance. It was (as I came to learn) the falsification of everything that society contained, but it was a special misrepresentation, different from our Italian brand, which engulfed us during the rest of the day. Just as for the psychoanalyst the patient's lies are as interesting as his truths, since all reveal something about him, so as a spectator belonging to another system of falsifications, I could learn something both from the scant bits of truth and the considerable misrepresentations that the Hollywood output gave me. I harbor no grudge, therefore, against that deceitful image of life; now I feel that I never mistook it for reality, but considered it only one among the many possible artificialities, though I would have been unable to explain this at the time.

There were also French movies in circulation, of course, and they turned out to be something entirely different, giving escapism another dimension, a special link between the places of my experience and the places of elsewhere (the effect called "realism," as I would understand later, consists of this). After having seen the Algiers Kasbah in *Pepé le Moko*, I looked with new eyes at the step-streets of our own old city. Jean Gabin's face was made of a different material, physiological and psychological, than that of American actors, whose faces would never have been raised from their plate, stained with soup and humiliation as at the beginning of *La Bandéra*. (Only the face of Wallace Beery in *Viva Villa* might be comparable, and perhaps that of Edward G. Robinson.) French cinema reeked of odors, while American cinema smelled of Palmolive, gleaming and antiseptic. The women had a carnal presence that fixed them in the memory as living women and at the same time as erotic phantoms (Viviane Romance is the actress I associate with this notion), whereas in Hollywood's star actresses eroticism was sublimated, stylized, idealized. (Even the most carnal of the American actresses of the time, the platinum-blonde Jean Harlow, was made unreal by the dazzling whiteness of her skin. In black-and-white, the power of white brought about a transfiguration of female faces, legs, shoulders, and cleavages; it made Marlene Dietrich not the immediate object of desire but desire itself, like an extraterrestrial essence.) I realized that French cinema spoke of more disturbing, vaguely forbidden things; I knew that in *Quai des brumes* Jean Gabin was not a veteran who wanted to emigrate and start farming in the colonies (this is what the dubbed Italian version tried to make us believe); instead, he was a deserter running away from the front, a story the Fascist censorship would never have allowed.

In other words, I could go on as long about French films of the thirties as about the American ones, but the discussion would extend to many other things besides cinema and besides the 1930s, whereas American cinema is self-contained then. I would almost say it has no before and no after: certainly it has no before or after in the story of my life. Unlike French cinema, the American cinema of that time had nothing to do with literature, and perhaps this is why it stands out so prominently, so isolated, in my experience: these memories of myself as spectator belong to my memories of the time before literature had touched me.

What was known as the "Hollywood firmament" constituted a system to itself, with its constants and its variables, a human typology. The actors represented models of character and ways of behaving. There was a possible hero for every temperament: for one who dreamed of a life of action Clark Gable stood for a certain brutality leavened by a merry braggadocio; and Gary Cooper, a sangfroid relieved by irony; for those who wanted to overcome obstacles by humor and savoir faire, there was the aplomb of William Powell, the discretion of Franchot Tone; for the introvert who masters his shyness there was James Stewart, while Spencer Tracy was the model of the open, fair-minded man who could make things with his hands; and there was even a rare example of the intellectual hero in Leslie Howard.

For actresses the range of physiognomies and characters was more limited: makeup, hairdo, expression all aimed at a unified stylization divided into two basic categories, blondes and brunettes. Within each category the stars went from the temperamental Carole Lombard to the down-to-earth Jean Arthur, from the broad and languid mouth of Joan Crawford to the thin and pensive one of Barbara Stanwyck. But in between there were a number of less and less distinct figures, with a certain interchangeability. Between the catalog of women found in American movies and the catalog of women encountered off-screen in everyday life there was no possibility of establishing a connection; I would say that where one ended the other began. (With the women in French films, on the contrary, this connection existed.) From the gamine unconventionality of Claudette Colbert to the spiky energy of Katharine Hepburn, the most important model suggested by the female characters of American cinema was the woman who rivaled a man in her resolve and stubbornness and wit and talent. For cool self-control in handling men, Myrna Loy was the one who showed most intelligence and irony. Now I discuss her with a seriousness that I would never have then associated with those carefree comedies of hers; but basically, for a society like ours, for Italian mores of those years, especially in the provinces, the independence and gumption of those American women could have been a lesson, which I somehow perceived. I had made Myrna Loy such a prototype, a female ideal—perhaps wifely, or perhaps sisterly, but anyhow a personification of taste and style—that it could coexist with the phantoms of carnal aggressiveness (Jean Harlow, Viviane Romance) and with those of exhausting and languid passion (Greta Garbo, Michèle Morgan) towards whom my attraction was tinged with fear, or alongside that image of physical happiness and vital spirits, Ginger Rogers, for whom I cherished a love doomed from the outset even in reveries because I couldn't dance.

There could be some question whether creating an Olympus of ideal and, for the moment, unattainable women is good or bad for a young man. It certainly had one positive aspect: it prevented you from being satisfied with what little (or much) you might encounter and it drove you to project your desires farther, into the future, the elsewhere, the difficult. The most negative aspect was that it did not teach us to see real women with an eye prepared to discover unfamiliar beauty which did not conform to the criteria; it did not teach us to invent new characters with the material that chance or search caused us to meet on our horizon.

For me movies were made particularly of actors and actresses, but I must not forget that for me, and for all Italian moviegoers, only half of each actor and actress existed: the figure, but not the voice, which was replaced by the abstraction of dubbing, by a conventional speech, alien and insipid, as anonymous as the printed titles that in other countries (at least in those where the spectator is considered mentally more quick) tell you what the mouths are communicating with all the sensitive power of individual pronunciation, a phonetic signal made by lips, teeth, saliva, formed chiefly by the different geographical backgrounds of the American melting pot, in a language which, to those who understand it, reveals expressive nuances and for those who do not understand it has an extra musical capacity (such as what we hear today in Japanese films or in Swedish ones). The conventionality of American movies thus came to me doubled (no pun intended) by the conventionality of the dubbing, which to our ears, however, became part of the film's magic, inseparable from those images. A proof that cinema's power was born silent; and speech—at least for Italian spectators—has always been considered a superimposition, like a printed caption. (For that matter, Italian films also seemed dubbed in those days, even if they weren't. Though I saw nearly all of them and remember them, I don't speak of them because they counted for so little, in any way; and in this discussion of cinema as another dimension of the world I could really find no place for them.)

Some of my assiduousness as a spectator of American movies came from a collector's obstinacy, which meant that all interpretations of an actor or an actress were like stamps in a series that I was pasting into the album of my memory, gradually filling in the blanks. So far I have mentioned only famous stars, but my collecting extended to the horde of character actors who at that time were an essential ingredient of every movie, particularly in the comic parts, men like Edward Everett Horton or Frank Morgan or, in "bad guy" parts, John Carradine or Joseph Calleia. The situation recalled the masks of the commedia dell'arte, where every role is foreseen; and when I used to read the names of the cast I knew in advance that Billie Burke would be a somewhat giddy lady, C. Aubrey Smith a gruff colonel, Mischa Auer the international idler, Eugene Pallette the millionaire. But I also expected some little surprise, seeing a familiar face in an unexpected role, or perhaps wearing different makeup. I knew the names of almost all of them, even the one who always played the fussy hotel clerk (Franklin Pangborn), and the one who always played the bartender with a bad cold (Billy Gilbert). Others, whose names I don't recall or never managed to learn, I remember by sight: the various butlers, for example, who were a separate and very important category in movies of the time, perhaps because it was already becoming clear that the age of butlers was over.

Mine was a spectator's erudition, you realize, not an expert's. I could never compete with today's professional scholars in the field (or appear on a TV quiz) because I have never been tempted to confirm my memories by consulting manuals, film archives, specialized encyclopedias. These recollections belong to a mental storeroom where written documents do not count but only the random accretion of images over the days and the years, a storeroom of private sensations which I have never wanted to mix with the storeroom of collection memory. (Among the critics of the time I used to follow Filippo Sacchi in the *Corriere della sera*, very acute and sensitive to my favorite players, and later "Volpone," actually Pietro Bianchi, in *Bertoldo*, the first critic to make a connection between cinema and literature.)

I should emphasize that this whole story is concentrated within the space of a few years. My passion had barely been able to develop and free itself from family repression when it was promptly stifled by government repression. All of a sudden (I believe it was in 1938), Italy decided to extend its policy of autarchy also to movies and placed an embargo on American pictures. It was not exactly a question of censorship: as usual, the censors gave or denied their license to individual films, and those that were not approved simply remained unseen by everyone. The propaganda of the regime (which at that time was adopting Hitler's racist line) accompanied the embargo decree with a crude anti-Hollywood campaign, but the real reason for the measure must have been commercial protectionism, to make room on the market for Italian (and German) movies. So they barred the four biggest American producers and distributors: Metro, Fox, Paramount, Warner (again I rely on my memory, on my obsession's precise recording). But films of other companies, such as RKO, Columbia, Universal, United Artists (which, even previously, had been distributed through Italian firms), continued to arrive as late as 1941, until Italy was at war with the United States, that is. I was still granted some occasional satisfactions (one of the greatest, in fact: *Stagecoach*); but my collector's greed had been dealt a death blow.

Compared to all the prohibitions and obligations Fascism had imposed, and to the still more serious ones it continued imposing in those prewar years and then during the war itself, the veto on American movies was certainly a minor or marginal privation, and I was not so foolish that I didn't realize that. But it was the first that directly affected me, who had not known other years than those of Fascism or felt needs other than those which my environment could stir and satisfy. This was the first time I was deprived of a right that I enjoyed: more than a right, it was a dimension, a world, a space of the mind; and I felt this loss as a cruel oppression, which contained all the forms of oppression that I knew of only by hearsay or by having seen other people suffer them. I still speak of this today as a lost happiness, because something thus disappeared from my life and was never to reappear. When the war ended, many things had changed: I had changed, and films had become something different, something else in themselves and something else for me. My biography as a spectator resumes, but it is the story of another spectator who is no longer only a spectator.

With so many other things on my mind, if I happened to recall the movies of the Hollywood of my adolescence, I found them poor stuff: it was not one of the heroic eras of the silent film or of the early sound period for which my first investigations of the history of cinema had kindled a desire. My memories of the life of those years had also altered, and many things that I had considered insignificant, day-to-day matters, now took on a meaning, tension, premonition. In short, as I reconsidered my past, the world of the screen seemed to me much more bland, more predictable, less exciting than the world outside. Of course, I must also say that it had been the gray and banal provincial life that drove me towards the celluloid dreams, but I know I am repeating a cliché that oversimplifies the complexity of the experience. It is pointless for me to explain today why and how the provincial life that surrounded me during childhood and adolescence was all made up of exceptions to the norm, and if it was sad and idle, the sadness and the idleness were in me, not in the visible aspect of things. Even Fascism, in a locality where mass phenomena did not apply, was a collection of individual faces, of the behavior of individuals, not a uniform covering like a coat of tar. But (to the disenchanted eye of a boy, looking at it, half-inside and half-outside) it represented an added element of contrast, a piece of the puzzle that, because of its irregular shape, was harder to fit in among the others, a film whose beginning I had missed and whose end I was unable to imagine. What then, in this context, had cinema been for me? I would say: distance. It fulfilled a need for distance, for expanding the borders of the real, for seeing immeasurable areas opening out, abstract as geometric entities, but also concrete, absolutely full of faces and situations and settings, which with the world of direct experience established their own (abstract) network of relationships.

Since the end of the war, cinema has been seen, debated, made, in a completely different way. Italian postwar cinema may well have changed our way of seeing the world (I cannot say to what extent), but it certainly changed our way of seeing cinema (any cinema, including the American). There is not one world inside the glowing screen in the dark hall and another world outside, heterogeneous, the two separated by a sharp break, ocean or abyss. The dark hall disappears, the screen is a magnifying glass held up to the everyday world outside, and it forces us to observe what the naked eye tends to skip over without pausing. This function has — or can have — its usefulness, small, or medium, or in some cases very big. But it does not satisfy that anthropological, social need for distance.

Then (to pick up the thread of private biography again) I soon entered and became part of the world of written paper, some margin of which borders on the world of celluloid. In an obscure fashion I immediately felt that, in the name of my old love for the movies, I had to maintain my status as pure spectator, and that I would forfeit its privileges if I crossed over to join those who make films. For that matter, I was never tempted. But since Italian society is narrow, you end up eating in a restaurant with movie-makers, everybody knows everybody else: a condition that robs the status of spectator (and of reader) of much of its fascination. There was also the fact that for a short time Rome had become an international Hollywood, and the barriers between the film industries of the various countries soon fell: in other words, the sense of distance was lost in every meaning of the word.

In any case, I continue going to the movies. The exceptional contact between the spectator and a filmed vision can always occur, through art or chance. In the Italian cinema much can be expected of the personal genius of the directors, but very little can be expected of chance. This must be one of the reasons why I have sometimes admired Italian cinema, often appreciated it, but never loved it. I feel it has taken more from my pleasure in movie-going than it has given. This pleasure cannot be judged only by the so-called "films d'auteur," to which I have a critical attitude of the literary sort; it must also consider the median or minor output, with which I try to reestablish a pure spectator's relationship.

I must mention then the contemporary satirical comedies that represented the average Italian production throughout the sixties. In most instances I find them loathsome, because the more the caricature of our social behavior is meant to be merciless the more it proves smug and indulgent. In other cases I find them enjoyable and good-humored, with an optimism that remains miraculously genuine; but then I feel that these movies do not lead us very far in the knowledge of ourselves. In short, to look ourselves straight in the eye is difficult. It is appropriate that Italian vitality should delight foreigners, but leave me cold.

It is no accident that a craftsmanlike product of constant quality and stylistic originality was born in our country with the "spaghetti Western," as a rejection of the area in which Italian cinema had asserted itself and then come to a halt. And as a construction of an abstract space, parody-distortion of a purely cinematographic convention. (But in this way it also says something about us Italians, our mass psychology, about what Westerns mean to us, and how we complement and adjust the myth to invest in it what we carry within ourselves.)

And so I, similarly, if I am to recreate for myself the pleasure of movies, have to depart from the Italian context and become a pure spectator again. In the cramped, smelly studio-cinemas of the Latin Quarter I can find the films of the twenties and thirties that I thought I had lost forever, or I can subject myself to the assault of the latest discovery, Brazilian perhaps or Polish, from backgrounds about which I know nothing. In short: I go and seek out either old movies that enlighten me about my own prehistory or movies so new that they can perhaps suggest what the world will be like after I am gone. And even in this sense it was always American films—I mean the very latest—that have something fresher to communicate to me: on superhighways, drug stores, faces old or young, on the way of moving from one place to another and of spending one's life.

But what cinema gives now is no longer distance: it is the irreversible feeling that everything is near, at hand, on top of us. And this close observation can be exploratory-documentary or else introspective, the two directions which today can define cinema's educational function. The first provides a strong image of the world outside us which for some objective or subjective reason we are unable to perceive directly; the other forces us to see ourselves and our daily existence in a way that alters something in our relationship with ourself. The work of Federico Fellini, for example, comes closest to this spectator's biography which

Fellini himself persuaded me to write; except that for him biography, in turn, has become cinema, the outside has invaded the screen, the darkness of the hall is poured into the cone of light.

That autobiography which Fellini has pursued uninterruptedly from *I vitelloni* till today affects me deeply not only because there is only a few years' difference in our ages and not only because we both come from seaside towns — he from the Adriatic and I from Liguria — where the life of idle young men is fairly similar (even if my Sanremo had many differences from his Rimini, being a border city and boasting a Casino, so we felt the gap between the bathing-beach summer and the "dead season" of winter perhaps only in the war years), but also because behind all the dreariness of days spent in cafés, the walk to the sea front, the friend who gets up in drag then drinks too much and starts crying, I recognize an unsatisfied young manhood of moviegoers, a provincial society that judges itself by movie standards, in continuous comparison with that other world which is cinema.

The biography of the Fellini hero — which the director picks up again from the beginning each time — in this sense is more exemplary than mine, because his young man leaves the provinces, comes to Rome, and moves to the other side of the screen, makes films, becomes cinema himself. The Fellini film is cinema turned inside out, the projector swallows the hall, and the camera turns its back on the set. But the two poles are always interdependent, the provincial city acquires a meaning as it is remembered from Rome; Rome acquires a meaning because it has been reached from the provinces. Between the human monstrosity of the one and the other there is established a common mythology, revolving around gigantic female deities like Anita Ekberg in *La dolce vita*. And unearthing and classifying this agitated mythology is the aim of Fellini's work, with the self-analysis of *8½* at its core, like a spiral crowded with archetypes.

To define the process more exactly, we must bear in mind that in Fellini's biography the reversal of roles from spectator to director is preceded by another reversal. From reader of weekly humor magazines, Fellini became a cartoonist and contributor to them. The continuity between Fellini cartoonist-humorist and Fellini film-maker is furnished by the Giulietta Masina character and by the whole special "Masina area" of his work, with that rarefied poetic quality that subsumes the figurative schematization of cartoons and goes on — through the village squares of *La strada* — to the world of the circus, the melancholy of clowns, one of the most insistent themes of the Fellini keyboard and most linked with a retrospective stylistic taste, corresponding, that is, to a childish, disincarnate, pre-cinema visualization of an "other" world. (This "other" world to which cinema gives an illusion of carnality that mixes its phantoms with the attracting-repelling carnality of life.)

And, again, it is not by chance that the film analyzing the Masina world, *Giulietta degli spiriti*, has as its declared figurative and chromatic source the colored cartoons of the *Corriere dei Piccoli*, the Italian children's magazine: the graphic world of printed, mass-circulation paper asserts its special visual authority and its close kinship with cinema from the very beginning.

In this graphic world, the humorous weekly, still virgin territory for cultural sociology, I believe (removed as it is from the routes between Frankfurt and New York), should be studied as a medium almost as indispensable as cinema in defining the mass culture of the Italian provinces between the two wars. And if it has not already been studied, the connection between humorous journalism and Italian cinema should also be investigated, not least because of the position it occupies in the biography of another and senior founding father of our cinema: Zavattini. It is the contribution of humorous journalism (perhaps even more than those of literature, figurative culture, art photography, and intellectual journalism) that gives Italian cinema an already tested kind of communication with the public, a stylization of figures and story.

But Fellini is not linked only with the zone of "poetic," "sophisticated," "angelic" humorism, where he found his place through his youthful pieces and cartoons; he belongs also with the more plebeian, Roman-dialect style that marked other cartoonists of the magazine *Marc'Aurelio*, among them Attalo, who portrayed contemporary society with unpleasant, deliberate vulgarity, with a line so crude and almost obscene that it forbade any consolatory illusion. The power of the image in Fellini's films, so hard to define because it cannot be fitted into the patterns of any figurative culture, has its roots in the overpowering, jarring aggressiveness of journalistic graphics. That aggressiveness capable of imposing, throughout the world, cartoons and comic strips that, the more they seem distinguished by an individual stylization, the more they prove effective in communicating at a mass level.

Fellini never lost this basis of popular communication even when his language became more sophisticated. For that matter, his frank anti-intellectualism has never flagged: for Fellini the intellectual is always a desperate case; in the best of instances, he hangs himself, as in *8½*, and when he runs amok, as in *La dolce vita*, he murders his children, then shoots himself. (The same scene in *Roma* is enacted in a period of classic stoicism.) According to Fellini's avowed intentions, arid and rationalizing intellectual lucidity is opposed to a spiritual knowledge, magical, a religious participation in the mystery of the universe. When we come to results, however, neither of these opposed terms seems to me to have a sufficiently strong cinematographic prominence. But instead, as a constant defence against intellectualism, Fellini retains always his sanguinary, spectacular instinct, his elementary truculence, the carnival or end-of-the-world atmosphere that his Rome, in ancient times or our own, unfailingly evokes.

What has often been called Fellini's baroque stems from his constantly forcing the photographic image in the direction that leads from the caricatural to the visionary. But he always keeps in mind a very precise depiction as the starting point, which must find its most communicative and expressive form. For those of us who belong to his generation this is particularly evident in the images of Fascism, which in Fellini, no matter how grotesque the caricature, always have the flavor of truth. Fascism, in the course of twenty years, had many different psychological climates, just as from year to year the uniforms changed. Fellini always finds the right uniforms and the right psychological climate for the years he is portraying.

Fidelity to truth should not be a criterion of aesthetic judgement, and yet when I see some films by young directors who like to reconstruct the Fascist period indirectly, as a historic-symbolic setting, I inevitably suffer. In the work of our most prestigious young filmmaker especially, everything regarding Fascism always has the wrong tone, perhaps justifiable conceptually but false as far as the images are concerned, as if he were unable to hit the target even by accident. Does this mean that the experience of a period cannot be transmitted, that a delicate texture of perceptions is inevitably lost? Or can it mean that the images through which the young conceive Fascist Italy, which are in particular those that writers have given (we have given), partial images that presupposed an experience shared by everyone, are no longer capable, once this common reference is gone, of evoking the historical consistency of a period? In Fellini's *Clowns*, on the contrary, the comic stationmaster, taunted by some kids on a train, has only to call a Fascist railway guard with his black moustache and, on the spectral train, the boys have only to raise their arms in a silent Roman salute, and the climate of the period is brought back completely, unerringly. Or it is enough to hear, over the sight of the audience in the little vaudeville theater in *Roma*, the lugubrious sound of the air-raid alarm.

The evocative precision achieved by the distortion of caricature is probably found in the images of religious education, which must have been a basic trauma for Fellini since it keeps returning, in the appearance of terrifying priests, with a downright physiological horror. (But here I am in no position to judge: I experienced only secular repression, which struck deeper and is thus less easy to be rid of.) To the presence of a repressive school-church Fellini opposes the vaguer presence of a church that conveys the mysteries of nature and man, a church without contours, like the dwarf nun who calms the madman in the tree in *Amarcord*, or which does not answer the questions of the man undergoing a crisis, like the ancient Monsignor who speaks of birds in *8½*, surely the most haunting, unforgettable image of the religious Fellini.

With visual repugnance Fellini goes a long way, but on the road of moral repugnance he comes to a stop, rejoins the monstrous to the human, to indulgent carnal complicity. Both the *Vitelloni*'s provincial town and film-making Rome are circles in hell, but they are also enjoyable Lands of Cockaigne. This is why Fellini succeeds in disturbing totally: he forces us to admit that what we would most like to drive away is intrinsically close to us.

As in the analysis of neuroses, past and present mingle their perspectives; as in the explosion of a hysterical attack, they become spectacle. Fellini makes cinema the symptomology of Italian hysteria, that special family hysteria that before him was depicted as a largely southern phenomenon. From that place of geographical crosscurrents, his native Romagna, he redefines that hysteria in *Amarcord* as the real unifying element of Italian behavior. The cinema of distance which had nourished our youth is definitively overturned, to become the cinema of absolute proximity. In the hard times of our lives everything remains there, anxiously present; the first images of eros and the premonitions of death come to us in every dream; the end of the world began with us and shows no sign of ending; the film of which we self-deceptively thought we were only spectators is the story of our life.

Annie Dillard as Holy the Firm

John Sokol © *1981*

Annie Dillard

Total Eclipse

1

It had been like dying, that sliding down the mountain pass; it had been like the death of someone, irrational, that sliding down the mountain pass and into the region of dread. It was like slipping into fever, or falling down that hole in sleep from which you wake yourself whimpering. We had crossed the mountains that day, and now we were in a strange place — a hotel in central Washington, in a town near Yakima.

I lay in bed. My husband, Gary, was reading beside me. I lay in bed and looked at the painting on the hotel-room wall. It was a print of a detailed and lifelike painting of a smiling clown's head, made out of vegetables. It was a painting of the sort which you do not intend to look at, and which, alas, you never forget. Some tasteless fate presses it upon you; it becomes part of the complex interior junk you carry with you wherever you go. Two years have passed since the total eclipse of which I write. During those years I have forgotten, I assume, a great many things I wanted to remember — but I have not forgotten that clown painting or its lunatic setting in the old hotel.

The clown was bald. Actually, he wore a clown's tight rubber wig, painted white; this stretched over the top of his skull, which was a cabbage. His hair was bunches of baby carrots. Inset in his white clown makeup, and in his cabbage skull, were his small and laughing human eyes. The clown's glance was like the glance of Rembrandt in some of the self-portraits: lively, knowing, deep, and loving. The crinkled shadows around his eyes were string beans. His eyebrows were parsley. Each of his ears was a broad bean. His thin, joyful lips were red chili peppers; between his lips were wet rows of human teeth and a suggestion of a real tongue. The clown print was framed in gilt and glassed.

To put ourselves in the path of a total eclipse, that day we had driven five hours inland from the Washington coast where we lived. When we tried to cross the Cascades range, an avalanche had blocked the pass.

A slope's worth of snow blocked the road; traffic backed up. Had the avalanche buried any cars that morning? We could not learn. This highway was the only winter road over the mountains. We waited as highway crews bulldozed a passage through the avalanche. With two-by-fours and walls of plyboard, they erected a one-way, roofed tunnel through the avalanche. We drove through the avalanche tunnel, crossed the pass, and descended several thousand feet into Central Washington and the broad Yakima Valley, about which we knew only that it was orchard country. As we lost altitude, the snows disappeared; our ears popped; the trees changed, and in the trees were strange birds. I watched the landscape innocently, like a fool, like a diver in the rapture of the deep who plays on the bottom while his air runs out.

The hotel lobby was a dark, derelict room, narrow as a corridor, and seemingly without air. We waited on a couch while the manager vanished upstairs to do something unknown to our room. Beside us on an overstuffed chair, absolutely motionless, was a platinum-blond woman in her forties wearing a black silk dress and a strand of pearls. Her long legs were crossed; she supported her head on her fist. At the dim far end of the room, their backs towards us, sat six bald old men in their shirtsleeves, around a loud television. Two of them seemed asleep. They were drunks. "Number six!" cried the man on television. "Number six!"

On the broad lobby desk, lighted and bubbling, was a ten-gallon aquarium containing one large fish; the fish tilted up and down in its water. Against the long opposite wall sang a live canary in its cage. Beneath the cage, among spilled millet seeds on the carpet, were a decorated child's sand bucket and matching sand shovel.

Now the alarm was set for six. "When I was at home," said _____, "I was in a better place." I lay awake remembering an article I had read downstairs in the lobby, in an engineering magazine. The article was about gold mining.

In South Africa, in India, and in South Dakota, the gold mines extend so deeply into the earth's crust that they are hot. The rock walls burn the miners' hands. The companies have to air-condition the mines; if the air-conditioners break, the miners die. The elevators in the mine shafts run very slowly, down and up, so the miners' ears do not pop in their skulls. When the miners return to the surface, their faces are white.

Early the next morning we checked out. It was February 26, 1979, a Monday morning. We would drive out of town, find a hilltop, watch the eclipse, and then drive back over the mountains and home to the coast. How familiar things are here; how adept we are; how smoothly and professionally we check out! I had forgotten the clown's smiling head and the hotel lobby as if they had never existed. Gary put the car in gear and off we went, as off we have gone to a hundred other adventures.

It was before dawn when we found a highway out of town and drove into the unfamiliar countryside. By the growing light we could see a band of cirro-stratus clouds in the sky. Later the rising sun would clear these clouds before the eclipse began. We drove at random until we came to a range of unfenced hills. We pulled off the highway, bundled up, and climbed one of these hills.

2

The hill was five hundred feet high. Long winter-killed grass covered it, as high as our knees. We climbed and rested, sweating in the cold; we passed clumps of bundled people on the hillside who were setting up telescopes and fiddling with cameras. The top of the hill stuck up in the middle of the sky. We tightened our scarves and looked around.

East of us rose another hill like ours. Between the hills, far below, was the highway which threaded south into the valley. This was the Yakima Valley; I had never seen it before. It is justly famous for its beauty, like every planted valley. It extended south into the horizon, a distant dream of a valley, a Shangri-La. All its hundreds of low, golden slopes bore orchards. Among the orchards were towns, and roads, and plowed and fallow fields. Through the valley wandered a thin, shining river; from the river extended fine, frozen irrigation ditches. Distance blurred and blued the sight, so that the whole valley looked like a thickening or sediment at the bottom of the sky. Directly behind us was more sky, and empty lowlands blued by distance, and

Mount Adams. Mount Adams was an enormous, snow-covered volcanic cone rising flat, like so much scenery.

Now the sun was up. We could not see it; but the sky behind the band of clouds was yellow, and, far down the valley, some hillside orchards had lighted up. More people were parking near the highway and climbing the hills. It was the West. All of us rugged individualists were wearing knit caps and blue nylon parkas. People were climbing the nearby hills and setting up shop in clumps among the dead grasses. It looked as though we had all gathered on hilltops to pray for the world on its last day. It looked as though we had all crawled out of spaceships and were preparing to assault the valley below. It looked as though we were scattered on hilltops at dawn to sacrifice virgins, make rain, set stone stelae in a ring. There was no place out of the wind. The straw grasses banged our legs.

Up in the sky where we stood the air was lusterless yellow. To the west the sky was blue. Now the sun cleared the clouds. We cast rough shadows on the blowing grass; freezing, we waved our arms. Near the sun, the sky was bright and colorless. There was nothing to see.

It began with no ado. It was odd that such a well-advertised public event should have no starting gun, no overture, no introductory speaker. I should have known right then that I was out of my depth. Without pause or preamble, silent as orbits, a piece of the sun went away. We looked at it through welders' goggles. A piece of the sun was missing; in its place we saw empty sky.

I had seen a partial eclipse in 1970. A partial eclipse is very interesting. It bears almost no relation to a total eclipse. Seeing a partial eclipse bears the same relation to seeing a total eclipse as kissing a man does to marrying him, or as flying in an airplane does to falling out of an airplane. Although the one experience precedes the other, it in no way prepares you for it. During a partial eclipse the sky does not darken — not even when 94% of the sun is hidden. Nor does the sun, seen colorless through protective devices, seem terribly strange. We have all seen a sliver of light in the sky; we have all seen the crescent moon by day. However, during a partial eclipse the air does indeed get cold, precisely as if someone were standing between you and the fire. And blackbirds do fly back to their roosts. I had seen a partial eclipse before, and here was another.

What you see in an eclipse is entirely different from what you know. (It is especially different for those of us whose grasp of astronomy is so frail that, given a flashlight, a grapefruit, two oranges, and fifteen years, we still could not figure out which way to set the clocks for Daylight Saving Time.) Usually it is a bit of a trick to keep your knowledge from blinding you. But during an eclipse it is easy. What you see is much more convincing than any wild-eyed theory you may know.

You may read that the moon has something to do with eclipses. I have never seen the moon yet. You do not see the moon. So near the sun, it is as completely invisible as the stars are by day. What you see before your eyes is the sun going through phases. It gets narrower and narrower, as the waning moon does, and, like the ordinary moon, it travels alone in the simple sky. The sky is of course background. It does not appear to eat the sun; it is far behind the sun. The sun simply shaves away; gradually, you see less sun and more sky.

The sky's blue was deepening, but there was no darkness. The sun was a wide crescent, like a segment of tangerine. The wind freshened and blew steadily over the hill. The eastern hill across the highway grew dusky and sharp. The towns and orchards in the valley to the south were dissolving into the blue light. Only the thin river held a trickle of sun.

Now the sky to the west deepened to indigo, a color never seen. A dark sky usually loses color. This was a saturated deep indigo, up in the air. Stuck up into that unworldly sky was the cone of Mount Adams, and the *alpenglow* was upon it. The *alpenglow* is that red light of sunset which holds out on snowy mountaintops long after the valleys and tablelands are dimmed. "Look at Mount Adams," I said, and that was the last sane moment I remember.

I turned back to the sun. It was going. The sun was going, and the world was wrong. The grasses were wrong; they were platinum. Their every detail of stem, head, and blade shone lightless and artificially distinct as an art photographer's platinum print. This color has never been seen on earth. The hues were metallic; their finish was matte.

The hillside was a nineteenth-century tinted photograph from which the tints had faded. All of the people you see in the photograph, distinct and detailed as their faces look, are now dead. The sky was navy blue. My hands were silver. All the distant hills' grasses were fine-spun metal which the wind lay down. I was watching a faded color print of a movie filmed in the Middle Ages; I was standing in it, by some mistake. I was standing in a movie of hillside grasses filmed in the Middle Ages. I missed my own century, the people I knew, and the real light of day.

I looked at Gary. He was in the film. Everything was lost. He was a platinum print, a dead artist's version of life. I saw on his skull the darkness of night mixed with the colors of day. My mind was going out; my eyes were receding the way galaxies recede to the rim of space. Gary was lightyears away, gesturing inside a circle of darkness, down the wrong end of a telescope. He smiled as if he saw me; the stringy wrinkles around his eyes moved. The sight of him, familiar and wrong, was something I was remembering from centuries hence, from the other side of death; yes, *that* is the way he used to look, when we were living. When it was our generation's turn to be alive. I could not hear him; the wind was too loud. Behind him the sun was going. We had all started down a chute of time. At first it was pleasant; now there was no stopping it. Gary was chuting away across space, moving and talking and catching my eye, chuting down the long corridor of separation. The skin on his face moved like thin bronze plating that would peel.

The grass at our feet was wild barley. It was the wild einkorn wheat which grew on the hilly flanks of the Zagros Mountains, above the Euphrates Valley, above the valley of the river we called *River.* We harvested the grass with stone sickles, I remember. We found the grasses on the hillsides; we built our shelter beside them and cut them down. That is how he used to look then, that one, moving and living and catching my eye, with the sky so dark behind him, and the wind blowing. God save our life.

From all the hills came screams. A piece of sky beside the crescent sun was detaching. It was a loosened circle of evening sky, suddenly lighted from the back. It was an abrupt black body out of nowhere; it was a flat disc; it was almost over the sun. That is when there were screams. At once this disc of sky slid over the sun like a lid. The sky snapped over the sun like a lens cover. The hatch in the brain slammed. Abruptly it was dark night, on the land and in the sky. In the night sky was a tiny ring of light. The hole where the sun belongs is very small. A thin ring of light marked its place. There was no sound. The eyes dried, the arteries drained, the lungs hushed. There was no world. We were the world's dead people rotating and orbiting around and around, embedded in the planet's crust, while the earth rolled down. Our minds were lightyears distant, forgetful of almost everything. Only an extraordinary act of will could recall to us our former, living selves and our contexts in matter and time. We had, it seems, loved the planet and loved our lives, but could no longer remember the way of them. We got the light wrong. In the sky was something that should not be there. In the black sky was a ring of light. It was a thin ring, an old, thin silver wedding band in the sky, or a morsel of bone. There were stars. It was all over.

3

It is now that the temptation is strongest to leave these regions. We have seen enough; let's go. Why burn our hands any more than we have to? But two years have passed; the price of gold has risen. I return to the same buried alluvial beds and pick through the strata again.

I saw, early in the morning, the sun diminish against a backdrop of sky. I saw a circular piece of that sky appear, suddenly detached, blackened, and back-lighted; from nowhere it came and overlapped the sun. It did not look like the moon. It was enormous and black. If I had not read that it was the moon, I could have seen the sight a hundred times and never thought of the moon once. (If, however, I had not read that it was the moon — if, like most of the world's people throughout time I had simply glanced up and seen this thing — then I doubtless would not have speculated much, but would simply have, like Emperor Louis of Bavaria in 840, died of fright on the spot.) It did not look like a dragon, although it looked more like a dragon than the moon. It looked like a lens cover, or the lid of a pot. It materialized out of thin air — black, and flat, and sliding, outlined in flame.

Seeing this black body was like seeing a mushroom cloud. The heart screeched. The meaning of the sight overwhelmed its fascination. It obliterated meaning itself. If you were to glance out one day and see a row of mushroom clouds rising on the horizon, you would know at once that what you were seeing, remarkable as it was, was intrinsically not worth remarking. No use running to tell anyone. Significant as it was, it did not matter a whit. For what is significance? It is significance for people. No people, no significance. This is all I have to tell you.

In the deeps are the violence and terror of which psychology has warned us. But if you ride these monsters deeper down, if you drop with them farther over the world's rim, you find what our sciences cannot locate or name, the substrata, the ocean or matrix or ether which buoys the rest, which gives goodness its power for good, and evil its power for evil, the unified field: our complex and inexplicable caring for each other, and for our life together here. This is given. It is not learned.

The world which lay under darkness and stillness following the closing of the lid was not the world we know. The event was over. Its devastation lay round about us. The clamoring mind and heart stilled, almost indifferent, certainly disembodied, frail, and exhausted. The hills were hushed, obliterated. Up in the sky, like a crater from some distant cataclysm, was a hollow ring. The ring was as small as one goose in a flock of migrating geese — if you happened to notice a flock of migrating geese. It was one 360th part of the visible sky. The sun we see is less than half the diameter of a dime held at arm's length.

The sight had nothing to do with anything. The sun was too small, and too cold, and too far away, to keep the world alive. The white ring was not enough. It was feeble and worthless. It was as useless as a memory; it was as off-kilter and hollow and wretched as a memory.

When you try your hardest to recall someone's face, or the look of a place, you see in your mind's eye some vague and terrible sight such as this. It is dark; it is insubstantial; it is all wrong.

The white ring and the saturated darkness made the earth and the sky look as they must look in the memories of the careless dead. What I saw, what I seemed to be standing in, was all the wrecked light that the memories of the dead could shed upon the living world. We had all died in our boots on the hilltops of Yakima, and were alone in eternity. Empty space stoppered our eyes and mouths; we cared for nothing. We remembered our living days wrong. With great effort we had remembered some sort of circular light in the sky — but only the outline. Oh, and then the orchard trees withered, the ground froze, the glaciers slid down the valleys and overlapped the towns. If there had ever been people on earth, nobody knew it. The dead had forgotten those they had loved. The dead were parted one from the other and could no longer remember the faces and lands they had loved in the light. They seemed to stand on darkened hilltops, looking down.

4

We teach our children one thing only, as we were taught: to wake up. We teach our children to look alive there, to join by words and activities the life of human culture on the planet's crust. As adults we are almost all adept at waking up. We have so mastered the transition we have forgotten we ever learned it. Yet it is a transition we make a hundred times a day, as, like so many will-less dolphins, we plunge and surface, lapse and emerge. We live half our waking lives and all of our sleeping lives in some private, useless, and insensible waters we never mention or recall. Useless, I say. Valueless, I might add — until someone hauls their wealth up to the surface and into the wide-awake city, in a form that people can use.

I do not know how we got to the restaurant. Like Roethke, "I take my waking slow." Gradually I seemed more or less alive, and already forgetful. It was now almost nine in the morning. It was the day of a solar eclipse in central Washington, and a fine adventure for everyone. The sky was clear; there was a fresh breeze out of the north.

The restaurant was a roadside place with tables and booths. The other eclipse-watchers were there. From our booth we could see their cars' California license plates, their University of Washington parking stickers. Inside the restaurant we were all eating eggs or waffles; people were fairly shouting and exchanging enthusiasms, like fans after a World Series game. Did you see — ? Did you see — ? Then somebody said something which knocked me for a loop.

A college student, a boy in a blue parka who carried a Hasselblad, said to us, "Did you see that little white ring? It looked like a Life-saver. It looked like a Life-saver up in the sky."

And so it did. The boy spoke well. He was a walking alarm

clock. I myself had at that time no access to such a word. He could write a sentence, and I could not. I grabbed that Life-saver and rode it to the surface. And I had to laugh. I had been dumbstruck on the Euphrates River, I had been dead and gone and grieving, all over the sight of something which, if you could claw your way up to that level, you would grant looked very much like a Life-saver. It was good to be back among people so clever; it was good to have all the world's words at the mind's disposal, so the mind could begin its task. All those things for which we have no words are lost. The mind—the culture—has two little tools, grammar and lexicon: a decorated sand bucket and a matching shovel. With these we bluster about the continents and do all the world's work. With these we try to save our very lives.

There are a few more things to tell from this level, the level of the restaurant. One is the old joke about breakfast. "It can never be satisfied, the mind, never." Wallace Stevens wrote that, and in the long run he was right. The mind wants to live forever, or to learn a very good reason why not. The mind wants the world to return its love, or its awareness; the mind wants to know all the world, and all eternity, and God. The mind's sidekick, however, will settle for two eggs over easy.

The dear, stupid body is as easily satisfied as a spaniel. And, incredibly, the simple spaniel can lure the brawling mind to its dish. It is everlastingly funny that the proud, metaphysically ambitious, clamoring mind will hush if you give it an egg. Each self is multiple, a mob.

Further: while the mind reels in deep space, while the mind grieves or fears or exults, the wordaday senses, in ignorance or idiocy, like so many computer terminals printing out market prices while the world blows up, still transcribe their little data and transmit them to the warehouse in the skull. Later, under the tranquilizing influence of fried eggs, the mind can sort through this data. The restaurant was a halfway house, a decompression chamber. There I remembered a few things more.

The deepest, and most terrifying, was this. I have said that I heard screams. (I have since read that screaming, with hysteria, is a common reaction even to expected total eclipses.) People on all the hillsides, including, I think, myself, screamed when the black body of the moon detached from the sky and rolled over the sun. But something else was happening at that same instant, and it was this, I believe, which made us scream.

The second before the sun went out we saw a wall of dark shadow come speeding at us. We no sooner saw it than it was upon us, like thunder. It roared up the valley. It slammed our hill and knocked us out. It was the monstrous swift shadow-cone of the moon. I have since read that this wave of shadow moves 1800 miles an hour. Language can give no sense of this sort of speed—1800 miles an hour. It was 195 miles wide. No end was in sight—you saw only the edge. It rolled at you across the land at 1800 miles an hour, hauling darkness like plague behind it. Seeing it, and knowing it was coming straight for you, was like feeling a slug of anesthetic shoot up your arm. If you think very fast, you may have time to think, "Soon it will hit my brain." You can feel the deadness race up your arm; you can feel the appalling, inhuman speed of your own blood. We saw the wall of shadow coming, and screamed before it hit.

This was the universe about which we have read so much and never before felt: the universe as a clockwork of loose spheres flung at stupefying, unauthorized speeds. How could anything moving so fast not crash, not veer from its orbit amok like a car out of control on a turn?

Less than two minutes later when the sun emerged, the trailing edge of the shadow-cone sped away. It coursed down our hill and raced eastward over the plain, faster than the eye could believe; it swept over the plain and dropped over the planet's rim in a twinkling. It had clobbered us, and now it roared away. We blinked in the light. It was as though an enormous, loping god in the sky had reached down and slapped the earth's face.

Something else, something more ordinary, came back to me along about the third cup of coffee. During the moments of totality, it was so dark that drivers on the highway below turned on their cars' headlights. We could see the highway's route as a strand of lights. It was bumper-to-bumper down there. It was 8:15 in the morning,

Monday morning, and people were driving into Yakima to work. That it was as dark as night, and eerie as hell, an hour after dawn, apparently meant that, in order to *see* to drive to work, people had to use their headlights. Four or five cars pulled off the road. The rest, in a line at least five miles long, drove to town. The highway ran between hills; the people could not have seen any of the eclipsed sun at all. Yakima will have another total eclipse in _____ . Perhaps in _____ , businesses will give their employees an hour off.

From the restaurant we drove back to the coast. The highway crossing the Cascades range was open. We drove over the mountain like old pros. We joined our places on the planet's thin crust; it held. For the time being, we were home free.

Early that morning at six when we had checked out, the six bald men were sitting on folding chairs in the dim hotel lobby. The television was on. Most of them were awake. You might drown in your own spittle, God knows, at any time; you might wake up dead in a small hotel, a cabbage-head watching TV while snows pile up in the passes, watching TV while the chili peppers smile and the mountain blows up and the moon passes over the sun and nothing changes and nothing is learned because you have lost your bucket and shovel and no longer care. What if you regain the surface and open your sack and find, instead of treasure, a beast which jumps at you? Or, you may not come back at all. The winches may jam, the scaffolding buckle, the air-conditioning collapse. You may glance up one day and see by your headlamp the canary keeled over in its cage. You may reach into a cranny for pearls and touch a moray eel. You yank on your rope; it is too late.

Apparently people share a sense of these hazards, for when the total eclipse ended, an odd thing happened.

When the sun appeared as a blinding bead on the ring's side, the eclipse was over. The black lens cover appeared again, back-lighted, and slid away. At once the yellow light made the sky blue again; the black lid dissolved and vanished. The real world began there. I remember now: we all hurried away. We were born and bored at a stroke. We rushed down the hill. We found our car; we saw the other people streaming down the hillsides; we joined the highway traffic and drove away.

We never looked back. It was a general vamoose, and an odd one, for when we left the hill, the sun was still partially eclipsed—a sight rare enough, and one which, in itself, we would probably have driven five hours to see. But enough is enough. One turns at last even from glory itself with a sigh of relief. From the depths of mystery, and even from the heights of splendor, we bounce back and hurry for the latitudes of home.

Stanley Elkin as The Conventional Wisdom

John Sokol © *1981*

Stanley Elkin

Where I Read What I Read

Once I spent a year in bed reading.

I have never been able to read on a beach. I have never been able to read on a park bench.

An illiterate traveler, I do not understand why the airlines stock all those magazines. Indeed, the only printed matter I can concentrate on in the sky are commands, the "No Smoking" and "Fasten Seatbelt" signs, "Return to Cabin." "Occupied" and "Libre" on the lav doors like news from the front.

And nothing in waiting rooms, doctors' or dentists', the lawyer's, the barber's crushed leatherette, hairs stuck between the pages like bookmarks.

I cannot read in hospitals, I cannot read in cars. I can't even bring myself to read in libraries. The idea of a reading or browsing room is, for me, no idea at all.

We read, I've told my classes, to die, not entirely certain what I mean but sure it has something to do with being alone, shutting the world out, doing books like beads, a mantra, the flu. Some perfect, hermetic concentration sealed as canned goods or pharmaceuticals. It is, I think, not so much a way of forgetting ourselves as of engaging the totality of our attentions, as racing-car drivers or mountain climbers engage them, as surgeons and chess masters do. It's fine, precise, detailed work, the infinitely small motor managements of diamond cutters and safecrackers that we do in our heads. Ideally it is. Which is probably why we remember, even as we forget where we put our glasses and car keys, where we left our umbrella, if not the page number — if a book's any good we never read the page number — then what side, the left or the right, a particular passage appears on, even its generalized location, top, middle, bottom. It's why serious readers are as unlikely to forget an author's name or the title of his book read years before as they are the names of their friends. For much the same reasons — absorption, absolutely paid attention — I can tell you the name of every movie house where I saw any movie and, because I'm self-centered, not only the year but the season, too, when anything out of the way ever happened to me. I can't guess your age and weight but I can reel off my own cumulative, flickering stats, systolic and diastolic, shoe size and shirt collar, like some show-biz polymath of self, and recall not only the prevailing conditions, the weather I mean, but all the f-stop circumstances surrounding every book I've ever read. April in Paris, Autumn in New York, Moonlight in Vermont.

You remember this stuff yourself. It makes us real and stories our lives — anecdoting in our anecdotage. What, you've amnesia? You don't recall where you were when Pearl Harbor was bombed, Kennedy killed, where you were standing for the heart attack?

I spent a year in bed, reading.

It was the '58/'59 academic year. In April 1959 I was to take the "pre-lims," the preliminary exams for my Ph.D. We called them pre-lims and, in a way, they were. I trained for them like some boxer in reverse. In bed, a month's worth of library books behind my heaped pillows in the headboard, Stanley Elkin's Five Foot Shelf, the perfect living arrangements for a graduate student. If a whaling vessel was Herman Melville's Harvard and his Yale, then a Sealy Posturepedic was my Stillman's Gym. Cookied and milked, sandwiched and Coked, I left the bed only for personal hygiene and to teach my MWF freshmen rhetoric classes, and was back in it shortly after noon and, still snacked and still snug, remained there reading my books, getting up my centuries, my sixteenth and eighteenth, my two American, perfecting my timing, till, well — till it was time to go to bed. And weighed in a year later nine pounds heavier, overweight, Baugh, Brooke, Chew, Malone and Sherburne my cut men, my trainers and seconds, in all the corners of my head, in perfect shape to go what I then thought was the distance.

It was a hell of a year. An idyll. I was twenty-eight, getting on toward twenty-nine. *Sic ibid op cit*, but it was swell. *I.e. e.g.*, it was! A shower, a change of sheets and Fanny Burney *et al.* beside me in the wilderness!

A few years earlier — this would have been late summer, the middle of September, 1955, I would have been twenty-five — I was in the Army — this would have been the U.S. Army, I would have been in basic training — and on bivouac in Fort Carson's Rocky Mountains.

I was, as I've said, twenty-five, already five to seven years older than most of the rest of my fellows, a two-year RA, which you could do in those days, on the seventeenth, eighteenth and nineteenth of the month — you see? you see what total recall I have for my life, what attention I pay, my perfect pitch for the data and small beer of personal circumstance, my life like an open book, some limited edition, *Reader*, only I've read? — in strictly the best physical condition of my life — I would have been six feet tall, I would have dropped sixteen pounds from the 192 I was when I was inducted, I would have weighed 176 pounds — but still giving my comrades-in-arms those five to half dozen to seven years, still spotting them their youth, my own bookish, already middle-aged young manhood against their Detroit and even meaner streeted, late-prime-time kidhood, my own already declining, slug-a-bed sperm count against their blockbuster, highly motile, St. Vitus marathon dancing ones. (These were the mid-*fifties* high Rockies, recall. Colorado Springs seemed to me cowpoke, an Army town. The Broadmoor Hotel was around then but, for my fatigue and khaki sensibilities, dislocated, anachronous, like some range Xanadu. I would have stared longingly at it from the bus.)

So there I was, shipshape, for me, but in heavy seas, force 10 winds (and the tops of the mountains *indeed* like waves, like the glaciers they'd been and some still were, displaced as stone like sinners in stories), worried about bivouac because the scuttlebutt had it how rough it all was, as years later I'd worry about those four centuries I was, as they put it in academe, responsible for, and as months later — this would have been December — I would arrange to have myself taken off orders to France only because I'd heard that you pulled two weeks of KP on the ship going over. In good shape but a nervous Nelly, I dreaded the nine-mile hike — this would have been on a Sunday — from the spot where they had to let you off the bus, where even a goddamn bus had to stop because it couldn't go another foot. Wow, I thought bookishly. Whew. Jeez.

Which was when the sergeant came by asking for volunteers to ride out — up? — to bivouac in a truck on Saturday. We'd have to help set up camp for the fellows. We would get Sunday off while the rest of the guys were chinning themselves up and down the Rocky Mountains. That was about it. I volunteered and packed a paperback copy of Thomas Mann's novellas and short stories into my knapsack, saving it for my Sunday off.

Sergeant Turner — he didn't give his first name — was an eleven-and-a-half-foot black man who either wore customized, armor-plated fatigues or had Permapress flesh with razor sharp military creases down the front of his thighs and shins. He wore a dark pistol on his hip but otherwise was the most unencumbered looking man I'd ever seen. Like a swimmer, say, only dressed. His crisp breast pockets were not only empty, they seemed never to have been unbuttoned. It was in his truck that we drove to the bivouac area, never mind what it said on the side and never mind either how he found it or how the marching Sunday teen-agers would find us. Maybe it hadn't *been* a bivouac area until Turner decided to park there. Maybe it hadn't even been America.

We set up a mess tent. He told us to blow up our air mattresses and set up our pup tents. He told us to hang around. And all *right* we thought when Turner went off forgetting to tell us what else to do. He said, "I'm going to get dinner." Maybe he knows a place, I thought. He came back, his pistol unfired, with three jackrabbits whose necks he had broken. (All of us thinking, What the hell, how bad can it *be*, maybe this is already it, maybe just eating Turner's home cooking is what they mean by setting up camp, maybe just *finding* this place is. Thinking, anyway how could just half a dozen men set up camp for a regiment? We ain't any developers, this is only 1955, there's barely even shopping centers yet.)

When it was almost dark he told us to dig a hole and bury the ammunition. He gave us its dimensions like God giving them to Noah. He may even have spoken in cubits.

All we had were our trenching tools and we worked most of the night on it, till three or four in the morning, and it was quite a hole, a hole the size of a boy's bedroom, and all that kept us going was the thought of that Sunday off, Turner periodically reminding us of our reward. "All right," he said, before he went off to sleep at midnight, "you men already been through Saturday. You're on your own time now. The quickest you get done the quickest you get to enjoy the rest of your Sunday." When the tallest of us could stand in the hole without sticking up out of it the hole was dug and we piled the cases of ammunition into it, covered it over with dirt, did our landscaping like responsible strip miners, and went off to pup tent.

I woke up at ten — this would have been a.m. — on perhaps the most beautiful day in the history of weather, the world at room temperature, the air so clear and fine one could see without glasses. I peed in the trees and washed in my helmet liner in water from a stream so crisp and sweet it might have been the headwaters of water itself, its source I mean, its sheer perfect wholesome, untrammeled, unsullied, thoroughbred, sanitate, unadulterate immaculate taps.

I could smell bacon frying from the mess tent. There were eggs. There were toast and jellies and dining car coffees.

After breakfast I got my air mattress and retrieved Thomas Mann from my knapsack. I wandered off a few hundred feet, out of sight of the mess and pup tents, and entered a thin pine forest, pine needles on a forest floor exactly like the one where the earth moved for Maria and Robert Jordan in *For Whom the Bell Tolls* — Professor Flanagan's course; this would have been March 1954 — and settled the air mattress against a tree at precisely the angle where my helmet would make a comfortable pillow for my head.

It moved for me, too. I had picked a spot at the very edge of the trees, with a view of the passes and mountains beneath me wide as beauty. It moved for me, too. I could have been the only man in the world. It moved and moved.

I opened my book and began to read "Mario the Magician." It was, to then, the most wonderful story I'd ever read, the finest ever written. Or maybe it was the circumstances, maybe it was the day. Maybe it was the company. Didn't I tell you we read to die, to be alone, to shut the world out? (But there it was, you say. There the world was, all before me, Colorado spread out like God's best shot, all ripe Nature's good old summertime. All right, maybe I did look up, sure I did, I looked up to take it in, but I am not by nature an eater of jackrabbit, not by nature a mountain man, not by nature, finally, by nature at all, and if I looked up to take it in — look, I was *there* for the view — it was as much Mann's novella I was trying to absorb as the scene before me, trying to rhyme the novelist's world with the world's one. I was astounded by how beautifully men could write, stunned by how they could imagine worlds so much more beautiful, if not more comfortable, than even this one, which, steeped with style, was so much more suitable, too, than even that laid-back graduate student cum teaching assistant bed with its crumbs and learning.) This was the happiest day of my life.

Which is when the scratching started, fellow civil engineers scurrying about the brush and whispering, "The son of a bitch wants us back! He says we didn't cover it with a tarpaulin." "Did he dig the fucker up?" "No, man, he found the tarpaulin." And another voice, this one official, or at least charged and calling with some increment of delegated authority, you know whose. I knew whose.

"Any guys still back in there start hauling ass! Sergeant Turner wants that hole dug up!"

"It's Sunday, man. He give us Sunday off."

"Tell him about it."

Which is when I picked my book up in one hand, my air mattress in the other, stuffed my pot on my head, and started running, the air mattress held out stiffly behind me like a cavalry flag, in the one direction still available to me. Which was down.

Perhaps that day I invented hang-gliding, broken field, down—Rocky running, the encumbered downhill, downforest dash. I may even have invented the principle of civil rights protests.

It wasn't fear which gave me grace, it wasn't even the senseless redundancy of digging up that goddamn Great Wall of Chinese Hole—Turner hadn't said a word about any tarpaulin—it wasn't even my outraged graduate scholar's sense of justice. It wasn't even gravity. It was simple invasion of privacy, a ruined read on the loveliest day in the world.

I didn't stop to catch my breath, I could have run all the way to Kansas.

I hadn't heard him call my name. I hadn't heard him at all. What it was, I think, were those engaged attentions, my Rocky Mountain High, my dual glimpse of what man could do, what glaciers and erosion, still hanging on from reading about Mario, still hanging on from looking up, only diffused now, spilling over into the viscerals and atavistics, frozen in my tracks as one of Turner's jackrabbits. I turned, looked up.

"You're AWOL," he said in a normal voice three or four hundred feet above me and not even counting his own personal extra eleven and a half feet. "You're A.W.O.L.," he spelled it out for me, "and stealing a U.S. government property air mattress."

I climbed Golgotha like a thief.

"Don't you want to dig?"

"No, Sergeant."

"All right," he said gently. "Those other boys be doing the digging. You read that book you reading. When they be done you can guard it till you be relieved."

This would have been just before one. They called me at two. (All they'd had to do was uncover the hole, spread the tarpaulin over the crates of ammo, and cover it up again. They'd have finished up sooner but were a man short, they said.)

I was relieved at midnight.

(Nor was this the last time the Army influenced my summer reading. The last time — this would have been August 1958 — was a year after I'd been separated. I was in the Reserves. I'd been teaching summer school at the University of Illinois in Champaign-Urbana and couldn't make it to Camp McCoy, Wisconsin, for the two-week training session with the rest of the outfit. They cut special orders for me, but, when I reported to McCoy, nobody, in effect, was home. Only a skeleton crew was on duty, the RA's permanently assigned there and a handful of civilians. The next cycle wasn't due in for a week — they were coming, I think, from Kansas City — and they didn't know what to do with me. They gave me a pass for the mess hall and my choice of a dozen two-story empty barracks buildings in which to stay. I was instantly alert, thirty-five months after I'd last seen Turner all senses still go — because I had the Francis Steegmuller translation of *Madame Bovary* in my suitcase, see — only thinking not "go" exactly, but actual "leave! get out!" Where, I asked carefully, should I report?

(Report?

(In the morning. In the morning, *Sir*! What were my duties? What covered hole in what ground would I be marching round and round, ready and by this time willing to kill the first son of a bitch who might take it into his head sometime to throw up over it or pick a daisy from it or just lie down on it.

(Duties?

(Thinking: This isn't any army, this is a nest of saboteurs, Reds probably or Canadian spies down from Lake Nipigon.

(But the fact of it was it was strictly don't call us, we'll call you, and I read all of *Madame Bovary* there, taking my time, stretching it out, moving from barracks to barracks and bed to bed to catch the sun.)

On Labor Day weekend in 1953 I was asked by my summer

employer, the Peacock Laundry and Dry Cleaners of North Clark Street, Chicago, Illinois, to accept as my last assignment for them the job of substitute watchman so that their real watchman could have the holiday off. I was to show up on Sunday evening and stay till they opened for business again the following Tuesday. They would give me twenty-five bucks, a half week's pay, and no trips to the vault, that chemical climate like the start of the world where I had to hold my breath for minutes and shove fur coats into storage with my eyes closed.

I had been taking Harrison Hayford's Contemporary English, Irish and American Lit. course at Northwestern University summer school and, though the course was over now, there was still one novel which I hadn't read—Joyce's *Ulysses*. I remember what Professor Hayford had told us, not to be intimidated by the book but just to allow that bold, black serpentine "S" which winds down from the top of its left hand first page to "tately, plump" at its bottom, to wash over us. For weeks now I had been showering in that giant "S" but could not get past the third page. This was the book I took with me to the Peacock Cleaners.

I don't read sitting up and there was no place for a night watchman to lie down. In the back, though, were long tables and I chose one of these, under a light like a fixture in a pool hall. There, in the dry cleaners, I took my last shower under the "S" and, pillowed on wet wash, began to read. I read for thirty-eight hours and finished the book and the course twenty minutes before the store opened up.

It wasn't until afterward, after I left the store, that I smelled the smells, tasted them, the naphthas and benzines, the agents and solvents, Clark Street and Dublin suddenly all mixed together, coating my mouth like sore throat, swabbing my throat like pus, stinging my eyes like chemical warfare. I had a headache that would last days, an olfactory hyperesthesia that would actually return full blown when I visited Dublin sixteen years later. Hey, I was like Bloom in Nighttown, like Proust in the cookie jar, the disparate impressions of laundry and literature like things bonded in genes.

These have been, I see now, a few from the fifties. Strange—to me strange—occasions from a decade when I read more books than I'd ever read in my life, when, as a student and soldier, I was more intellectually engaged than I'd ever been before or since. More intellectually engaged, sadly, than I ever will be again. I began to teach and write in the sixties, have been at it since, and, while I still read of course, I no longer catch up. Merely — at best — to keep up. Which, as anyone knows, is not the same thing.

I would hope that some day someone will read one of my books with just a particle of that sense of occasion which I brought to Flaubert and to Mann and to all the rest. I haven't said it here, am almost ashamed to own up, but once I opened books slowly, stately, plump imaginary orchestras going off in my head, like overtures, like music behind the opening credits in films, humming the title page, whistling the copyright, turning myself into producer and pit band, usher and audience, reclined, positioned as a dreamer, who could read in a barracks but not on a bench.

They were wondrous times, I think, and begin to understand my watchman circumstances, and all the things that happened back in those days and those nights when I was never bored.

Jeffrey Fiskin as Disputing Taste

John Sokol © 1982

Jeffrey Fiskin

Disputing Taste

The story and the occasion of its telling are inextricably bound.

This would be the third day. We had begun in the north, Mendocino, with John Parducci, the sort the English call a man of character. He scrambled around his vast redwood vats with a length of rubber hose for his wine-thief. He muttered vague imprecations on all journalists and salesmen as he dared us with an enormous goblet of red wine.

I, the neophyte, kept a discreet silence. Philip, the Eleusinian, simply declared the wine a tough, young zinfandel. It was the "tough" that got Parducci. He liked "tough." The rest of our visit went smoothly.

From winery to winery, we made our way south through Sonoma and across the valley to Napa. The towns come closer together. The winemakers are less hermetic. They and their wines become, as Philip noted, more civilized if less distinct. The while, I kept a discreet silence.

However, on the third day, at the fifteenth winery, I was ready to speak. I had tasted nearly a hundred wines in as many hours. What days before had been hidden was now revealed. A pinot noir tastes and smells more or less like a pinot noir. The younger wines are, the more they taste like grape juice. Indeed, I was ready to speak.

The opportunity came after we had tasted all the young cabernets in cask, one in oak from Limousin, one in oak from Nevers, one from this vineyard, one from that vineyard and all the permutations thereof.

We were invited to the house and offered, amidst whispers and sly smiles, some secret elixir served from a medicine bottle, the kind used for cough syrup.

I swirled, sniffed and sipped. I *was* ready to speak. "A young cabernet!" I announced proudly.

Philip's wince was the first clue. The faces of the winemakers clarified the problem. Any idiot would have known it was a young cabernet. That, clearly, was not the point.

Philip quickly breached the chasm of my return to discreet silence. "Cabernet, of course . . . and something else."

Now you've done it too, I thought. California's boutique wineries never blend. At this stage the stuff was grape juice, raw and unfiltered. The best you can hope to tell is what grape was used.

Undaunted by my silent warnings, Philip continued, "A bit softer than a plain cabernet."

Soft, my ass. It was probably *aqua regia*.

I took a quick look around to make sure the exits weren't blocked. We were in deep shit.

Philip swirled, sniffed and sipped again. "Almost as if . . . as if there were . . . No. Couldn't be."

The board of inquisitors leaned closer and with one voice dared Phil to be hung for a sheep. "What?"

"Well, it reminds me a little of an Haut Brion."

Good thinking, Phil, a little brown nose never hurt.

"As if . . . as if . . . No. Well . . . As if there were a bit of merlot blended in. No more than five percent."

It was the shy, fatuous grin coupled with the mathematical precision of five percent that destroyed them. The rest of our visit went smoothly. 97% cabernet, 3% merlot.

Driving down the hill from the winery, Philip could not long endure my accusatory squint.

"What?" he asked.

"You know damn well 'what'! That stuff tasted like cabernet. Period."

"True. But we had already tasted all their cabernets. *And* it was in a medicine bottle, so it must have come up from the lab. Likely experimental. *And* four years ago they planted an acre of merlot. *And* it takes about four years for young vines to produce usable grapes. *And* if you're going to experiment with a blend for the first time, you would probably try one that the French have had success with for a few centuries at least. *And* you would be circumspect enough to blend in ever so little the first time. Say less than five percent."

He tried to smile but the guilt had already overtaken him. He came down with stomach flu that night.

I went alone to the next winery on notice to cajole a taste of the vintner's famous hobby wines if possible. Unfortunately, the owner was not familiar with Phil's theory on the civilizing influence of Napa. He was one crusty son-of-a-bitch.

Walking from the house to the chais (an aluminum-sided garage actually), he tested me for political bias. Sadly, on the topic of Mexican labor I was found wanting. He might have dismissed me then and there, but he chose a subtler excommunication. I was to fall on my own sword in battle.

The chais was dark, cool, spartan and clean. Rows of oak barrels, old and new, lined the walls with military precision. My host drew off two glasses of red wine and thrust them at me, both of them.

"Whaddayathink?"

I thought, Phil will just have to come back here on his own. But I swirled and sniffed on the off chance I could discover something useful.

No luck. Two identical three-week-old pinot noirs. No difference. None whatsoever. I tasted them. No help. I wondered whether Phil knew what this fellow had planted four years ago. I looked around the garage, hoping for a sign. The weight of responsibility bore down. The shades of journalists, salesmen and immigrant laborers cursed me.

"Whaddayathink?"

And then I saw it. Right there. A wine-taster's epiphany. The two barrels from which the wine had been drawn brooded dumbly across the room. One was stately, new, fresh, yellow oak. The other was smudged and black and old.

I turned away for a moment, switched glasses from hand to hand, then turned back to face my antagonist.

"I'm not sure."

I waited for his triumphant smile. Then:

"But there seems to be more wood in one. Of course that's hardly possible. Two new pinot noirs aged exactly the same length of time. Still . . . this one seems to have more oak. But then I am new at all this."

I offered him one of the glasses, presumably the one with more oak. He shunted them aside.

"You'd be surprised," he said, "how many of you guys couldn't tell the difference. It's about time somebody showed up who knows his stuff. You ever hear about my hobby wines?"

We sampled his legendary hobby wines for the remainder of the afternoon and argued politics.

Phil was feeling better when I got back. He sipped from the medicine bottle of hobby wine I'd brought and told me the story. It was a dream he'd had while I was gone.

The occasion for the dream-story was the purchase sometime during the last century of a château in Bordeaux. To celebrate, the new owner held a small but elegant dinner to which he invited the owners of the two contiguous châteaux, grand gentlemen with impeccable pedigrees in the wine trade.

They dined lavishly and drank deeply of every available vintage drawn from the château's estimable library of past efforts. Finally, keeping with the traditions of his new home, he asked them down to his cellar, each to choose a bottle as a parting gift.

Wandering the mossy subterrànea, they passed one cask with a particularly elaborate boss carved above the spigot but otherwise unmarked. All the other casks announced their contents in chalked shorthand.

"What have we here?" asked M. duMesnil.

The host looked to his steward for the answer.

"We don't know. Been a mystery for years. Anyway, there's not much left of whatever it is."

"You're in luck then," said duMesnil. "You have M. de la Renaudie's remarkable palate at your service."

"No, no!" responded M. de la Renaudie. "It is your incomparable discernment that is the pride of our little village, M. duMesnil."

The two gentlemen demurred, each to the other, in that fashion for a few moments while their host directed his steward to draw two small glasses from the wood.

Monsieurs duMesnil and de la Renaudie swirled, sniffed and sipped in unison and, likewise, in unison pronounced, "Cabernet sauvignon."

Then de la Renaudie added, "And cabernet franc."

"And malbec," concluded duMesnil.

They smiled for each other and nodded to their host.

Again they swirled, sniffed and sipped together. In unison again, "The vintage of the comet, 1858."

"My dear de la Renaudie, you astound me!"

"Ah no, it is you, most admirable duMesnil, who are astounding."

Swirl, sniff, sip.

"And the cabernet is from the northern vineyard, I think," suggested de la Renaudie.

Then duMesnil, "And the malbec from the south?"

"No doubt!"

The host couldn't help asking after the cabernet franc.

DuMesnil replied coldly that there was only one planting of cabernet franc. De la Renaudie bowed in agreement. "To the west."

Swirl, sniff, sip.

Their brows furrowed in unison. A cloud.

Together, "And something . . . um . . . off."

Swirl, sniff, sip.

Together, "Hmph."

Swirl, sniff, sip.

"Something vaguely metallic?" offered duMesnil.

"I think not. Rather an animal taste," corrected de la Renaudie.

Swirl, sniff, sip.

"No. Definitely metallic. Surely you agree."

"Forgive me, duMesnil, but I cannot. The hint is clearly animal."

"I suggest you taste it again, de la Renaudie."

"I would if any doubt remained."

"Your stubbornness has served you poorly in the past. As has your palate. Witness your last vintage."

"I became satisfied with that wine the instant that stick of wood you call a tongue failed to appreciate it. Had you liked it, I would have withdrawn the entire year's production."

The host attended neither the duel nor the funerals. He did have his steward empty the offending cask lest the unpleasantness ever be repeated.

Some time later, during the cleaning, a workman found, at the bottom of the cask, an old key someone had lost through the bunghole. It was on a worn leather thong.

Phil added a footnote to our tasting trip later that evening. He had found an interview in the late edition of the local paper with Harry Waugh, heir to the wine-trade writing tradition of Andre Simon. The interviewer had begun by asking Mr. Waugh about his storied feats of blind-tasting and wine identification.

"Mr. Waugh, have you ever identified a wine incorrectly?"

Waugh thought for a moment before answering.

"No, I don't believe so. At least not since lunch."

Phil's reading of Waugh's line was impeccable. It left me feeling empty all the same. The tasting week, cask and bottle, had been a fine technical education for my vocabulary as well as my palate. Clever, discerning, well-spoken Phil had been a preceptor of Lisztian virtuosity. Yet the whole experience lacked moral dimension, discounting Phil's stomach flu of course.

I remembered Huysman's Des Esseintes who, having learned the syntax of perfumes, inundated with the effluvia of stephanotis, lavender, frangipane, plum and vanilla, threw open his window, scattered his vials of scent to the winds and tried to inhale a breath of fresh air. But the breeze brought back bergamot, jasmine, cassia and rose. Somehow I had inherited his spiritual lethargy.

We flew to Southern California ending our week together at a wine auction held in the Grand Salon of the Queen Mary. We arrived in time for the pre-auction tasting, moved carefully among the three hundred other guests and thoughtfully chose the three dozen wines we wanted to taste among nearly a hundred offered. Pace had been one of the week's lessons. I followed Phil's lead, but deferred less now. He, in turn, was quite willing to entertain my considerations. I presumed that meant there was rather less to serious wine-tasting than his dream-story suggested. Just another arcana, like the rest. My lethargy obtained. Still the dream nagged at me though I didn't yet understand why.

The jewel of the collection was an 1885 Chambertin from Bouchard Père. The opening was surrounded by appropriate pomp. A venerable from the English wine trade presided as the Queen Mary's own retired wine steward uncorked the bottle. A ceremonial hush prevailed until the wine master sipped and pronounced the wine old but sound. Then all hell broke loose. The assembled faithful reached out their glasses, hundreds, ours among them, like so many well-dressed begging poor. What might have been a thoughtful Oriental tinkling was drowned by our pleas. A second bottle was opened to restore calm. Most of us got a dash of the precious amber.

Behind the faded color, nearly topaz, within the waning charm, there was a clue. Nothing like Proust, mind you, but a clue. As duMesnil and de la Renaudie had done, I swirled, sniffed, sipped. There wasn't much to say. The wine was old but sound. I tried to recall the historical 1885. All that came to mind was Rudolf's suicide at Mayerling, which, in fact, occurred four years later. Old but sound. Swirl, sniff, sip. Phil was beaming in beatitude. I was musing on a lovesick archduke in an Austrian hunting lodge. Not even that. I was remembering Charles Boyer. Swirl, sniff, sip.

"What do you think?" Phil asked.

"I don't know. I don't have anything to compare it to."

"I agree. Incomparable!"

Phil beamed. The clue remained elusive.

I called Phil a few weeks later.

"How were the '58's? the 1858's."

"You mean what did people say about them? Just a minute."

I waited, listening to the white noise of long distance.

Phil came back on the line. "Well, here's Andre Simon writing about a dinner in 1935: '. . . a perfect bottle of the most perfect wine imaginable; so great and so simple withal; so gentle and sweet, on the brink of the grave, of course, but unafraid and with the quiet majesty of the sun that has all but left a cloudless sky and will have disappeared into the sea in another second or two.'"

"They didn't mention that."

"Who?"

"DuMesnil and de la Renaudie. From your dream."

"Know why? DuMesnil's the name of a girl I know whose family collects art. The de la Renaudies I stayed with in France."

"I meant in the dream."

"Just kidding. But the dream was about distinction."

"So is what Simon wrote," I remarked testily.

"Then I have a suggestion. Spend more time with Simon and less time worrying about my dreams."

I have tried to resurrect the memory of the 1885 Chambertin but all I
remember is Philip beaming. Topaz, Boyer, old but sound, and Philip
beaming. Nothing else. I have had older wines since. I've had some
truly superb wines as well, a '45 Mouton comes to mind, but I'm afraid
it's hopeless. I haven't a clue. No, that's not quite true. I do have a clue
somewhere in my cellar, clues, bottles, annotations, where it's cool.

Robert Fitzgerald as Spring Shade

John Sokol © *1981*

Robert Fitzgerald

No Castles, No Cathedrals

1

On my way to and from school with my short pace I passed through the nearby State House four times a day. In the lofty interior dusk there were gleams from polished marble floors crisscrossed by perforated rubber carpeting, and glints of varnish from canvas murals, huge and somber, showing episodes from frontier days, ceremonial meetings between feathered Indians and explorers in buckskins. At the center, four naves crossed and daylight came down from the dome. An odor of stale cigar smoke and cuspidors filled the place.

In good weather we sometimes saw the governor pass our house on foot on his way to his office in the State House. His mansion occupied a block on our street not far away, a big white house with a two-story pillared portico above a porte cochere on a curving drive. The paunchy sauntering man in the Panama hat was Governor Len Small. According to a story I heard years later, at the close of his term of office he won from the *Illinois State Journal* a solicitous headline: DID YOU LEAVE ANYTHING, LEN? A small boy stood in some awe of this mythical figure, as of the great building he headed for, which dominated our neighborhood from the northwest.

At the end of a long rise you saw a façade of heavy piers and arches of gray limestone making a high loggia, on which rose a great porch of polished columns bearing an architrave and pediment. This mass of the forward or eastern wing was repeated in wings to left and right, south and north, and mansard roofs, each topped by two open cupolas, surmounted all three. The more slender central mass, as high again, in façades of more closely spaced columns, rose to a gaunt dome of weathered copper, lifting its lanterna at an enormous height above the city.

At twelve or so I cherished *The Beloved Vagabond* for brave mumming and wandering on the roads of France. What stirred me most in the novel was the vagabond's exploit of sketching, on a café table in Paris, a fantastic work of architectural genius, an affair of towers and domes that he called the *palais de dipsomanie*. I did not know what that meant, but I imagined something like our State House. The Chicago architect who designed it in 1868 had in fact modeled the porches on the temple of Jupiter Stator in Rome. He thought he had improved on St. Paul's and on the Capitol at Washington by omitting the peristyle, and the truth is that his impure and ungainly building had more height and majesty. It towered and bulked and cut off the winter sunset, the sheer cliff of it going aloft in arches and verticals in one great pile, to house the elect of Illinois and beyond that to represent the dignity of the Republic, heir to all ages and builders.

"No castles, no cathedrals, and no kings," wrote Emerson of America in 1833, "Land of the forest . . ." Well, here was our castle and our cathedral. As to the forest, all over that town the elm trees with small fine leaves and soaring trunks and boughs over streets and lawns cooled and darkened the summer air. A dozen years later, when my grandmother was dying in 1934, my aunt and I flew from New York to be with her. From Chicago in a Ford trimotor, made all of corrugated metal, we rose to what seemed then a great altitude, a couple of miles perhaps, and at that height we eventually looked down on Springfield for the first time from the air. On the pale expanse of prairie we saw many dark square miles of wooded land, and the dome of the State House in its clearing jutted up in that forest.

2

An architectural enchantment of a more general kind came over me with the discovery of perspective as an excitement of sense and spirit. Looking, say, from the State House eastward on a long avenue flanked by business buildings, on a clear day the masses withdrawing in sunlit planes and blue verticals of shade seemed subject to an exquisite astringent power, the magic of space itself that made things so beautifully and sharply dwindle. Then the eye could luxuriate in drawings or etchings of cityscapes and architectural monuments, especially etchings by Whistler and by Joseph Pennell. At the public library I chanced on Ruskin's little book on the art of drawing, so serenely didactic, and soon I spent hours with sketch pad and pencil. Not only buildings but figures and natural forms acquired a new beauty that could be studied in the hope of rendering it by line, and illustrators could be compared for veracity and style. One picture never lost the power to terrify me: Kipling's drawing, in the last of the *Just So Stories*, of the giant animal that came out of the sea. The story had such charm that it tempted rereading, but I could not face the animal—a mountain of inspired bestiality—and closed my eyes to turn the page opposite which it appeared.

With some pleasures of the eye a boyish prurience began to mingle. *Redbook* magazine, for example, which I sometimes picked up for my bedridden father at a newsstand, published on several pages, in soft rotogravure, portraits of beauties whose deep decolletage dreamily bared their double rondure of bosom. Now and then there were fleeting exposures in movies. In *Kismet*, cameras in soft focus and careful cutting made the most of Mae Murray's white body and long ethereal hair in a harem bathing scene. For several years I concealed a passion for one unlikely movie figure, an actress named Thelma Todd, who appeared in comic shorts with Martha Raye of the capacious mouth. As a comedienne Thelma seemed to throw her beauty and sexuality away, but this only enhanced her power. Of all crushes of this kind, the most ineffable overcame me at a stage performance at the Majestic Theater of *Trelawney of the Wells*, John Drew's last touring vehicle. In many scenes of that play Miss Helen Gahagan performed twenty feet from my privileged seat, all sparkle and grace, all Edwardian silks and flounces and expanses of snowy bosom and shoulders, mighty and adorable, a true goddess.

There were excitements less dignified than these. In the Sunday supplement of the *Chicago Herald and Examiner*, regular attention in tones of scandal was given to the activities of libertines and chorus girls, Roman orgies of the rich, and at a certain stage these reports with their crude enticing illustrations became something that I waited and looked for, weakly fascinated, vaguely ashamed. Naked girls in champagne baths were a standby of those editors. One Sunday I had this supplement open on the floor in my bedroom while I pored, chin in hand, over the latest champagne-bath story, when a strange sympathetic process took place in my body, and in my disorientation afterward I both knew and did not know that it meant the passing of childhood.

Modest frame houses and lawns were the rule in our neighborhood. The front yard of our house ran thirty feet to a terrace that sloped to the cement sidewalk. Beyond the sidewalk there was again a plot of grass, perhaps four feet wide, bounded by the curb. The walk directly in front of the house divided to pass on either side of a maple tree whose branches shaded the front bedroom windows. On this walk fell tender maple keys in spring and the pointy yellow translucencies of maple leaves in autumn. In midsummer heat waves the light armchairs of wicker or woven straw on the porch would be carried to the lawn after supper and placed to catch any air that stirred, as the locust choir sawed away in the big trees.

The moon always rose over Mr. Brubaker's cornpatch, visible behind his white brick cottage across the street and down the block to the east. Beyond this place ran the Chicago & Alton Railroad tracks, south toward St. Louis and north toward Chicago. Since the crossing was only a few blocks from the C & A station, both incoming and outgoing trains would be going slowly as they passed, their wheels on the rail junctures making a sedate rhythm, clank clank . . . clank clank. Sometimes with hissing of airbrakes and shock of couplings they would halt completely before jerking and moving on, flatcars or box-cars of the east and west — the Pennsylvania Railroad, the New York Central, the Wabash Railroad, the Burlington Route, the Chesapeake & Ohio, the Southern Pacific, the Atchison, Topeka & Santa Fe. When a passenger train went by you could often see, through open side doors of the mail car just behind the engine and coal car, canvas bags on long racks and light-blue-uniformed men sorting mail into them.

Our house was clapboard, painted battleship gray. Of what the gray painting covered there was a revelation one day when men appeared with ladders and removed the paint, waving hoarse torches that blew transparent flame along sections of wall until the old gray coating liquified and could be scraped off with tools like palette knives; then the timber showed through, unevenly toasted, black and brown. Next day the painters on their ladders, dipping brush in pail, drawing brush over pail's lip to measure the saturation, applied fresh gray fluid in long slapping strokes.

Three steps, oblong blocks of cement, went down from the front porch. One step bore the number 215 imprinted in the cement. Be-

tween the ground and the clapboarding of the house proper there was a
wooden lattice perhaps thirty inches high along the front and under the
porch, signifying that the basement did not extend that far. The porch
was not in fact an addition built on to the house but was like an open
front room, not very deep, to the left of the front door; that is, the porch
ceiling made part of the floor of the bedroom above. Going in the front
door you entered a square room, more than a hall, with an armchair to
your left, two glass-enclosed bookcases against the wall behind it, a
short flight of stairs going back to a landing with a window above it in
the left wall, the stairs and banister then proceeding left to right to the
ceiling.

On a table in the crook of the stairs rested telephone and lamp.
There was a sofa beside the table. To the right you entered the parlor,
whose bay windows overlooked the front yard. Also to the right, and to
the rear of the parlor, was the dining room, and, behind swinging
doors, the pantry. The plain kitchen table that stood in the pantry bore
evidence of prolonged and assiduous whittling, as by someone with a lot
to think over slowly — or by someone waiting for work: the initials A L,
very deeply carved. My grandfather had bought this table at auction
when the firm of Lincoln and Herndon was dissolved.

In the parlor against the near wall stood the upright piano, a
Knabe, and piano bench, with a floor lamp beside it. The bay with
three windows, duplicated upstairs in the bedroom where my father
lay, was pretty well filled by a couch. A Persian rug, dark and thick, lay
in the front room, another in the parlor. A fireplace with a small coal
grate, quite superfluous, occupied one corner of the parlor; heat, in
fact, came from a big radiator on the far wall. If you shuffled on the
rug, your index finger, pointed at the radiator, would enjoy the thrill of
a tiny spark before touching. On the parlor rug, on Sunday after Mass,
you could spread out the colored funny papers, the Katzenjammer
Kids and Slim Jim, and tire your elbows reading.

4

In this room my Uncle Ed always gave the hour after dinner to reading
the *Illinois State Register*, the evening paper. Under the center fixture
brightly lit he would sit, neatly folding and refolding the paper, giving
attention to the local news, the business news, and the syndicated col-

umn that he chuckled over and called "Odd McIntyre." His fine profile was Barrymore-like and grave under the thinning hair to which he took military brushes several times a day. Before he came to make a household with his mother and my invalid father, he had managed theaters in Racine and Duluth for the Orpheum Circuit; now he kept up with show business by reading *Variety* every week. He was a valetudinarian who went in for well-cooked vegetables, half rubbers, and long winter underwear woven of silk and wool. Sobriety and skepticism were his style. When I acted up he would treat me to one of his silences, fixing me with his bored blue eyes.

My grandmother favored the morning paper, the *Illinois State Journal*, and always read it slowly after breakfast. She was devoted to a serial story called "The Married Life of Helen and Warren." The thin gold frame of her glasses left a bruised indentation on the soft bridge of her nose. Her soft cheeks were finely wrinkled, sometimes made fragrant by a touch from her powder puff. She remembered that when she was a little girl in Galway her father one day took her on his knee and told her that Mr. Lincoln had been shot. She had a shrewd gray eye and a reputation in the family for being a good businesswoman. On the second or third of the month if Mrs. Brown, the florist, had forgotten her rent, Grandmother would telephone her considerately and send me downtown to collect it among the glassed-in refrigerators and the humid plants. She never ignored an appeal from a mission, so drifts of tawdry holy cards piled up in her desk drawer, and prayers were being offered for her intentions at many far and desolate places.

More than once I happened on what I remember as a kind of ritual encounter in the parlor. My Uncle James has dropped in, between jobs, as so often, and my grandmother is trying to resist an appeal for money. He is pacing back and forth, running his hand through his pompadour; she is seated with lips compressed and distressful breathing. To my mind she is entirely too upset by the plea from her youngest, Jim, who had played baseball at Fordham, who always joked about the Jebbies, who when I was a very small boy had defined "ammunition" for me as buttered toast. "Ma, give me two dollars," he repeats, and he, too, is upset, his ruddy face looks ruddier than usual. It is only two dollars that he always wants, the happy-go-lucky fellow. Is she stingy, is he humiliated? "God have mercy on us all, what will become of us?" she will say in the end, putting two bills in his hand, and off he will go to buy whatever two dollars can buy.

5

At one point or another in the room by the front door, depending on the season and sunniness and time of day, a furry bar of orange and purple light appeared, a treasure without a body, precarious, given to fading. One might not otherwise have noticed the small colored glass panel high in the front window. The bookcases in this room contained all volumes of *The Book of Knowledge*. They also contained novels by men with three names — Albert Payson Terhune, James Oliver Curwood, Edgar Rice Burroughs. Then there were *Rhymes of a Red Cross Man, Dere Mabel*, a book on the Lafayette Escadrille, and *Over the Top*, a book on the British in the trenches by a Yank named Arthur Guy Empey. *Treasure Island, The Adventures of Tom Sawyer*, and *Moby Dick* were there in illustrated editions, and something I soon cared for even more: *Henry Esmond*, closely printed in a cheap yellow binding. The weightiest books were nineteenth-century volumes from my grandfather's library: *The Great Cryptogram*, for example, and *Battle Field and Bivouac*, a narrative of campaigns by the U.S. Cavalry in the 1870s against the Sioux. In this there were photographs of generals, Custer and Crook, and of Indian scouts, and fold-in maps of skirmish points in the Black Hills and on the Great Plains.

In winter, the radiator against the front wall could dry gloves, wet from making snowballs — knit gloves that dried to become themselves and leather gloves that shrank into parched stiff little paws.

The interior world and the outside world greatly differed. Although a matter of a few small rooms, the interior contained the far away and long ago: it contained the voyages of the Pequod and the Hispaniola. Accessible in the interior, to be borrowed for oneself, were Esmond's style and Jim Hawkins' and Ishmael's. Here people took refuge, slept, and dreamed; here they fortified themselves with food and put on their defensive dress, and felt themselves to be most safely what they were, beings with limited needful bodies and frail nagging souls and memories, who depended on one another. Swing a heavy door and step through, and you walked into the large and alien wind, blowing from who knows where over the wild-scented earth and its vegetation, or down paved ways amid strangers. Not to mention the steady wind of time. The house and practically everything in it and all those who lived in it except me have now vanished from the face of the earth, and so have the eight or nine other houses on that block. In their place is a new expensive State building, very glassy, set in broad lawns, and a parking lot on the railroad side.

6

A light-boned boy's metabolism must be nearly as wondrous as that of birds who have so much energy to burn. The excess could not be expended in playgrounds during school recesses but demanded exertion or exploring and roaming, in the great hours After School. During one whole autumn, my friend Dan O'Connell and I would head at four o'clock for a weedy junkyard on the far side of the railroad tracks between Capitol Avenue and Monroe Street, to take possession there of the wreck of a flivver. Dan wore for a time, as I did, a leather cap with ear flaps, shaped like an aviator's helmet. He was lusty and debonair. His favorite chant, which he could make mysteriously brazen or suggestive, was "Ja da, ja da, jada jada jing jing jing." At his father's shoe store on the Court House Square, Dan and I had been privileged one day to see and handle heroic accouterments of the Great War: sheathed in thick military khaki, the bayonet and gas mask that his older brother had brought home from France. The abandoned chassis in the vacant lot became our two-seater pursuit plane, flown on scouting or combat missions above the German lines. It had a machine gun synchronized to shoot through the propeller. When tired of battle in the air, we could go to a movie at one of the second-string movie houses beyond the Square: Bill Hart in a Western, or hairbreadth Harry Houdini sweating through a serial of escapes.

My likeliest companion on the Fourth of July, Halloween, and every day in summer was my near neighbor Henry Barber, a skinny boy, black-haired and brown-eyed, who wore glasses and tooth braces and lived in a big red brick house half a block away. In a darkened room on the south side of the first floor lived Henry's Grandpa, a very old man, white-bearded, with a black silk skull cap, who as Henry Rankin had been an office boy in the firm of Lincoln and Herndon in the 1850s and had written a life of Lincoln. When we were playing in the yard, if Henry went to Grandpa's window and rapped, the old face would appear smiling and the old fingers would push through an aperture in the window sash a card bearing four or five large gray pills. These apparently contained nothing but sugar, and were regarded as a treat both by Grandpa and Henry.

On summer days Henry's mother sometimes hired us to root out dandelions from the lawn. Supplied with paring knives and a bucket, squatting in the grass, we hitched around cross-legged from one dandelion colony to another while swapping the fantasies and conjectures of boyhood. Henry was double-jointed and could do amazing things with his thumbs. Sunny parts of the lawn on a hot day would redden our faces and bedew Henry's upper lip with sweat, but we could always knock off in favor of mumbly-peg in the shade, and there we would rest, jesting and gurgling, filled with tasty hosewater.

In my eighth grade year, in the fall of 1923, when Henry was in the ninth grade or junior high school, he went to a college football game in Urbana. Sitting with me on his front steps next day, he told me of watching the game from a seat almost on a level with the players and close enough to see how gigantic they were. "Here was the calf of this guy's leg," he said, "like this"—and he made a hoop with his arms to show the girth, bigger around than he was. We were, just the same, getting big enough to foresee being really big, and for my birthday that fall I received my first regulation football.

Flat in its box lay the heavy pigskin with a hard pebbly surface, tan, unmarred, and clean, giving off a strong leather smell. Into it you were to fit the smooth stout rubber bladder, with its tube sticking out of the aperture. Then the rawhide lace would be passed in loose loops through the eyelets and the serrated tip of a football pump pushed and turned to the sticking point in the tube. As you pumped, the football filled and hardened until you could force no more air into it. Pinching the tube then, you withdrew the pump, folded the tube over and tied it with a doubled and redoubled rubber band before shoving it under the edge of distended leather and pulling the lace tight, its superfluous length tucked back under the crisscrossing.

With my heel I dented the ground beside the mulberry sapling on the left side of the front yard and placed the ball with one nose in the dent and the other in the air at a slight angle backward. Measuring a few steps behind the expectant ball, I loped forward to the place kick. If squarely booted in the right spot, the ball would soar away, on a trajectory rising twenty or thirty degrees, end over end in a backward tumble, crossing the street and dropping on the terrace or lawn opposite, a flight of perhaps forty yards. I practiced this time and again.

I also practiced the dropkick, a synchronized movement in which only two steps were taken as the ball, held well forward, was dropped and the kick executed just as it hit the ground. Had not Charley Brickley of Harvard dropkicked goals from midfield? Punting was another matter. For a punt you set the ball afloat high in front of you and kicked it in the air, on your whole instep, making a louder sound, a "boom" in the language of the sports writers. What you hoped for was a high, spiraling flight, giving your tacklers time to get downfield. I practiced punting in the middle of the street to keep away from the trees on either side. By practice I thought I would acquire prowess. At twelve, at thirteen, at fourteen, my tradition told me that what counted was not inborn ability but training and guts and a certain magic of equipment. I had a book on football by a man named Daly who had coached at West Point. "Football is war," he said, and roused me. "Go out there to fight and keep it up all afternoon."

The following year I was taken to see the Michigan-Illinois game, pitting a famous passing quarterback, Benny Friedman, against a famous broken-field runner, Red Grange. I saw two masses of giant heroes, regularly forming and breaking into melee on the gray November field. On end sweeps to the right three powerful blockers ran low ahead of Grange with his piston-driving stride, and all three most often hurled themselves one after another in vain against the Michigan left end, a towering Swede named Benny Oosterbahn, who, striving with great hands, would put them all aside and snag the runner.

On some Sunday afternoons when for one reason or another nothing athletic was afoot — no tennis, no biking, no sledding, no company — I might have liked to stick with my book, whatever it might be; but my father's program for me called for an hour outdoors, even in the dead of winter. I owned, and favored, a soft camel's hair cap that in zero weather could be pulled down over mouth and chin, leaving an opening for nose and eyes. In this, and in mackinaw and gloves and overshoes if needed, I stepped out on winter Sundays for exercise: if the front walk needed shoveling, for that. Once while I was banging away with a sharp spade at an ice crust, a very tall, very stately and stooped old man in overshoes and a fur cap came by and smiled at me as I stood aside for his careful steps. He had long drooping moustaches, perfectly white. When I came in, my father, who from his bedroom window had seen the old man approach, said he was De Witt Smith, and that as a boy he had been a muleteer on the Santa Fe Trail.

More often, my exercise consisted of a two-mile walk. I would turn south on Second Street and keep a steady pace past Edwards, Cook, Lawrence, Canady, Scarritt, toward South Grand Avenue. Few walkers or cars broke the stillness, only my own feet crunching or scuffing. If any wind blew, nose and cheeks would feel it and after a while, from numbness, would feel less. The low sun shone overhead on creaking elm and maple boughs. On South Grand Avenue I would walk eastward to Fifth or Sixth Street, then turn again left and northward on the return leg, down streets even quieter and more deserted, passing now several dark mansions of an older day, mansarded and turreted, deep on barren snow-sheeted lawns with fountain bowls and stained figures of nymphs or stags. You could see for a long way through the open winter vistas of bare trees.

In the course of this walk one afternoon I suffered, very suddenly, an entirely new sense of everything. I found myself unfamiliar. Nothing that I saw in this condition seemed familiar. Dimensions were felt to be arbitrary and precarious: the many trees, near and far, looked both like trees and like bunches of twigs fixed in the ground. It was as though the world had been made, or remade, in that instant: space, light, surfaces, bodies, all breathless with coming-to-be. Everything had become pure spectacle, subject to an unformulated but dazzling question: why all this, instead of nothing at all? The walker had become pure witness, disburdened of every interest and even every sensation but the overwhelming one of being there. And yet everything existed tenuously, as though it might as well not. I finished my walk; the strangeness faded; I said nothing; workaday facts remained unchanged. But once and for all they had been called in question.

John Fowles as The Ebony Tower

John Sokol © 1981

Wistman's Wood

John Fowles

Antaeus is distinguished for its publishing of original writing, and I feel a bit of a cheat in sending something that has already been published (in a book called *The Tree*, inspired by the work of the distinguished French-Hungarian photographer, Frank Horvat). But it is the nearest I have got, suspect will ever get, to a brink most writers sooner or later discover on the edge of their universe — where words end. To be more exact, where the gap between what one is trying to say and the words one has to say it with becomes so great that wisdom must be silence. I do not regard this as tragic, but simply in the nature of things; as it is in nature itself and our relations with it. For me Wistman's Wood stands, among other things, for any fictional text also. Somewhere one must always in the end leave it, failed; but at least knowing that having failed is a universe better than never having gone, or returned, in the first place.

JOHN FOWLES

We park by a solitary row of granite buildings. To the east and behind it is a small half-hidden valley with two tall silent chimneys and a dozen or so ruined stone sheds scattered about a long meadow through which a stream runs. The valley is bowered, strangely in this most desolate of Southern English landscapes, by beech trees. Its ruins are now almost classical in their simplicity and seeming antiquity — and one is truly old, a medieval clapper bridge, huge slabs of rock spanning the little stream. But the rest were not designed, nor the beeches planted, to be picturesque. In Victorian times gunpowder for quarry-blasting was made and stored here. The stone sheds and chimneys were scattered, the trees introduced, the remote site itself picked, for purely safety reasons. Most contemporary visitors to Powder Mill Farm, on the southern fringe of the barren, treeless wastes of northern Dartmoor, are industrial archaeologists, summoned by this absurdly — in regard to its former use — Arcadian and bosky little valley behind. But we are here for something far more ancient and less usual still.

We set off north-west across an endless fen and up towards a distant line of tors, grotesque outcrops of weather-worn granite. Though it is mid-June, the tired grass is still not fully emerged from its winter sleep; and the sky is tired, a high grey canopy, with no wind to shift or break it. What flowers there are, yellow stars of tormentil, blue and dove-grey sprays of milkwort, the delicate lilac of the marsh violet in the bogs, are tiny and sparse. Somewhere in the dark and uninhabited uplands to the north a raven snores. I search the sky, but it is too far off to be seen.

We cross a mile of this dour wasteland, then up a steep hillside, through a gap in an ancient sheep-wall, and still more slope to climb; and come finally to a rounded ridge that leads north to an elephantine tower, a vast turd of primary rock, Longford Tor. At our feet another bleak valley, then a succession, as far as the eye can see, of even bleaker tor-studded skylines and treeless moorland desert. My wife tells me I must have the wrong place, and nothing in the landscape denies her. I do, but not with total conviction. It is at least thirty years since I was last in this part of the Moor.

We walk down the convex slope before us, into the bleak valley, and I begin to think that it must indeed be the wrong place. But then suddenly, like a line of hitherto concealed infantry, huddled under the steepest downward fall of the slope near the bottom, what we have come for emerges from the low grass and ling: a thin, broken streak of tree-tops, a pale arboreal surf. For me this secret wood, perhaps the strangest in all Britain, does not really rise like a line of infantry. It rises like a ghost.

I can't now remember the exact circumstances of the only other time I saw it, except that it must have been late in 1946, when I was a lieutenant of marines in a camp on the edge of Dartmoor. This was not part of our training area, and I can't have been on duty. It was winter, there was ice in the air and a clinging mist, and I was alone. I think I had been walking somewhere else, trying to shoot snipe, and had merely made a last-minute detour to see the place, perhaps to orient myself.

At least it lived up to the reputation that I had once heard a moorland farmer give it: some tale of an escaped prisoner from Princetown a few miles away found frozen to death there — or self-hanged, I forget. But it had no need of that kind of black embroidery. It was forlorn, skeletal, almost malevolent — distinctly eerie, even though I am not a superstitious person and solitude in nature has never frightened me one-tenth as much as solitude in cities and houses. It simply felt a bad place, not one to linger in, and I did not go into the trees; and I had never gone back to it, though often enough on Dartmoor, till this day. In truth I had forgotten about it, in all those intervening years, until I began writing about my father and his suspicion of the wild. One day then its memory mysteriously surged, as it surges itself from the moorland slope, out of nowhere. Its name is Wistman's Wood.

I do not know who Wistman was—whether he was some ancient owner or whether the word derives from the old Devonshire dialect word *wisht*, which means melancholy and uncanny, wraithlike; and which lies behind one of Conan Doyle's most famous tales. There would never have been a hound of the Baskervilles, were it not for the much older Wisht Hounds of Dartmoor legend.

Wistman's Wood may be obscurely sited, but it is no longer, as it was in the 1940s, obscurely known. The rise of ecology has seen to that. In scientific terms it is an infinitely rare fragment of primeval forest, from some warmer phase of world climate, that has managed to cling on—though not without some remarkable adaptations—in this inhospitable place; and even more miraculously managed to survive the many centuries of human depredation of anything burnable on the Moor. Culturally it is comparable with a great Neolithic site: a sort of Avebury of the tree, an *Ur*-wood. Physically it is a half-mile chain of copses splashed, green drops in a tachist painting, along what on Dartmoor they call a clitter, a broken debris of granite boulders—though not at all on true tachist principle, by chance. These boulders provide the essential protection for seedlings against bitter winter winds and grazing sheep. But the real ecological miracle of Wistman's Wood is botanical. Its dominant species, an essentially lowland one, should not really be here at all, and is found at this altitude in only one other, and Irish, site in the British Isles. Here and there in the wood are a scatter of mountain ashes, a few hollies. But the reigning tree is the ancient king of all our trees: *Quercus robur*, the Common, or English, Oak.

We go down, to the uppermost brink. Names, science, history . . . not even the most adamantly down-to-earth botanist thinks of species and ecologies when he or she first stands at Wistman's Wood. It is too strange for that. The normal full-grown height of the common oak is thirty to forty metres. Here the very largest, and even though they are centuries old, rarely top five metres. They are just coming into leaf, long after their lowland kin, in every shade from yellow-green to bronze. Their dark branches grow to an extraordinary extent laterally;

are endlessly angled, twisted, raked, interlocked, and reach quite as much downwards as upwards. These trees are inconceivably different from the normal habit of their species, far more like specimens from a natural bonzai nursery. They seem, even though the day is windless, to be writhing, convulsed, each its own Laocoön, caught and frozen in some fanatically private struggle for existence.

The next thing one notices is even more extraordinary, in this Ice Age environment. It is a paradoxically tropical quality, for every lateral branch, fork, saddle of these aged dwarfs is densely clothed in other plants—not just the tough little polypodies of most deciduous woodlands, but large, elegantly pluming male ferns; whortleberry beds, grasses, huge cushions of moss and festoons of lichen. The clitter of granite boulders, bare on the windswept moors, here provides a tumbling and chaotic floor of moss-covered mounds and humps, which add both to the impression of frozen movement and to that of an astounding internal fertility, since they seem to stain the upward air with their vivid green. This floor like a tilted emerald sea, the contorted trunks, the interlacing branches with their luxuriant secondary aerial gardens . . . there is only one true epithet to convey the first sight of Wistman's Wood, even today. It is fairy-like. It corresponds uncannily with the kind of setting artists like Richard Dadd imagined for that world in Victorian times and have now indelibly given it: teeming, jewel-like, self-involved, rich in secrets just below the threshold of our adult human senses.

We enter. The place has an intense stillness, as if here the plant side of creation rules and even birds are banned; below, through the intricate green gladelets and branch-gardens, comes the rush of water in a moorland stream, one day to join the sea far to the south. This water-noise, like the snore of the raven again, the breeding-trill of a distant curlew, seems to come from another world, once one is inside the wood. There are birds, of course . . . an invisible hedgesparrow, its song not lost here, as it usually is, among all the sounds of other common garden birds, nor lost in its own ubiquity in Britain; but piercing and peremptory, individual, irretrievable; even though, a minute later, we hear its *prestissimo* bulbul shrill burst out again. My wood, my wood, it never shall be yours.

Parts of all the older trees are dead and decayed, crumbling into humus, which is why, together with the high annual humidity, they carry their huge sleeves of ferns and other plants. Some are like loose brassards and can be lifted free and replaced. The only colour not green or bronze or russet, not grey trunk or rich brown of the decaying wood, are tiny rose-pink stem-beads, future apples where some gall-wasp has laid its eggs on a new shoot. But it is the silence, the waitingness of the place, that is so haunting; a quality all woods will have on occasion, but which is overwhelming here—a drama, but of a time-span humanity cannot conceive. A pastness, a presentness, a skill with tenses the writer in me knows he will never know; partly out of his own inadequacies, partly because there are tenses human language has yet to invent.

We drift from copse to copse. One to the south is now fenced off by the Nature Conservancy to see what effect keeping moorland sheep, bullocks, and wild ponies from grazing will have. It has a much denser growth at ground level, far more thickety, and is perhaps what the wood would have looked like centuries ago, before stock was widely run on the Moor; and yet now seems artificial—scientifically necessary, aesthetically less pleasing, less surreal, historically less honest beside the still open wood, "gardened" by what man has introduced. There is talk now of wiring off the whole wood like this, reserving it from the public, as at Stonehenge. Returning, we come on two hikers, rucksacks beside them, lying on their backs inside the trees, like two young men in a trance. They do not speak to us, nor we to them. It is the place, wanting it to oneself, and I am prey to their same feeling. I persuade my wife to start the long climb back. I will catch up.

I go alone to the most detached and isolated of the copses, the last and highest, to the north. It grows in a small natural amphitheatre, and proves to be the most luxuriant, intricate, and greenly beautiful of the chain. I sit in its silence, beneath one of its most contorted trees, a patriarchal gnome-oak. The botanist in me notices a colony of wood-rush, like a dark green wheat among the emerald clitter; then the delicate climbing fumitory *Corydalis claviculata*, with its maidenhair-fern leaves and greenish-white flowers. A not uncommon plant where I live in Dorset; yet now it seems like the hedgesparrow's song, hyperdistinct, and also an epitome, a quintessence of all my past findings and knowledge of it; as with the oaks it grows beneath, subsuming all other oaks. I remember another corydalis, *bulbosa*, that they still grow in the garden at Uppsala in honour of the great man who named the genus.

From somewhere outside, far above, on top of Longford Tor, I hear human voices. Then silence again. The wood waits, as if its most precious sap were stillness. I ask why I, of a species so incapable of stillness, am here.

I think of the photographer Frank Horvat, of a recent afternoon we spent together discussing our shared love of trees, then photography in general and his eminently French and lucid philosophy of it. I envied him a little, out of my own constantly shifting and confused feelings about my own art; as dense and raveled as this wood, always beyond my articulation or rational comprehension, perhaps because I know I came to writing through nature, or exile from it, far more than by innate gift. I think of my father and, wrily, of why I should for so many years have carried such a bad, unconsciously repressing mental image of Wistman's Wood — some part or branch of him I had never managed to prune out. It is incomprehensible now, before such inturned peace, such profound harmlessness, otherness, selflessness, such unusing . . . all words miss, I know I cannot describe it. A poet once went near, though in another context: *the strange phosphorus of life, nameless under an old misappellation.*

So I sit in the namelessness, the green phosphorus of the tree, surrounded by impenetrable misappellations. I came here really only to be sure; not to describe it, since I cannot, or only by the misappellations; to be sure that what I have written is not all lucubration, study dream, *in vitro*, as epiphytic upon reality as the ferns on the branches above my head.

It, this namelessness, is beyond our science and our arts because its secret is being, not saying. Its greatest value to us is that it cannot be reproduced, that this being can be apprehended only by other present being, only by the living senses and consciousness. All experience of it through surrogate and replica, through selected image, gardened word, through other eyes and minds, betrays or banishes its reality. But this is nature's consolation, its message, and well beyond the Wistman's Wood of its own strict world. It can be known and entered only by each, and in its now; not by you through me, by any you through any me; only by you through yourself, or me through myself. We still have this to learn: the inalienable otherness of each, human and non-human, which may seem the prison of each, but is at heart, in the deepest of those countless million metaphorical trees for which we cannot see the wood, both the justification and the redemption.

I turned to look back, near the top of the slope. Already Wistman's Wood was gone, sunk beneath the ground again; already no more than another memory trace, already becoming an artefact, a thing to use. An end to this, dead retting of its living leaves.

Gail Godwin as Violet Clay

John Sokol © *1981*

Gail Godwin

My Face

The day has turned out well. More importantly for our purposes, so has my hair. Some years ago I stopped trying to subdue it into the current fashion, and it has since rewarded me by catching the light and air and using them to frame my face for command performances like today.

The photographer arrives on the noon bus and wants to begin work right away. Out of a cleverly packed kit he brings forth cameras, lights, meters, a tripod, and even a white umbrella. During a session of warm-up shots I pose self-consciously on a chaise longue while he tells me how he went to photograph Auden once and, after only two frames, the great poet rose and said, "All right. That's enough, young man."

"Oh God!" I cry, forgetting "my face" for a few seconds. "What did you do?"

"I was lucky that day. Words saved me. I said, 'But Mr. Auden, in my profession I don't get a chance to revise.' He looked at me for a minute and then said, 'All right,' and sat down again. The only trouble was, he sat down too fast and fell off the chair. But we did some good pictures, and after the session was over he said, 'If you'll come back again, young man, I'll cook you a chicken dinner.'"

I move to my desk, to recline against the deluxe sprawl of my new IBM and the fading rhododendron blossoms outside the window. The photographer has set up a spotlight and opens the white umbrella. The combination, he explains, makes the face soak up the light. It "fills out the face" with a youthful luminosity. If the need ever arises, he tells me, I can substitute a piece of white poster paper. "Put it on a surface just below your face and it will send up the light in a nice way."

Last week a different photographer walked me into the woods and told me to get comfortable on a rock I had sat down on, in a patch of dappled shade. She retreated on tiptoe and lurked some distance away where she crouched and *waited*, like a nature lover stalking a shy animal. The woods grew still. My hair engaged in a little dance with the breeze. A gnat cruised loudly past my face. What is she waiting for,

I thought, watching the face of the photographer. She pursed her lips, she hummed to herself, she smiled mysteriously, she squinted her eyes. I grew almost bored. Then I relaxed and began thinking my own thoughts. Click, she went then. Click. Click.

This photographer stands on a chair behind the white umbrella and asks: "When do you look most like you *like* to look?"

And I think of myself, alone sometimes in this house, how I'll take little intermissions at the bathroom mirror, arranging my face until it suits me. There *is* a look I like. But has anybody ever seen it? If someone did, would that person say, "Ah, what an interesting woman," or, if he/she knew me, "Ah, yes, that's Gail." Or: "Why is that woman posing?" Or: "Why on earth is Gail making that strange face?"

One time, when I was little, I was watching my mother put the finishing touches on the face she was taking out into the world that day. Suddenly I saw her mirror image compose itself into a frightening look. Her eyes widened and gazed into some sorrowful romantic distance; her nostrils dilated; her full lips spread into a weird close-mouthed smile. I knew that, to her, this was her favorite image of herself; I could tell by a kind of relaxed triumph that came over her. "Stop that!" I cried. "Stop looking like that," for, as long as she did, my mother was lost to me.

As I think these thoughts, the photographer who evoked them with his question takes about a dozen pictures. Later, when I am going over his contacts, I search in vain for my secret favorite look that I have been able to create at the bathroom mirror. What did I expect: that he would be able to evoke the look by getting me to *recall* the look? There are other looks — by which I mean acceptable versions of my face — but I don't see that one. Or perhaps it's there, but it looks different turned around. After all, the mirror shows us the reverse of the self others see. Stand in front of the mirror with someone whose face you know well. His face in the mirror will not look quite the same. It may even look strange to you. Yet this is the face he sees every day. What would be strange for him would be to see his face as *you* see it at its most familiar.

It is not because I am beautiful, or notorious, or even because my face is unusual, that two professional photographers have chosen to ride four hours on the bus, at their own expense, to imprint its image on a dozen rolls of film. No, it is merely because I am an American author soon to have another book published.

I don't know exactly when this practice began of making the contemporary writer a visual object, but it has occurred during my lifetime. During my youthful reading, I rarely knew what the writers looked like—except for the highly visible Hemingway, with his white beard and bare, stocky chest. There was still, I recall, a certain impish elusiveness about writers. They effaced themselves from your imagination, leaving the field free for their characters and *their* stories. As late as 1970, when my first novel was being published and the editor called to ask did I want my picture on the jacket, I replied at once, "Oh, I don't think *my picture* will help the book." I distinctly remember feeling that I would forfeit some of the mystery of a new fictional voice if my face appeared on the book.

My face did not appear on my second novel, either. This novel was about a beautiful woman, so beautiful that stronger, unbeautiful people need her for their various purposes and thus make her their prisoner. The cover artist wisely chose not to depict the particular face of any beautiful woman. If my face had appeared on the back of the book, some skeptical reader might surely have inquired: "What does *she* know about the problems of being extraordinarily beautiful?"

At the editor's suggestion, my third novel did carry my photograph. I was a little disappointed at the one he chose from the contact sheets, but he seemed to feel it would "go well with the book." The heroine of that novel was a woman of 32, intelligent, romantic, and insecure. When she catches a glimpse of her face in a tilted mirror above her beautiful grandmother's coffin, it shocks her. ("It always did when she faced a mirror unexpectedly. It was too alert, too tense, too transparent in what its owner felt.") The photo the editor chose was that of an intelligent-looking woman in her thirties with a closed mouth that stops just short of a smile; she has large, rather dreamy eyes, but their effect is diminished by the pronounced worry line that slashes her brow. My mother hated that picture; she couldn't understand why I would allow anyone to publish a picture that "makes you look old, and not even pretty." The picture startled her: in it, her daughter was lost to her.

Though I have learned not to agonize every time I come across some face of mine that fails to do justice to my wit, charm, and profundity, I still harbor a deep desire for invisibility. In my second novel, Francesca, the beautiful woman, goes to work briefly as the amanuensis (really the cleaning girl) for the ugly "M," a writer who has shaved her head. "M" tells Francesca that she shaved her head so that she would stop looking in the mirror and notice more things about the world.

What "M" meant, of course, was that for an artist there is great value in being invisible. Only when you can stop looking at yourself do you become capable of filling other bodies. Keats, praising this trait in Shakespeare, called it Negative Capability.

Yet, in our present-day literary culture, so very visual and star-struck, we have come to expect the face as part of the fare. So accustomed are we to a novelist's or poet's physiognomy that we may even catch ourselves thinking of the face itself as author of the book; never mind that the face, whatever its lineaments, often distracts, distorts, raises false hopes, or otherwise undermines the fiction or poetry. (It is symptomatic of a monumental distraction when a *New York Times* reviewer squanders five out of eleven paragraphs discussing the face of the author on the back of the novel he is supposed to be reviewing, and then digresses further into a mini-essay about jacket photos.)

And one wonders what Jane Austen's comments might have been, had she looked down from Writers' Heaven several months ago and observed the confusion attendant on a paperback release of her early writings. In the first place, she might not have been all that pleased to have her juvenilia published; in the second place, there is her *name*—she who always signed her works "by A Lady"; in the third place, there is a *picture of the author*, in a little oval vignette, above the title, *Love and Freindship* (sic) . . . but wait a moment, who *is* this beautiful, full-bosomed woman in her low-cut gown? One thing for certain: It's not our Jane. But it took the president of the Jane Austen Society to point this out to the embarrassed publisher, who then tracked the error down to the New York Public Library. Which had been housing an incorrectly labeled impostress in Jane's file: a portrait of Sarah Austin, a nineteenth-century translator. (Now plain Jane, thin lips pursed, wearing her house cap and high-necked frock, has been instated in her rightful place; but one wonders about that filing error: wishful thinking on somebody's part? After all, Jane has turned out to be a star, and oughtn't a star to look like that pretty lady in the low dress?)

It is time to go through my contact sheets and select one image of myself to appear on the back of my new novel and another image to serve as my "publicity" photo. As I crouch, with magnifying glass over these myriad me's, ruminations and emotions as varied as the poses play through my mind.

1. Would even Lord Byron have been able to face his contact sheets without spasms of self-loathing?

2. A quote from a painter in my fourth novel: "They say people make their faces after a certain age, but it is also true that before a certain age people's faces help to make them." If, as a teen-ager, I had had my decade's version of, say, Brooke Shields' face, what would I be doing today? Beautiful faces effortlessly open the secrets of other hearts and minds. An alternative route to these secrets — which I always knew I wanted — is via the effort of imagination. If you are beautiful, the world comes to you; but if you have imagination, you can summon the world.

3. Only once in my life has my face opened doors. This was when my favorite uncle William lay dying in the hospital. An extremely popular figure in the community, his room was being besieged by friends, acquaintances, old girlfriends, highway patrolmen, preachers, other judges and lawyers, and a few curiosity seekers. The doctor gave orders that no one but family (and the Reigning Girlfriend) be admitted, and then only for brief sessions. All who were admitted had to be screened by the nurse on duty at the time. But never I. "You can go on in," all the nurses who had never seen me before would say, "anyone can see *you're* one of them."

I have the Godwin face. I have many of my mother's expressions (her sad-romantic gaze; her "polite" look, which is an incongruous combination of silly, pursed mouth and wide, furious eyes; her weird, close-mouthed smile and flaring nostrils when she is being beautiful), but it is the face of my father's family, his lineal features that I see in my photographs — just as, sometimes amused, sometimes alarmed, I see myself in old photographs of his family. There is a sister, in her eighties now, whose girlhood snapshots could pass for some of mine, and, what is even more scary, I have only to sit beside her — queenly, sarcastic old doyen — at a family reunion, and have a preview of myself, at age eighty-three, holding court, as she answers questions about her house ("Yes, it's on the market, but so far nobody's been able to afford it"), accepts compliments on her daughter's food ("Well of course Christine's table is full of good things; she learned *something* at my house") and on her own skin ("Yes, I've got the pure Powell skin of our mother's family; poor Mose and William got the old sallow Godwin skin.") As I watch her (just now an obsequious cousin has flung himself to his knees beside her and cries, "Hail, Matriarch!") I think: well, I have the nice Powell skin, too, and I also have the large, slashed brow and forehead that will soon make the top part of my face look like a *patriarch*, as hers does now; and I, too, have the long, heavy cheeks that are one day going to shake like an angry bulldog's when I'm on my soapbox, but she *has* lasted (as I intend to), and she still works every day (as I intend to), and she does add to a party (as I hope I shall, at her age).

4. A quote from my heroine's friend in my third novel: "You are the type of person who will never be able to see your own face. Your face is a series of impressions, of moods. It will always give more pleasure to others than to yourself."

5. An unvoiced expletive as I X out with a black crayon a certain frame. ("P.S. If there are any frames that you would not like to be seen, please X out on contact sheet," the Photographer-with-the-White-Umbrella has instructed.) Oh, Thomas Pynchon was so shrewd! But it is too late for me to refuse to pose, to steal my image back from old high school files. It is too late for me to be the wise, invisible genie-author, laughing over the reader's shoulder.

I will also never look like a star. (If my work should last, what high-cheekboned, swan-necked, smooth-browed impostress will some visual idealist sneak into my file?) What many a reader will see while reading my books is—let's face it—a younger version of Aunt Thelma posing as my mother. All I can do, at this stage, is to be myself (so the encroaching old face will at least signify the intrinsic me) and to use the black crayon when it is offered: try not to be caught in public with my eyes squeezed shut, with a drink in my hand, or simpering like a fool.

6. A frequent quote from my grandmother: "Fools' names and fools' faces are often seen in public places."

Though the writer in me aspires to the invisibility that will grant me the freedom to imagine myself into anybody, to become Nobody watching and describing the parade of life, the egoist in me hankers for that instant, visible glamour which reveals me a Somebody the moment I enter a room. And, to a degree, the American consumer in me retains a childlike faith in the miracle-working properties of products which, if dotted at the strategic pulse points, thrown across the shoulder or buttoned or belted in the latest fashion, or slathered on my pure Powell skin, will make a roomful of strangers stand up and chant in chorus: "Who *is* that woman who just came in?"

At home alone with my muse, I wear a uniform of old tan corduroys with the wales rubbed smooth, and any old sweater or shirt. But when I go into the city, I start worrying the day before about how to dress that woman who will always startle me from at least one plate-glass window. One day, I keep vowing, when I have purchased all the right things, I will be able to see Somebody striding along beside me in that window and glimpse at last a glamorous version of myself.

Like the majority of people, my attitude towards my looks wobbles wildly between vanity and despair. But, providentially, my vocation always saves me. In my study, I am invisible. I'm a free-floating consciousness able to go anywhere and see anything without being observed in return. Even when I'm thinking well or lost in the contemplation of other lives, I am temporarily "refined out of existence."

Not long ago, in a moment of anxious vanity ("If I start *today*, I can keep what I have") I sent off to California for an eighteen-dollar book on face-lifting through exercise. ("For women and men over twenty-one," the tactful subhead explained.) Back came a pink volume weighing several pounds and sealed in plastic. I tore off the plastic, read the grudging praise of a prominent plastic surgeon (after all, this book was going to take away some of his business, wasn't it?), and began leafing through the exercises, turning first to my "trouble spots": LOWER CHEEKS, JOWLS, SCOWL.

I began to despair. Knowing my aversion to boredom and routine, could I count on myself to devote fifteen minutes a day for the rest of my life to making faces at myself in a mirror?

Furthermore, it seemed that, to do these exercises properly *and safely*, I would have to order more stuff: the author's patented exercise cream, to keep from pulling the skin out of shape; a pair of special cosmetic gloves to keep my fingers from slipping on the cream; and a little spatula-like implement to provide "cheek resistance" for the cheek exercises.

Knowing, at this point, that I would probably never open this book again, I transferred my interest to the one really ghoulish aspect of the book and lost myself in its contemplation. On each page where the pretty model was doing her exercise to iron out crows' feet, guard against turkey neck, or restore youthful fullness to the lips, there was an inset of an older woman's face — rather, that part of her face that was in shambles because she had failed to do this particular exercise.

The photos were all of the same poor woman, and I found myself imagining her life. Who was she? (I should point out that she was not grotesque; if you saw her on the street, if you noticed her at all, you would think: just a plain woman, late sixties/early seventies, who hasn't had an interesting life or taken very good care of herself.) But how had she come to lend her face to these pictures? Did anyone tell her beforehand, "You are going to represent the face women don't want to have"? Was she paid well? More money, or less, than the pretty model? Did they just pick her off the street (a California bag lady, glad for the cash), or was she, perhaps, a very well-to-do model whose speciality was admonitory photographs? Was she — it was possible — *the author's mother*? ("Hey, Mom, I have a terrific proposition for you. It will benefit thousands of women, put bucks into our joint account, and you and I will always know I *love* your dear face just the way it is.")

Where was "I" at this moment? Somewhere in California, in a room I was beginning to furnish. Where was the American female, fourth decade, of the incipient bulldog demeanor? Invisible.

I watched Bill Moyers interviewing Dame Rebecca West, age 89, at her home in London. Before and during the interview, the network flashed portraits and photographs of the author in her earlier incarnations: baby sister, young militant, companion of H. G. Wells, banker's wife, woman of accomplishment receiving her honor from the Queen. In all of these stills, you could trace a family resemblance, a continuity-in-retrospect, to the living female Knight on the screen, in her long gown and her pearl choker which tugged at her neck like a self-imposed leash. She was "being good" tonight, but not too good. She made the camera wait while she took her time formulating her answers or remembering the past; she exerted no effort to impress, she even went so far as to demur, or agree politely, if the interviewer switched topics suddenly, or put words into her mouth. She seemed, much of the time, to have become invisible to herself: she was just one big, fluid, rapid mind browsing confidently among whatever ideas were put before her. At one point, because she is hard of hearing, she *lunged* towards Moyers to catch the tail end of his remark, and — for a second — her large head was transformed into a lionlike figure: she became visually, on camera, a sort of mythical beast, heraldic of her accumulated strengths.

Since then, I have been planning *my* heraldic visage; it's much more fun than doing the exercises in the pink book. I've been imagining little scenarios to go with my eighty-year-old mastiff-face. Here is one:

I will have worked very hard at my craft, and because its attendant exercises in Negative Capability have become the priority of my life, I will have rendered myself invisible to me (for large portions of a given day) and visible to others in the various guises they will create for me. To some, I will be a wrinkled old lady (but not as wrinkled as Auden, if I keep using my creams); but to those who see me as a Lady of Letters, my face will have become emblematic of my style ("Don't you just love the thoughts that roam that gashed forehead of hers? And the way her cheeks *quiver* with sensitivity or *rumble* with a wicked wit!")

When the young photographers come, one of them will be after a certain distinctive pouch nobody has quite done justice to on film; another will try to make me shut my eyes or giggle and spill my drink; while another, aspiring to Mythical Photography, will wait for the appearance of my beast in the lens.

I will pose some, wearing a gown of lavender-gray (no jewelry), and reclining among my books and memory artifacts on some dramatic but comfy piece of furniture. One owes an audience a few stage props.

I will get rid of the boring ones quickly by a polite sarcasm or succinct withdrawal of my Presence. ("You look *tired*, young woman." "That will do, young man.")

But if they are swift-witted and charming and very agreeable to me, I will let them tarry while I ruminate aloud, until, through the fissures and gravitational drifts of my old face, they can glimpse the shapes and visions behind it.

I may write something sweet into the flyleaf of one of my books for them. And invite them to stay for supper.

Nadine Gordimer as The Conservationist

John Sokol © 1981

Nadine Gordimer

The Bolter and the Invincible Summer

My writing life began long before I left school, and I began to leave school (frequently) long before the recognised time came, so there is no real demarcation, for me, between school and "professional" life. The quotes are there because I think of professional life as something one enters by way of an examination, not as an obsessional occupation like writing for which you provide your own, often extraordinary or eccentric, qualifications as you go along. And I'm not flattered by the idea of being presented with a "profession," *honoris causa;* every honest writer or painter wants to achieve the impossible and needs no minimum standard laid down by an establishment such as a profession.

This doesn't mean that I think a writer doesn't need a good education in general, and that I don't wish I had had a better one. But maybe my own regrets arise out of the common impulse to find a justification, outside the limits of one's own talent, for the limits of one's achievement.

I was a bolter, from kindergarten age, but unlike most small children rapidly accustoming their soft, round selves to the sharp angles of desks and discipline, I went on running away from school, year after year. I was a day scholar at a convent in the Transvaal goldmining town where we lived and when I was little I used to hide until I heard the hive of voices start up "Our Father" at prayers, and then I would walk out of the ugly iron gates and spend the morning on the strip of open veld that lay between the township where the school was and the township where my home was. I remember catching white butterflies there, all one summer morning, until, in the quiet when I had no shadow, I heard the school bell, far away, clearly, and I knew I could safely appear at home for lunch. When I was a little older, I took refuge for hours in the lavatory block, waiting in the atmosphere of Jeyes' Fluid for my opportunity to escape. By then I no longer lived from moment to moment, and could not enjoy the butterflies; the past, with the act of running away contained in it, and the future, containing discovery and punishment, made freedom impossible; the act of seizing it was merely a desperate gesture.

What the gesture meant, I don't know. I managed my school work easily; among the girls of the class I had the sort of bossy vitality that makes for popularity; yet I was overcome, from time to time, by what I now can at least label as anxiety states. Speculation about their cause hasn't much place here, which is lucky, for the people who were around me then are still alive. Autobiography can't be written until one is old, can't hurt anyone's feelings, can't be sued for libel, or, worse, contradicted.

There is just one curious aspect of my bolting that seems worth mentioning because it reveals a device of the personality that, beginning at that very time, perhaps, as a dream-defence, an escape, later became the practical subconscious cunning that enabled me to survive and grow in secret while projecting a totally different, camouflage image of myself. I ran away from school; yet there was another school, the jolly, competitive, thrillingly loyal, close-knit world of schoolgirl books, to which I longed to belong. (At one time I begged to go to boarding school, believing, no doubt, that I should find it there.) Of course, even had it existed, that "School Friend" world would have been the last place on earth for me. I should have found there, far more insistently, the walls, the smell of serge and floor polish, the pressure of uniformity and the tyranny of bell-regulated time that set off revolt and revulsion in me. What I did not know—and what a child never knows—is that there is more to the world than what is offered to him; more choices than those presented to him; more kinds of people than those (the only ones he knows) to which he feels but dares not admit he does not belong. I thought I *had* to accept school and the attitudes there that reflected the attitudes of home; therefore, in order to be a person I had to have *some* sort of picture of a school that would be acceptable to me—it didn't seem possible to live without it. The English novelist Stevie Smith once wrote that all children should be told of the possibility of committing suicide, to console them in case they believed there was no way out of the unbearable; it would be less dramatic but far more consoling if a child could be told that there is an aspect of himself he *does not know is permissible*.

The conclusion my bolting school drew from the grown-ups around me was that I was not the studious type and simply should be persuaded to reconcile myself to the minimum of learning. In our small town many girls left school at fifteen or even before. Then, after a six-weeks course at the local commercial college, a girl was ready for a job as a clerk in a shop or in the offices of one of the gold mines which had brought the town into being. And the typewriter itself merely tapped a mark-time for the brief season of glory, self-assertion and importance that came with the engagement party, the pre-nuptial linen "shower," and culminated not so much in the wedding itself as in the birth, not a day sooner than nine months and three weeks later, of the baby. There wasn't much point in a girl keeping her head stuck in books, anyway, even if she chose to fill the interim with one of the occupations that carried a slightly higher prestige, and were vaguely thought of as artistic — teaching tap-dancing, the piano, or "elocution."

I suppose I must have been marked out for one of these, because, although I had neither talent nor serious interest in drumming my toes, playing Czerny, or rounding my vowels, I enjoyed using them all as material in my talent for showing off. As I grew toward adolescence I stopped the home concerts and contented myself with mimicking, for the entertainment of one group of my parents' friends, other friends who were not present. It did not seem to strike those who were that, in their absence, they would change places with the people they were laughing at; or perhaps it did (I do them an injustice) and they didn't mind.

All the time it was accepted that I was a candidate for home-dressmaking or elocution whom there was no point in keeping at school too long, I was reading and writing not in secret, but as one does, openly, something that is not taken into account. It didn't occur to anyone else that these activities were connected with learning, so why should it have occurred to me? And although I fed on the attention my efforts at impersonation brought me, I felt quite differently about any praise or comment that came when my stories were published in the children's section of a Sunday paper. While I was terribly proud to see my story in print — for only in print did it become "real," did I have proof of the miracle whereby the thing created has an existence of its own — I had a jealous instinct to keep this activity of mine from the handling that would pronounce it "clever" along with the mimicry and the home concerts. It was the beginning of the humble arrogance that writers and painters have, knowing that it is hardly likely that they will ever do anything really good, and not wanting to be judged by standards that will accept anything less. Is this too high-falutin' a motive to attribute to a twelve-year-old child? I don't think so. One can have a generalised instinct toward the unattainable long before one has actually met with it. When, not many years later, I read *Un Coeur Simple* or *War and Peace*—O, I knew this was *it*, without any guidance from the list of the World's Hundred Best Books that I once tried to read through.

I started writing at nine, because I was surprised by a poem I produced as a school exercise. The subject prescribed was "Paul Kruger" (President of the Transvaal Boer Republic), and although I haven't been asked to produce any juvenilia here, in view of what has happened between people like myself and our country since then, I can't resist quoting, just for the long-untasted patriotic flavour:

> "Noble in heart,
> Noble in mind,
> Never deceitful,
> Never unkind . . ."

It was the dum-de-de-dum that delighted me, rather than the sentiments or the subject. But soon I found that what I really enjoyed was making up a story, and that this was more easily done without the restrictions of dum-de-de-dum. After that I was always writing something, and from the age twelve or thirteen, often publishing. My children's stories were anthropomorphic, with a dash of the Edwardian writers' Pan-cult paganism as it had been shipped out to South Africa in Kenneth Grahame's books, though already I used the background of mine dumps and veld animals that was familiar to me, and not the European one that provided my literary background, since there were no books about the world I knew. I wrote my elder sister's essays when she was a student at the Witwatersrand University, and kept up a fair average for her. I entered an essay in the literary section of the Eisteddfod run by the Welsh community in Johannesburg and bought with the prize chit *War and Peace, Gone With the Wind*, and an Arthur Ransome.

I was about fourteen then, and a happy unawareness of the strange combination of this choice is an indication of my reading. It was appetite rather than taste that I had; yet while it took in indiscriminately things that were too much for me, the trash tended to be crowded out and fall away. Some of the books I read in my early teens puzzle me, though. Why Pepys' Diary? And what made me plod through *The Anatomy of Melancholy*? Where did I hear of the existence of these books? (That list of the World's One Hundred Best, maybe.) And once I'd got hold of something like Burton, what made me go on from page to page? I think it must have been because although I didn't understand all that I was reading, and what I did understand was remote from my experience in the way that easily-assimilable romance was not, the half-grasped words dealt with the world of ideas, and so confirmed the recognition, somewhere, of that part of myself that I did not know was permissible.

All the circumstances and ingredients were there for a small-town prodigy, but, thank God, by missing the encouragement and practical help usually offered to "talented" children, I also escaped the dwarf status that is clapped upon the poor little devils before their time (if it ever comes). It did not occur to anyone that if I wanted to try to write I ought to be given a wide education in order to develop my mental powers and to give me some cultural background. But this neglect at least meant that I was left alone. Nobody came gawping into that private domain that was no dream-world but, as I grew up, the scene of my greatest activity and my only disciplines. When school-days finally petered out (I had stopped running away, but various other factors had continued to make attendance sketchy) I did have some sort of show of activity that passed for my life in the small town. It was so trival that I wonder how family or friends can have accepted that any young person could expend vitality at such a low hum. It was never decided what I should "take up" and so I didn't have a job. Until, at twenty-two, I went to the Witwatersrand University, I led an outward life of sybaritic meagreness that I am ashamed of. In it I did not one thing that I wanted wholeheartedly to do; in it I attempted or gratified nothing (outside sex) to try out my reach, the measure of aliveness in me. My existential self was breathing but inert, like one of those unfortunate people who has had a brain injury in a motor accident and lies unhearing and unseeing, though he will eat when food comes and open his eyes to a light. I played golf, learnt to drink gin with the R.A.F. pupil pilots from the nearby air station during the Second World War, and took part in amateur theatricals, to show recognisable signs of life to the people around me. I even went to first aid and nursing classes because this was suggested as an "interest" for me; it did not matter to me what I did, since I could not admit that there was nothing, in the occupations

and diversions offered, that really did interest me, and I was not sure —
the only evidence was in books — that anything else was possible.

I am ashamed of this torpor, nevertheless, setting aside what I can
now see as probable reasons for it, the careful preparation for it that my
childhood constituted. I cannot understand why I did not free myself in
the most obvious way, leave home and small town and get myself a job
somewhere. No conditioning can excuse the absence of the simple act
of courage that would resist it. My only overt rejection of my matchbox
life was the fact that, without the slightest embarrassment or conscience,
I let my father keep me. Though the needs provided for were modest,
he was not a rich man. One thing at least I would not do, apparently — I
would not work for the things I did not want. And the camouflage
image of myself as a dilettantish girl, content with playing grown-up
games at the end of my mother's apron strings — at most a Bovary in the
making — made this possible for me.

When I was fifteen I had written my first story about adults, and
had sent it off to a liberal weekly that was flourishing in South Africa at
the time. They published it. It was about an old man who is out of
touch with the smart, prosperous life he has secured for his sons, and
who experiences a moment of human recognition where he leasts ex-
pects it — with one of their brisk young wives who is so unlike the wife
he remembers. Not a bad theme, but expressed with the respectable
bourgeois sentiment which one would expect. That was in 1939, two
months after the war had broken out, but in the years that followed, the
stories I was writing were not much influenced by the war. It occupied
the news bulletins on the radio, taking place a long way off, in countries I
had never seen; later, when I was seventeen or eighteen there were
various boyfriends who went away to Egypt and Italy and sent back
coral jewellery and leather bags stamped with the sphinx.

Oddly enough, as I became engaged with the real business of
learning how to write, I became less prompt about sending my efforts
off to papers and magazines. I was reading Maupassant, Chekhov,
Maugham and Lawrence now, also discovering O. Henry, Katherine
Anne Porter and Eudora Welty, and the stories in *Partisan Review*, *New
Writing* and *Horizon*. Katherine Mansfield and Pauline Smith, although
one was a New Zealander, confirmed for me that my own "colonial"
background provided an experience that had scarcely been looked at,
let alone thought about, except as a source of adventure stories. I had
read "The Death of Ivan Ilyich" and "The Child of Queen Victoria"; the

whole idea of what a story could do, be, swept aside the satisfaction of producing something that found its small validity in print. From time to time I sent off an attempt to one of the short-lived local politico-literary magazines — meant chiefly as platforms for liberal politics, they were the only publications that published poetry and stories outside the true-romance category — but these published stories were the easy ones. For the other I had no facility whatever, and they took months, even years, to cease changing shape before I found a way of getting hold of them in my mind, let alone nailing words down around them. And then most of them were too long, or too outspoken (not always in the sexual sense) for these magazines. In a fumbling way that sometimes slid home in an unexpected strike, I was looking for what people meant but didn't say, not only about sex, but also about politics and their relationship with the black people among whom we lived as people live in a forest among trees. So it was that I didn't wake up to blacks and the shameful enormity of the colour bar through a youthful spell in the Communist party, as did most of my contemporaries with whom I share the rejection of white supremacy, but through the apparently esoteric speleology of doubt, led by Kafka rather than Marx. And the "problems" of my country did not set me writing; on the contrary, it was learning to write that sent me falling, falling through the surface of "the South African way of life."

It was about this time, during a rare foray into the nursery bohemia of university students in Johannesburg, that I met a boy who believed that I was a writer. Just that; I don't mean that he saw me as Chosen for the Holy Temple of Art, or any presumptuous mumbo-jumbo of that kind. The cosmetic-counter sophistication I hopefully wore to disguise my stasis in the world I knew and my uncertainty of the possibility of any other, he ignored as so much rubbish. This aspect of myself, that everyone else knew, he did not; what he recognised was my ignorance, my clumsy battle to chip my way out of shell after shell of ready-made concepts and make my own sense of life. He was often full of scorn, and jeered at the way I was going about it; but he *recognised the necessity*. It was through him, too, that I roused myself sufficiently to insist on going to the university; not surprisingly, there was opposition to this at home, since it had been accepted so long that I was not the studious type, as the phrase went. It seemed a waste, spending money on a university at twenty-two (surely I should be married soon); it was suggested that (as distinct from the honourable quest for a husband) the real reason why I wanted to go was to look for men. It seems to me now that this would have been as good a reason as any. My one preoccupation, outside the world of ideas, was men, and I should have been prepared to claim my right to the one as valid as the other.

But my freedom did not come from my new life at university; I was too old, in many ways, had already gone too far, on my own scratched tracks, for what I might once have gained along the tarmac. One day a poet asked me to lunch. He was co-editor of yet another little magazine that was then halfway through the dozen issues that would measure its life. He had just published a story of mine and, like many editors when the contributor is known to be a young girl, was curious to meet its author. He was Uys Krige, an Afrikaans poet and playwright who wrote in English as well, had lived in France and Spain, spoke five languages, was familiar with their literature, and translated from three. He had been a swimming instructor on the Riviera, a football coach somewhere else, and a war correspondent with the International Brigade in Spain.

When the boy (that same boy) heard that I was taking the train to Johannesburg for this invitation — I still lived in the small town — he said: "I wouldn't go, if I were you, Nadine."

"For Pete's sake, why not?"

"Not unless you're prepared to change a lot of things. You may not feel the same, afterwards. You may never be able to go back."

"What on *earth* are you talking about?" I made fun of him: "I'll take the train back."

"No, once you see what a person like that is like, you won't be able to stand your ordinary life. You'll be miserable. So don't go unless you're prepared for this."

The poet was a small, sunburned, blond man. While he joked, enjoyed his food, had an animated discussion with the black waiter about the origin of the name of a fruit, and said for me some translations of Lorca and Eluard, first in Afrikaans and then, because I couldn't follow too well, in English, he had the physical brightness of a fisherman. It was true — I had never met anyone like this being before. I have met many poets and writers since, sick, tortured, pompous, mousy; I know the morning-after face of Apollo. But that day I had a glimpse of — not some spurious "artist's life," but, through the poet's person, the glint off his purpose — what we are all getting at, Camus' "invincible summer" that is there to be dug for in man beneath the grey of suburban life, the numbness of repetitive labour, and the sucking mud of politics.

Oh yes — not long after, a story of mine was published in an anthology, and a second publisher approached me with the offer to publish a collection. The following year I at last sent my stories where I had never been — across the seas to England and America. They came back to me in due course, in hard covers with my name printed on the coloured jacket. There were reviews, and, even more astonishing, there was money. I was living alone in Johannesburg by then, and I was able to pay the rent and feed both myself and the baby daughter I had acquired. These things are a convenient marker for the beginning of working life. But mine really began that day at lunch. I see the poet occasionally. He's old now, of course; a bit seamed with disappointments, something of a political victim, since he doesn't celebrate his people's politics or the white man's colour bar in general. The truth isn't always beauty, but the hunger for it is.

John Haines as Stone Harp

John Sokol © 1981

John Haines

Out of the Shadows

It was early in July. I was on my way to Cabin Creek, eight miles distant by trail in the Redmond drainage. I intended to make a quick overnight trip to secure our hunting cabin for the season and to see what the prospects might be for blueberries later that summer.

For company I had brought with me our youngest dog, a female husky named Moppet. She was nearly two years old, a quiet, alert and intelligent animal. Glad to be along, to have been chosen, she trotted ahead of me on the trail, the thick gray and white plume of her tail swinging from side to side.

I was carrying my big pack basket containing a small ax, some food, and an old sweater to wear in the evening. I was also carrying one of the two rifles I owned, an ancient 8mm Mannlicher carbine I had inherited from an old resident in the country. It had once been a fighting weapon of the German Army in World War I. It had a scarred stock and a worn barrel, but was compact and light and easy to carry.

We had left home early to take advantage of the morning coolness. Now, five miles out, with the sun high at our backs on the open, sloping bench above Redmond Creek, the mid-morning was clear and warm. As always here, the trail was wet underfoot, the moss and the dark sod still soaking from the spring runoff. Mosquitoes and small gnats rose out of the moss; a continual and shifting cloud of them swarmed about us.

As we walked along, skirting one dark pool of meltwater after another, I was thinking of many things: of the summer before me, of the fishing about to begin, the hoped-for success of the summer garden, and not too far ahead another hunting season. I took casual note of the places where in the winter just past I had set my traps: a shelter of twigs and sticks fallen together, and every so often under the lower boughs of a spruce tree standing near the trail a rusty marten trap was hanging, wired to its toggle stick.

It was a typical summer day in the subarctic backcountry. I was alone with a dog in a country that with its creeks, ridges and divides, and with the high, brown slope of Banner Dome visible to the north, was as familiar to me as any suburban backyard. On the changing features of the landscape I seemed to see written my own signature of use.

We rounded the steep spruce-clad prow of the hill above Glacier Creek and stopped briefly at a cache I kept there below the point of hill. Here, three years before and late in the fall, we had camped in a tent while hunting moose. The ground poles of our tent were lying where we had left them under the trees. It was not hard for me to visualize things as they had been then: the gray slope of the canvas tent, smoke from the stovepipe and snow in the wind. For a few weeks that tent had been home. Moppet was not yet born. Now I looked up at the narrow platform of the cache fixed solidly in the three spruces above me. A half dozen traps were hanging from a spike in one of the supports. The ridge pole of the tent and the rest of its framework were pitched together and standing upright against the cache to keep them dry. I saw that everything was as I had left it when I stopped here with the dogs and sled on the last snow of the season.

We left the cache and went on down the trail toward the creek. The brush was thick, of dense, small-statured black spruce interspersed with thickets of alders. The trail wound about so that at no time could I see more than thirty feet ahead of me. Moppet was now out of sight somewhere ahead and probably waiting for me at the crossing.

As I came out of the woods and onto the open bench above the creek, I saw Moppet sitting at the edge of the steep slide down which the trail led to the creek bottom. Her ears were pricked sharply forward, and she was staring intently at something in the creek.

When I came up to her, I saw what she was watching. Down in the creek and less than twenty yards away, the shoulders and back of a large brown creature showed above the heavy summer grass and clumps of ice-cropped willows. It was moving slowly downstream at the far edge of an island that divided the creek.

At first I thought the animal was a young moose feeding on the fresh grass or on some waterplants in the shallow streamcourse. And yet there was something about its size and bulk and the way that it was moving that was not quite familiar. And then the creature's head came into partial view, and I saw how the brown hump of its shoulders rippled as it moved. It was a bear, larger than any bear I had yet seen in that country. One look at that heavy square head and the shoulder hump, and I knew we had met a grizzly.

No more than a minute passed as I stood there with Moppet at my feet, watching the big bear in the grass below us. I was glad now that I had not brought one of our other dogs who would have immediately rushed barking into the creek after the bear. I was grateful for this quiet and obedient animal sitting at my feet with her hair stiffened on her shoulders and her nose twitching.

Where I stood at that moment I had an easy shot broadside into the bear's chest or shoulders. I could perhaps have killed it then and there. But I did not want to leave a dead bear to rot in the creek, and we were too far from home to pack out more than a small portion of the meat.

In the brief time that we stood there, I quickly went over my choices. We could not proceed down into the creek and follow the trail across to the opposite bank; the bear was by now directly in our path. We could stay where we were and let the bear go on downstream if that was its intention. But would Moppet remain quiet long enough?

I thought of easing away from the scene, of moving upstream far enough to cross without disturbing the bear. It would have to be done quickly and quietly. At any moment the bear might discover us, or the noise of our retreat might alarm it. There were no trees large enough to climb in an emergency, and there was no hope of outrunning an aroused bear in that wet and spongy ground. My one advantage lay in the fact that we were above the bear and that it had not yet discovered us.

But the bear soon left me no choice. Something in our unseen presence on the bank above the creek, some sound, some prickling sense that it was not alone, seemed to change the bear's intentions. It stopped feeding. Its head came up, and it began to move more rapidly through the grass. As it did so, it turned in our direction. It was now in full view, no more than fifty feet away, and closing the distance between us.

In my sudden alarm that grizzly loomed larger and more of a threat than any black bear or bull moose I had ever met with. I was ready to fire, but in those swift moments I thought I might be able to frighten the bear, and by some noise of movement scare it back into the woods. Still holding my rifle, I raised my arms over my head. In what seems now to have been a ridiculous gesture, I waved my arms and did a small dance on the moss; I yelled and hooted and hoped. But the sudden noise, coming out of the stillness, seemed only to panic the animal. It broke into a loping run, heading directly toward us, and had already reached the bottom of the bank below us. I had no choice now. I put the rifle to my shoulder, took hurried aim at the heavy chest of hair below that big head, and fired.

At the sound of the gunshot the bear abruptly stopped a few feet below. It rose on its hind legs and stood at full height in front of us. In a rush of images I saw the stocky, upright length of its body, a patch of pale fur on its underthroat, the forepaws raised in a defensive gesture; I saw the blunt muzzle and the suddenly opened jaws. The bear seemed to tower infinitely. It growled loudly, swung its head to one side, and tried to bite at its chest. I was ready to fire again, and at that moment I might have put a shot squarely into its thick neck or broad upper chest. But for some reason in those tense seconds I again held my fire.

The bear dropped back to the ground. It turned away from us and ran back through the grass and brush in a tremendous, lunging gallop, scattering leaves and splashing water. I watched it climb the bank on the opposite side of the creek and disappear. A heavy crashing came from the dry alders on the far side, and then all was still.

I stood at the top of the bank with my rifle half-raised, listening. Over everything in that sudden stillness I was aware of my heart as a loud pounding above the calm trickle of water in the creek below. I heard a low whine, and glanced down. All this time Moppet had remained crouched and quiet at my feet. But now she rose with her fur bristling, searching the air with her nose, trying to catch some scent of that enormous creature so suddenly discovered and now vanished.

I moved away from the trail and walked a short distance upstream to where a bulky, crooked spruce grew at the edge of the bank. It was as large as any tree in the vicinity, and for some reason I felt more comfortable standing close to it. I removed my pack and set it on the ground beside me. I placed my rifle against the tree while I searched in my shirt pocket for tobacco and papers. In those days I was an occasional smoker. With trembling hands I rolled a cigarette, lit it, and smoked in silence.

It had all happened so quickly. Perhaps no more than three minutes had elapsed since I had first seen the bear. Now that I had some space in which to think, I realized that I had been extremely lucky. Had the bear not stopped, a second shot might have killed it, but if not there would have been no way I could have escaped at least a severe mauling.

Somehow in that blur of excitement and indecision I knew that I would not turn and run. Out of whatever stubborn sense of my own right to be there, or simply from an obscure pride, I would stand my ground, fire my shot, and from then on fend off the wounded bear as best I could, using my rifle for a club. In that event I would most likely have been killed, or I would have been so badly maimed that I could never have made it home without help, and there was no help any-where near. Days might have passed before anyone came looking for me.

I stood there and smoked, gradually coming to some calm in myself. I could hear nothing from the woods on the far side of the creek. There was not the slightest movement to be seen in the brush growing upon that low bank, nothing at all in the grass below. From time to time I gazed up or down the creek as far as I could see above the willows and alders. Nothing.

I did not know how badly hit that bear was. Perhaps it was now lying dead over there. Or it might only be wounded, lying in the brush near the trail, gathering its strength and waiting for me to pass. At such times events and probabilities seem magnified; fear has a thousand faces.

I finished my cigarette, and picked up my pack and my rifle. I knew that I would have to go down into the creek and search the sand and grass for blood. Whatever I found, I would follow the bear's path across the creek and into the woods. I wanted above all to be on my way to the cabin and out of any further trouble. But first I had to be sure of that bear.

I waited another few minutes. Then, with Moppet at my heels, I returned to the trail, and we began our descent into the creek.

At the bottom of the bank I easily found the place where the bear had stood up after I fired at him. His big tracks were pressed deeply into the wet sand, the long toenails and the pad marks clearly outlined at the edge of the small channel.

Slowly and quietly I began to trace the bear's path through the grass. Stopping frequently to look around me over the grass and through the brush, I followed as well as I could the paw marks in the sand and the muddy sod. Where I could not see his tracks, I guided myself by the bent and broken grasses in the deep trough of the bear's passage. As I walked, half-crouched, searching the ground, I examined with care every blade of grass and every leaf on the willows. But I found no sign of blood.

We went on through the grass and brush. Across the far channel we found the trail, climbed the shallow bank and entered the woods. Moppet remained at my heels, at times pressing closely against my leg. Though I tried quietly to coax her, she would not go ahead but stayed close behind. The fur on her shoulders and neck was stiffened, and as she looked from side to side into the woods a muted and anxious throaty sound came from her, half growl and half whine.

Once up the bank and into the woods, we stopped. It was spooky as hell under that shadowy, sun-broken canopy of leaves. I searched the woods around me for the slightest movement and listened for any sound: a wounded breathing, a growl, anything. Nowhere in all that wilderness could I hear a sound above the muted purling of water in the creek behind me, and the song of a fox sparrow somewhere in the watercourse.

We walked on, following the trail where it skirted the edge of a narrow ravine holding a wayward tributary of the creek. To cross the ravine I had built a rough bridge out of spruce poles. On the far side the trail turned upstream and continued through a swamp toward Cabin Creek.

When Moppet and I had crossed the bridge, I stopped again. Here an old game trail, deeply cut into the moss, intersected our sled trail and took its narrow, twisting way downstream. I hesitated. Nothing I had seen so far convinced me that the bear was at all wounded, but I was still not satisfied. I stepped into the game trail and began a careful circuit of the downstream woods into which I had seen the bear vanish. As quiet as it was, as eerily still, I felt that somewhere in that dim tangle of alders, willows and dwarf birch the bear must be lying and listening to our movements. As in an episode of warfare, a pervasive uneasiness seemed to divide the shadows and the sunlight. I had that acute sense of being watched and listened to by an invisible foe. Each twig-snap and wave of a bough seemed a potential signal.

After about twenty minutes of what I considered to be a reasonably careful search, I returned to the trail. I now felt, from the lack of any bloodsign or other evidence, that the bear had not been badly hit. I decided not to pursue the search any further. With Moppet following me, I went on through the swamp, climbing steadily toward the saddle that divided Glacier from Cabin Creek. We went carefully, every so often stopping to look back down the trail behind us. We were well away from the creek before Moppet would put aside her fear and go ahead of me.

It seemed to me now that I had merely grazed the underside of the bear's chest. I had fired downhill at a running target, and had aimed low. Moreover, the front sight of the old carbine had been damaged years ago and repaired with solder in a makeshift fashion. The gunsight was uncertain at best.

So obviously I had fired too low, and the bear had suffered no more than a nasty sting from the heavy 230-grain bullet I was using. Had the bear been solidly hit, there would surely have been blood somewhere, and there would by now be a dead or dying bear in the woods. As we came down off the hill on the last half-mile stretch to the cabin I began to feel a great deal easier, satisfied that I had not left a badly wounded animal behind me, and glad too that we had gotten off from the encounter ourselves with no more trouble.

We spent the night at the cabin. I fed Moppet and cut some firewood. In the late afternoon I did a few needed chores about the cabin. On going to the creek for a bucket of water, I found a few unripe blueberries among the bushes overhanging the deep, wet moss hummocks beside the creek. The berries were scattered and it did not seem to me that they would be worth a trip later to pick them. As the evening light deepened over the hills and the air grew cooler, a thrush sent up its spiraling song from the aspens on the hillside across the creek. Mosquitoes whined at the screen door. Otherwise, things were very quiet there on the hill above Cabin Creek.

The following morning I secured the cabin for the remainder of the summer. I set a strong barricade over the door, and closed and nailed heavy shutters over the two windows. In the late morning Moppet and I set out for home.

As we came down through the swamp near Glacier, Moppet once more dropped behind me and refused to go ahead. I walked quietly with the rifle safety off and my hand half-closed on the trigger. Again I watched the brush and listened to either side of the trail for the slightest sound. There was nothing but the quiet sunlit air of a summer day.

We crossed the creek, striding the small channels and pushing aside the grass, and on the far side we climbed the bank again. When we came to the top, I looked down. There, squarely in the trail and almost exactly where I had stood the day before when I fired at the bear, was a fresh mound of bear dropping. Nearby lay the spent shell from my rifle.

I looked closely at the dropping. It contained a few unripe blueberries, seeds and other matter. It was still wet, though not warm. Moppet sniffed at it, and the grizzled hair once more rose on her neck and shoulders. For a moment my uneasiness returned, that vague, shivery sense of being watched and followed. The bear was still around, alive and well. Dangerous? I had no way of knowing.

The bear had probably not run far on the previous day, but had found a place in which to lie and lick its wound, baffled as to the source of its sudden hurt. It had heard us pass on the trail, had heard every sound of my passage in the brush, had followed every detail of my search. Perhaps much later in the evening it came out of its hiding place, out of the late cool shadows, and returned to the trail. It had stood where we were standing now, with its great, shaggy head down, sniffing the moss, the wet, black sod, trying to place in its dim sense of things an identity it would carry with it for the rest of its life.

I looked back down into the grass and brush of the creek from which we had just come. I turned and looked ahead of me to where the stubby black spruce wood closed in around the trail. If the bear was still somewhere in that dense green cover, nursing its hurt and its temper, waiting for revenge, it would have its chance.

But nothing vengeful and bloody came out of the woods to meet us as we went on up the trail. The walk home by Redmond, the long uphill climb to the homestead ridge passed without further incident. We came down off the hill as on many another occasion, to the sunlit vista of the river and the highway, to the sound of the dogs' furious barking. I had a good story to tell, and Moppet was petted and praised for her wise behavior.

In many subsequent hikes over the trail to Cabin Creek, in hunting forays along the benches above Glacier, we never saw that bear again. Now and then in late summer and early fall a blue mound of dropping in the trail gave evidence of a bear in the country, and that was all.

Never before or since have I been so rattled on meeting an animal in the woods. Years later, when I began to think of writing these pages, I rehearsed for myself another outcome to the adventure. I described in detail how the bear, badly hit in its lungs, had waited in the brush on the far side of the creek. When Moppet and I went by on the trail, the bear suddenly lunged from its hiding place with a terrible, bubbling roar and struck me down.

In that instant of confusion and shock I was joined to the hot blood and rank fur at last. All my boyhood dreams of life in the woods, of courage and adventure, had come to this final and terrifying intimacy.

Following the initial shock, as I lay sprawled by the trail with the bear standing hot and wounded above me, I managed to regain a grip on my rifle. Though stunned and, as it seemed, half blinded, I raised the short muzzle of that ancient weapon and got off one last shot into the bear's throat. And with the sound of that shot in my ears, I lost consciousness.

In what may have been an hour or only minutes, I returned to a dazed sense of myself. I sat up, struggling to free myself of the things that seemed to hold me: my pack harness, torn clothing, and bits of broken brush. I seemed to look at myself and my surroundings from a great distance through a sun-dazzled semidarkness. I was still alive, though in the numbed, head-ringing silence I knew I was hurt, badly cut and bitten about my face and body. Moppet was gone. A short distance away from me the bear lay dead.

Somehow, maimed, stiffened and bleeding, using a dry stick for a crutch, I found my way home. Patched and scarred, I wore my changed face as an emblem of combat, and walked in my damaged body to the end of my days, survivor of a meeting terrible and true.

Elizabeth Hardwick as Sleepless Nights

John Sokol © *1981*

Elizabeth Hardwick

Cross-town

In the evening there was a moon in the eastern sky outclassing every miracle. It hung over Lexington Avenue where the stores were at last closed and where many little shoes and blouses were enchained for the night's sleep. Sometimes while waiting for a taxi at 79th Street, after midnight, it is possible, with a certain amount of effort or with a little too much wine, to imagine the city returned to trees, old footpaths and clear, untroubled waters, returned to innocence and nautical miscalculations and ancestral heroics. The sound of a rubber-soled footstep — what is that but the oars of Verrazano slipping into New York Bay, silently, to see what is there, what can be deftly unlocked without rousing a soul? A lot was there; the pirates soon and the merchants in league with them and Captain William Kidd, the first embezzling stockbroker — and a great deal more.

Many voyages over the amiable waters of the Bay and the Hudson, seeing the shore rich with hints. As for me, I do not miss the carriages or lament the old New York horse-droppings in front of the mansions in the West Thirties. And not old New York itself with money made before the Civil War and the interesting names which librarians love. Still, there was an impudent dinner on horseback in Sherry's restaurant with the riders and their mounts amid standing palms and the sylvan scenes on the wallpaper. You can find it on a postcard and imagine the outrageous clanging of the hooves on the marble tiles — and the Italians brought in at dawn to repair them.

Even now today the patroons have the tables set for sixty a block or so away. The plates that hold the thin goblets filled with an unsugared, lightly liquored dessert are of black and gold lacquer from China; and in a suite, perhaps in more than one, in the Waldorf Towers there is one of the many, many Renoirs that have made the emigration, and also an unfortunate Buffet, and also a Sienese primitive, or so they say, so they believe. Taste, arrangements, one of a kind. A huge piece of mineral, shaped like an obelisk, from the South American underground and weighing a ton, one of the earth's outstandingly large beauties, has been crated and pulleyed from continent to continent and now stands in an entrance hall. All to the good since you cannot be a great world city without many, many surprises.

Goddesses in flowing, liquid dress, winged helmets, carrying sheaves of grain; kinky-haired Medusas, so slim and dark; and the beautiful Athenas, makers of dresses and perfumes and rouge and nail polish in all the hues. Now the earth-tones and soon again a stirring of pastels light as petals on the grass. Goddesses on the arm of plain, unimpressive gods, running to shortness, but shrewd as trolls down in the ground where the minerals are or looking under the waves where the viscid oils lie with all their interest shaming the ladies' little vials on the dressing table.

Under the moon the taxi makes its way through the dark park and a cassette of Rachmaninoff passes perhaps over the buried imprint of his own footsteps. The gaseous piano, fortissimo, sounds like a new invention as it executes a sudden, jolting pedaling at the stoplight.

Here, back once more awaiting the appearance of the nightman, my neighbor can be seen walking her dog. A snub-nosed animal, the dog, with a strange dry body like tanned hide, a dog such as you can see wandering in poor countries, on the back streets of the West Indies. Maybe it was such a dog that killed Verrazano when he went on from the East River and the Hudson to the Caribbean; such a dog and not the natives at all. Well, as we say today, that is what you pay for New York City.

Nod to the neighbor. Friend is the correct word in this case because, as everyone has noted, neighbor has no special resonance in Manhattan. Oh, blight, the same cannot be said for neighborhood. And it cannot be said of the peculiar, blinding possibility of the painter and his wife in their large, light apartment on Seventh Avenue in midtown where they live in an anxious stasis similar to the comfortable house arrest offered to the families of the deposed.

The painter possesses an unfashionable and genuinely modest talent. He and his wife are soon to be sixty years old and of him it could be said that he has been too well-brought-up in New Haven and Yale to quit. They have very little cash and yet they spin around like a top, dizzied by the remarkable whirl of their assets. Their apartment (indeed, indeed a steal at $300,000.00 everyone says) and the small house they have had for thirty years in the town of Gloucester, Mass. (worth, worth, you better believe, Sir, at least $150,000). Remember the view and the spread of the rocky harbor and the memory of Fitzhugh Lane and so on and so on.

On Monday mornings the wife goes down to the basement with her laundry and sits through the cycles of washing and drying with a nodding patience. He often puts on his Irish woolen cap and his tweed jacket and with some abashment takes the shopping cart out of the closet and goes off with a list to the supermarket. If they speak of all-year-round in Gloucester there is defeat in it — the dead winter, the sailing boats hauled in, the nudity flown. It would not do, no, even though they are little engaged in the city's art affairs. The painter had his friends who were older than he and are now gone, such men as Edwin Dickinson and Leon Kroll. Pleasant to be a son and that is what he still feels when he goes off to the Childe Hassam exhibition at the National Academy on Fifth Avenue.

The painter studies, has studied and yet after thirty-five years the landscape of his heart is still the New Haven and Fisher's Island of his youth. A gallery on Newbury Street in Boston has some of his paintings of shingled summer houses and girls in white on the lawn. They are brought out and sometimes they touch a buyer's heart, like an old photograph, and so there is money from time to time — not much because the sentiments of the buyer are clouded by the fact that the painter's name is not known, except *here* and *there*, a curious fate for a name. Perhaps there is a little money from legacies, very likely for someone carefully brought-up. Anyway, he is known to his brother, a lawyer with an insurance firm in Hartford, as my brother who is an artist and lives in New York City; and his wife is spoken of by her sister in Florida as the brave one who married an artist and lives in New York. So they go on in the ideal, gently backward, greatly puzzled by the cost of things and the mirage of assets. . . . Off to sleep, genteel couple. The city is yours.

My friend and the dog go to the other side of the street. Not up to a great deal of talk at midnight. Yet how often she is on the street in the late night, sometimes at one end of the block and then again at the other. It is troubling. When she goes off to work the next morning, the dog howls if a footstep comes near the door of her apartment. He is said to be very quiet when Garland, such is her name, is at home.

In bed at last, ready to read. "Five women in nightgowns were shot in a damp field." No, not the morning paper. It is the Russian Revolution, St. Petersburg, in Victor Serge's *The Conquered City*. The next line explains: "After the killings the men had taken an hour to remove their red stars and sew on the nationalist cockades."

New York. Even when you have been here so long, can it be your autobiography? Not the scene of first love, disillusionment, parents, family, formation. Everything instead is confirmation. Has my reservation, my appointment been confirmed? Perhaps yes and maybe not.

The cold winds blow from the north, from empty space with fir trees like great chandeliers of ice. Then the hellish season and the water vapors as heavy as a fur cloak in the summer air. So, if you come from Siberia you may one day be hit by a blast of memory and feel the cold of an icy cave; but soon you can walk about the dusty street and scarcely forget San Juan stifling in the breeze of a hundred torrid melodies.

"The City Hall, in the Southern part of Manhattan Island, is in lat. 40° 42' 43" N. and long. 74° 0' 3" W. Average number of hours of sunshine ranges from 150 in November to 271 in June." That was many years ago, but some things don't change. And what is meant by hours of sunshine?

See the photograph of the grandmother in Kiev, wearing a fur hat; and large areas of the city with slave memories, rebellious fires on Minetta Street; and sugar cane and favelas under the Southern Cross. This is not Berlin or Paris and we are not a folk here. Here it is something else.

The Croats are furious from time to time and throw a bomb. It seems that we should liberate them. Who else?

It's all over, Boris. That was the last line of the dramatic crime serial that preceded the evening news. As for the news, after the fires and the gunshots, a victimless crime. It appears that a Columbia graduate student, or one once a graduate student, has stolen a 1630 edition of Galileo from a London library. When he tried to pass it on to a dealer there was a smart detective sitting behind the desk. Imperishable Galileo among the treasures of the earth. A Kazak rug, American rococo furniture attributed to Meeks, dolls, quilts, a diamond necklace — nothing out of stock at the auction houses.

When a dreadful crime takes place, the accused and the victim become for the time allotted them quite interesting and that is bad news for both. Biographers of soul and body arouse themselves — reveille. Off the researchers go to the reform school, seeking résumés, recommendations from psychiatrist and warden, plotting the flight of the spotted bird. If all goes well, all will go well; if not, beware. And here is the father of the accused opening the door with a shotgun in his hand. And somewhere else the mother, whose Mrs. has been followed by several names different from that borne by the accused. I haven't heard from him in thirteen years. He's not in trouble, is he? That is one genre, and the old frogs in the pond move about in a sluggish repetition.

Money and the natural wish for change, a nice change, occasionally require crime for the removal of the unchanging. A stir in the great mansion on the bluffs of a rich town in the Northeast and here a dozen tubs of blue agapanthus guard the sides of the driveway and the turf is as green and rich and imperishable as some vile shag on a bathroom floor. Three handsome cars are in the garage and the waves of the sea just beyond the light curtains of the master bedroom are as gratifying as waves of one's own anywhere else in the world. The coast is not unlike Biarritz.

What a fool he or she, already so rich, was to fall under the domination of the law and what with the blue flowers and the silvered mirrors and the crime and the amphibious lawyers — what can vengeance be like when so miserably deserved? And out of the index cards and the coughing tapes your biography will be preserved and in this, having caught the public eye, you will be trapped in the universal, the toneless data. No matter. Many consolations. You will share this internment, the fatality of being interesting to someone, with generals, scientists, flamboyant artists and other criminals. In a way you haven't fared worse than Michelangelo.

Only writers have the possibility of autobiography, this singularity, this exercise of option by way of adjectives and paragraphs. No wonder statesmen and public figures need all the help they can get from the files, the recorded meetings, the secretaries and extraordinary machinery. For others, the unaided, there are aesthetic problems — what will "work." My life would make a book, the hairdresser said. That is true, true. There is incident, suspense, narrative and then, too, there is the "I" and here the hairdresser insists that what went on there is nobody's business.

There is some dispute about Rousseau. Perhaps he did not abandon his children to the foundling hospital. What a base lie. Not to have abandoned the children, all five of them. But of course he sent the children to the foundling hospital. Everything we know about him and Thérése Le Vasseur makes it "work." That is if there actually were children born. There's always that.

A bit of my past nudged the present a month or so ago. There was a time when I used to run into people from home on the streets of New York and members of my family used to come in on the C&O and we would go to *Oklahoma!* and to the Latin Quarter, a large Hungarian sort of place with a large menu featuring the splendid oxymoron, baked Alaska, and a long, florid floor show. But no more, not for what you might call that sort of American.

A couple from Louisville telephoned me and spoke of the extraordinary decision they had made. They had sold their house on a street named Keithshire Drive. The old Indian names of Chinoe Road and the countrified Tate's Creek were never in fashion in the suburbs. They had sold their house and come here to New York to an apartment on York Avenue, and for life. The wife is forty-five and the husband is forty-seven. Fred and Dorothy. Fred worked for one of the Louisville distilleries, J. W. Dant, and he has some kind of position with the New York offices of another whiskey producer. They call this a hardship post, he said, but we are pleased as punch.

Hardship post. I have heard that phrase before, from a United States foreign service officer. He was referring to Calcutta. So, welcome Fred and Dorothy.

They are in three white rooms on the twelfth floor and they have brought with them, have transferred, their sideboard and gateleg tables and corner cupboard. A mahogany whatnot stands in the hall and on it are fluted bottles, saucers from Czechoslovakia and "Mama's cut glass." How happy they appeared, how pleased to be going up and down the gold-flecked elevator, which let out on long, narrow corridors with gold-flecked carpeting.

We sat together drinking Bourbon and names from years ago came into the conversation. Bob and Jack and Nancy and their stories, which were for the most part not out of luck. Everyone was pretty good. And just then a surly man rang the doorbell, a man who had been announced at apartment 12F and yet rang the bell of apartment 12H in error. Somehow all the bells and corridors and letters of the alphabet bore down in their awesome multiplication and a silence spread over our recital of place names and streets and the little villages at home named Athens, Paris and Versailles that lie between the larger towns.

And now a phonograph was playing overhead and the bass rhythm was like the light hammering of many nails in sequence, as if putting down a carpet.

The husband walked with me down the corridor to the elevator and on the way someone was playing phrases of Maria Callas' "Casta Diva," playing over and over, picking up the arm and putting it down with a scratch. A new world, Fred? Yes, it is, that it is. Now he bent towards me and it was true he still had the look, the look of fraternities and the football team and tall boys from the Kentucky mountains slipping the ball into the basket, and Coach Rupp, all of it. And also back there in the apartment in Dorothy's eyes there were lilacs and a pair of cardinals caught on the bush for a moment in the Japanese style, and fields of tobacco plants and horses standing in the dry winter fields.

Now, listen, Fred said. Dorothy has been in a life-threatening situation, but all is well, all is well.

Ah, York Avenue, the thoroughfare of hospitals. These two, he with his fair husband-face and she with her fair wife-face, were two intrepid warriors appearing out of the sky like defiant airplanes rushing through the stars, and as they said, for life.

Downstairs the garden of rocks and undying foliage in the lobby, the mirrors, the crystal chandelier and the radio on the doorman's desk playing Caribbean music. Nothing amiss here. All bright and warm and, yes, filled with hope. In front of New York Hospital the limousines stopped at the entrance and then went on to look for an empty waiting spot on the avenue. And nothing much else new from home.

What obstinacy in the air. A whole city built on obstinacy. Don't yield. The schoolchildren with their satchels crossing the city when it is barely light on a winter morning—obstinate little roots. Some are in parochial-school uniforms, green stockings and plaid skirts, and they themselves are like little nuns, postulates, hanging on. Others are being bussed to private schools. Children of professors, actors, lawyers, officials. And no matter how carelessly they are dressed in housepainter overalls or little-boy lumberjack costumes, there is no doubt they will be the inheritors of whatever there is—along with the others, loitering, wandering, disappearing under the turnstiles at the subway entrance, swiftly out of sight as the coin seller calls, Hey you, stop.

Surely it was thinking about himself and the meaning of his life that brought Rousseau to paranoia. He entered the "auto," the powerful mobile and drove over the landscape of his biography with miraculous speed and no care for distance. Almost at the end of his recollections, his apologia, which he read aloud to the Count and Countess d'Egmont, Prince Pignatelli, the Marchioness de Mesmes, and the Marquis de Juigne, he utters a firm summation. *I have always suspected M. de Choiseul of being the hidden author of all the persecutions I had suffered in Switzerland.*

William Harrison as In a Wild Sanctuary

John Sokol © *1981*

William Harrison

Why I Am Not an Autobiographical Writer

My life as a writer probably began in the Astor Theater across the street from my father's barber shop in a seedy neighborhood in Dallas. The telephone poles leaned in odd directions there on Bishop Avenue, slanting this way and that, wires crossing the sky. The Texaco station on the corner wore its mounds of dried grease. The barber shop smelled of bay rum and talcum.

On Saturday nights my father worked late, then joined my mother and me in the popcorn darkness of the old movie house. She would give him the homemade sandwich wrapped in loud tissue paper. He would eat some of my popcorn and a candy bar, then fall asleep while Gary Cooper, Fred Astaire or Spencer Tracy flickered before our eyes. He would slump beside us, eyes closed, mouth slightly open, with a smear of chocolate on his barber's smock.

In the Astor Theater, for me, the world announced itself: the grim war images on Movietone News, the glamour of Carole Lombard, the art of *Citizen Kane*—which my mother liked and my father didn't, sparking off the first discussion of aesthetics ever held in my presence. Beyond that little movie house our overgrown lawns and frame houses awaited me; my school was a red brick calamity; our lives seemed excruciatingly modest and I felt certain that the world beyond, the one in the movies which was both more real and more perfectly imagined, was somehow more various and more mysteriously important than we were.

My mother's scrapbooks. Aunts, faraway cousins, birthday cards, school notices, newspaper clippings, photos and snippets of inspirational poetry: she pasted everything into those pages. Mixed in with the usual family-album items were pictures and words of Churchill, Bogart, King George, Di Maggio, Garbo, Roosevelt, Barrymore, Dempsey and hundreds of others. I seemed to know these people.

One evening while my father listened to Joe Louis doing battle over the radio, my mother and I sat at the kitchen table talking about the Lindbergh kidnapping—which was still on her mind. Because I was so young she showed me a drawing of the Lindbergh house, telling me how the colonel and his wife sat at dinner—here, see, downstairs—while a kidnapper carried the sleeping baby down a ladder from the upstairs bedroom. That drawing, accompanied by a note in my mother's handwriting stating that Bruno Hauptmann was convicted for the crime on circumstantial evidence, became part of the family's documents.

Texas. This was also a state of mind.

Because of its oil and money, it always managed to set itself squarely on the world's stage. Celebrities came to Texas and put on ten-gallon hats. There were movies about Texas cowboys. Texaco stations like the one up the street from the barber shop were also in places like Mexico City and London.

I assumed that I was on stage, too—not in the spotlight, yet present.

At the university there were girls in cashmere sweaters, football, Russian novels and seriousness. But most of all there was journalism; I became a newspaperman in spirit, believing like a fanatic in the devices of a more objective prose. A good reporter, I asserted, looked around for something of consequence: the story on his beat. The reporter was a camera, yet more: his eye should be so sharp, I proclaimed, that it pierced all sentimentalities, postures, clichés, and lies. This ideal writer, I knew, should never talk about himself; for him, the first person pronoun should always be a natural embarrassment.

Oddly enough, my view holds. I find that I have little patience with authors who confess, who pose as prophets of the flesh in their insipid fantasies, who sentimentalize their domestic complaints in long novels or who abandon storytelling altogether for an esoteria of games and posturings.

"Pour out your heart!" cry the authors and critics of recent years.

Yet one needn't write just in order to engrave his signature on existence; history both current and past has lots of stories and signatures to record. More is needed of a wordsmith than just his introspective scrawl.

Fame is a vanity of assassins.

It is also an American poison.

The writers I admire have learned to sit quietly in the dark, content and creative in that little movie house inside themselves.

Travel. All rivers flow to the heart of both darkness and light. The writer travels like Marlow, wrapped in awe and irony, never imagining that he could possibly transform his destination; yet if his eyes are open, if he really sees, he can transform everything in his vision.

The lover knows he loves, not because he examines himself in the experience, but precisely because he fails to do so.

In my years of teaching at the university I've held strong and sometimes furious views on politics and religion, and I've lived through the usual amount of personal griefs and upheavals. Even so, my students and I have discussed books, hundreds and hundreds of books, writing techniques, ideas and aesthetics.

The teachers I admire don't hide from their students, but have magical ways and rough tricks by which they fold themselves into their subjects and disappear.

In more than twenty years of writing these are the first boldly personal words — pronouns and all — I've written; I find that I can only just barely make my peace with them, as one suffers an old snapshot of himself when he was photographed too skinny, too pensive, too odd.

But a last observation.

Mine has always been the greater vanity; I have believed that other people's stories have been mine to tell.

Hermann Hesse as Steppenwolf   *John Sokol © 1979*

Hermann Hesse

Translated from the German by Rika Lesser

The Jackdaw

It has been a long time since, as a returning visitor to Baden to take the cure, I have gone there with the expectation of being surprised. The day will come when the last stretch of the Goldwand will be built over, the lovely spa park converted into factories, but I will not live to see this. And yet on this visit, on the ugly, lopsided bridge to Ennetbaden, a wonderful and charming surprise awaited me. I am in the habit of allowing myself a few moments of sheer pleasure each day when I stand on this bridge — it lies but a few steps from the spa hotel — and feed the gulls with some small pieces of bread. They are not at the bridge at all hours of the day, and when they are there one cannot talk to them. There are times when they sit in long rows on the roof of the city baths building, guarding the bridge and waiting for one of the passersby to stop, take some bread out of his pocket, and throw it to them. When someone tosses a bit of bread up into the air, the youthful and acrobatic gulls like to hover over the head of the bread-thrower as long as they can; one can watch each one and try to make sure that each gull will get its turn. Then one is besieged by a deafening roaring and flashing, a whirling and clattering swarm of feverish life; beleaguered and wooed, one stands amid a white-gray winged cloud, out of which, without pause, short, shrill shrieks shoot. But there are always a number of more prudent and less athletic gulls who keep their distance from the tumult and who leisurely cruise down below the bridge and over the streaming waters of the river Limmat, where it is calm and where some piece of bread, having escaped the clutches of the vying acrobats up above, is always sure to fall. At other times of day, there are no gulls here at all. Perhaps they have all gone on an outing together, a school or a club excursion; perhaps they have found an especially rich feeding place further down the Limmat; in any event, they have all disappeared together. And then there are other hours when, to be sure, the whole flock of gulls is at hand, but they are not sitting on the rooftops or thronging over the head of the feeder; rather, they are swarming and raising a din importantly and excitedly just above the surface of the water a bit downstream. No amount of waving or bread-tossing will help, they don't give a hoot, busy as they are with their bird games, and perhaps their human games: gathering the tribes together, brawling, voting, trading stocks, who knows what else. And even with baskets full of the most delectable morsels you would not be able to draw them away from their uproarious and important transactions and games.

This time when I got to the bridge, seated on the railing was a black bird, a jackdaw of extremely small stature, and when it did not fly away at my nearer approach, I stalked it, more and more slowly inching closer to it, one small step after the other. It showed neither fear nor suspicion, only attentiveness and curiosity; it let me get within a half step of it, surveyed me with its blithe bird eyes, and tilted its powdery gray head to one side, as if to say: "Come now, old man, you certainly do stare!" Indeed, I was staring. This jackdaw was accustomed to having dealings with humans, you could talk to it, and a few people who knew him had already come by and greeted him, saying: "Salut, Jakob." I tried to find out more about him, and since that time I've collected quite a bit of information, all of it contradictory. The main questions remain unanswered: where the bird made its home and how it came to be on intimate terms with human beings. One person told me the bird was tamed and that he belonged to a woman in Ennetbaden. Another said that he roamed freely, wherever it suited him, and sometimes he'd fly into a room through an open window, peck at something edible, or pluck to shreds some knitted garment left lying around. A man from one of the French-speaking cantons, obviously a bird specialist, asserted that this jackdaw belonged to a very rare species, which, as far as he knew, could be found only in the mountains of Fribourg, where it lived in the rocky cliffs.

After that, I would meet the jackdaw Jakob almost every day; now by myself, now with my wife, I would greet him and talk to him. One day my wife was wearing a pair of shoes whose uppers had a pattern cut out of the leather, allowing a bit of stocking to shine through the holes. These shoes, and especially the little islands of hose, interested Jakob a great deal; he alit on the ground, and with sparkling eyes he took aim and pecked at them with gusto. Many a time he would sit on my arm or my shoulder and peck at my coat, my collar, my cheeks, and my neck, or tear at the brim of my hat. He did not care for bread;

still, he would get jealous and sometimes downright angry if you shared it with the gulls in his presence. He accepted and adeptly picked walnuts or peanuts from the hand of the giver. But best of all he liked to peck, pluck, pulverize, and destroy any little thing — a crumpled ball of paper, a cigar stub, a little piece of cardboard or material; he'd put one of his feet on it and rashly and impatiently hack away at it with his beak. And time and again one perceives that he does all this not for his sake alone but on behalf of the onlookers, some of whom always and many of whom often gather around him. For them he hops about on the ground or back and forth on the railing of the bridge, enjoying the crowd; he flutters onto the head or shoulder of one of the members of the audience, alights again on the ground, studies our shoes, and forcefully pecks at them. He takes pleasure in pecking and plucking, tearing and destroying, he does all this with roguish delight; but the members of the audience must also participate, they must admire, laugh, cry out, feel flattered by his show of friendliness, and then again show fear when he pecks at their stockings, hats, and hands.

He has no fear of the gulls, who are twice as large and many times stronger than he; sometimes he flies on high right in their midst. And they let him be. For one thing, he who scarcely touches bread is neither a rival nor a spoilsport; for another, I suppose that they, too, consider him a phenomenon, something rare, enigmatic, and a little bit uncanny. He is alone, belongs to no tribe, follows no customs, obeys no commands, no laws; he has left the tribe of jackdaws, where once he was one among many, and has turned toward the human tribe, which looks on him with astonishment and brings him offerings, and which he serves as a buffoon or a tightrope walker when it suits him; he makes fun of them and yet cannot get enough of their admiration. Between the bright gulls and the motley humans he sits, black, impudent, and alone, the only one of his kind; by destiny or by choice, he has no tribe and no homeland. Audacious and sharp-eyed, he sits watching over the traffic on the bridge, pleased that only a few people rush past inattentive, that the majority stop for a while, often a long while; because of him they remain standing, and gaze at him in astonishment, racking their brains over him, calling him Jakob, and only reluctantly deciding to walk on. He does not take people more seriously than a jackdaw should, and yet he seems unable to do without them.

When I found myself alone with him — and this happened only rarely — I could talk to him a little in a bird language which as a boy and youth I had partly learned from years of intimate discourse with our pet parrot and had partly invented on my own; it consisted of a brief melodic series of notes uttered in a guttural tone. I would bend down toward Jakob and talk things over with him in a fraternal way in my half-bird dialect; he would throw back his lovely head; he enjoyed both listening and thinking his own thoughts. But unexpectedly the rogue and the sprite would come to the fore in him again; he would alight on my shoulder, dig in his claws, and rapping like a woodpecker he would hammer his beak into my neck or cheek, until it was too much for me and I would shrug myself free, whereupon he would return to the railing, amused and ready for new games. But at the same time he would survey the footpath in both directions with hasty glances, to see if more of the tribe of humans were on the march and whether there were any new conquests to be made. He understood his position to a tee, his hold on us great clumsy animals, his uniqueness and chosen-ness in the midst of a strange ungainly people, and he enjoyed it enor-mously, tightrope walker and actor, when he found himself in the thick of a crowd of admiring, moved, or laughing giants. In me, at least, he had gained favor, and those times when I came to pay him a visit and did not find him I was disappointed and sad. My interest in him was a good deal stronger than in the majority of my fellow human beings. And much as I esteemed the gulls and loved their beautiful, wild, fer-vent expressions of life, when I stood in their fluttering midst, they were not individuals; they were a flock, a band, and even if I looked back to examine one of them more closely as an individual, never again would I recognize him once he had escaped my field of vision.

I have never learned where and by what means Jakob was es-tranged from his tribe and the safe harbor of his anonymity, whether he himself had chosen this extraordinary destiny — as tragic as it was radiant — or whether he had been forced to do so. The latter is more plausible. Presumably he was quite young when perhaps he fell wound-ed or unfledged from the nest, was found and taken in by people, cared for and raised. And yet our imagination is not always satisfied with the most plausible explanation, it also likes to play with the remote and the sensational, and so I have conceived of two further possibilities beyond the probable one. It is conceivable, or rather, imaginable that this Jakob was a genius who from an early age felt himself to be very different, striving for an abnormal degree of individuality, dreaming of accomplishments, achievements, and honors which were unknown in jackdaw life and the jackdaw tribe, and thus he became an outsider and loner who, like the young man in Schiller's poem "The Lay of the Bell," shunned the coarse company of his companions and wandered about himself until through some lucky chance the world opened for him a door to the realm of beauty, art, and fame, about which all young geniuses have dreamed since time out of mind.

The other fable I've made up about Jakob is this: Jakob was a ne'er-do-well, a mischiefmaker, a little rascal, which in no way rules out his being a genius. With his impudent attacks and pranks, he had at first bewildered and at times delighted his father and mother, siblings and relatives, and finally the whole of his community or colony. From early on, he was considered to be a little devil and a sly fellow, then he became more and more impertinent, and in the end he had so provoked his father's household against him, as well as the neighbors, the tribe, and the government, that he was solemnly excommunicated and, like the scapegoat, driven out into the wilderness. But before he languished away and perished, he came into contact with human beings. Having conquered his natural fear of the clumsy giants, he drew closer to them and joined them, enchanting them with his cheerful disposition and his uniqueness — of which he himself had long been aware. And so he found his way into the city and the world of human beings, and in it a place for himself as a joker, an actor, a main attraction, and a wunderkind. He became what he is today: the darling of a large public, a much-sought-after *charmeur* — particularly of elderly ladies and gentlemen, as much a friend to humans as one contemptuous of them, an artist soliloquizing at the podium, an envoy from a strange world — one unknown to clumsy giants, a buffoon for some, a dark admonition for others, laughed at, applauded, loved, admired, pitied, a drama for all, an enigma for the contemplative.

We the contemplative — for doubtless there are many others besides myself — turn our thoughts and conjectures, our impulse to understand the fabulous, not solely toward Jakob's enigmatic lineage and past. His appearance, which so stimulates our imagination, compels us to devote some thought to his future as well. And we do this with some hesitation, with a feeling of resistance and sadness; for the presumable and probable end of our darling will be a violent one. No matter how much we may want to imagine a quiet natural death for him, something on the order of his dying in the warm room and good care of that legendary lady in Ennetbaden to whom he supposedly "belongs," all probability speaks against it. A creature that has emerged from the freedom of the wild, from a secure place in a community and a tribe, and has fallen into the company of human beings and into civilization, no matter how adeptly he may adapt to the foreign surroundings, no matter how aware he may be of the advantages his unique situation provides, such a creature cannot completely escape the countless dangers concealed in this very situation. The mere thought of all these imaginable dangers — from electric current to being locked up in a room with a cat or dog, or being captured and tormented by cruel little boys — makes one shudder.

There are reports of peoples in olden times who every year chose or drew lots for a king. Then a handsome, nameless, and poor youth, a slave perhaps, would suddenly be clad in splendid robes and raised to the position of king; he would be given a palace or a majestic tent-of-state, servants ready to serve, lovely girls, kitchen, cellar, stable, and orchestra; the whole fairy tale of kingship, power, riches, and pomp would become reality for the chosen one. And so the new ruler would live amidst pomp and circumstance for days, weeks, months, until a year had elapsed. Then he would be tied and bound, taken to the place of execution, and slaughtered.

And it is of this story, which I read once decades ago and whose authenticity I have neither occasion nor desire to verify, this glittering and gruesome story — beautiful as a fairy tale and steeped in death, that I must sometimes think when I observe Jakob, pecking peanuts from ladies' hands, rebuking an overly clumsy child with a blow from his beak, taking an interest in and somewhat patronizingly listening to my parrotlike chatter, or plucking up a paper ball before an enraptured audience, holding it fast with one of his clawed feet — while his capricious head and his bristling gray headfeathers simultaneously appear to express anger and delight.

Donald Justice as Night Light

John Sokol © *1981*

Donald Justice

Piano Lessons: Notes on a Provincial Culture

So now it is vain for the singer to burst into clamor
With the great black piano appassionato. The glamour
Of childish days is upon me . . .

D. H. LAWRENCE

A piano lesson in those days cost fifty cents and lasted for half an hour. At such a price my parents, though far from well-off, could afford a weekly lesson for me all through the Depression years. Even then I may have guessed that these lessons represented some ambition for gentility, at least on my mother's part; and my father was generally pleased to indulge these fancies of hers. But they may have meant something beyond even that for her, I think, some dream of impossible success. Mother had studied piano herself years before and could still play certain favored hymns with a noisy and happy confidence. Often, it seems, it is the mother — or the mother's side of the family — to which the child's first cultural or artistic stirrings and strivings may be traced back, and this was certainly true of my own history.

Sometimes the half hour allotted to a lesson would stretch out to an hour or more, if no other pupil happened to be scheduled. Often, with Mrs. L and Mrs. K, my last two teachers, no one would be. It must have been clear to everyone, themselves included, that they were dedicated less to teaching than to whatever small sums their teaching could bring in. Nor were they embarrassed by this obvious fact. Times were hard and we understood. Afternoons with them I remember now as always hot and summerlike, time going by at a slow pace, drawn out endlessly towards dusk like a long ritardando, expressively rendered. Even in the winter months the electric fan might have to be set on the floor beside us, where it turned sometimes with a click like a metronome's. Iced tea or lemonade, hot-weather favorites, I might have had for the asking, but I never liked either one. I preferred plain ice water, a tall glass of which usually rested on top of the yellow Schirmer editions of Czerny and Chopin stacked on the closed lid of the baby grand. Fan turning, water glass in place, teacher close beside me, I would run through the scales, the exercises, again and again.

My first piano teacher, a Mrs. Snow, had formed an ideal for me no later teacher would match. Only last week, looking through one of my mother's albums, I came across a snapshot of her. Under a corner of sky now brown and faded she stands with smiling pupil, unidentified, in front of a cottage above whose entrance a signboard reads: MUSICLAND. She wears a choker of beads and clutches a crushed handkerchief. I had forgotten her double chin. The snapshot is not in color—too ancient for that—but the color of the flowered chiffon dress she is wearing in the picture does all the same come back to me, a half-bleached-out coppery or rust tone; and now suddenly her very body odor, to which I must have grown so accustomed as a child, comes back as well, rich and muffled, quite distinctive. Sometimes there are these delicate little intimacies between teacher and pupil, never spoken of.

I cannot help feeling that there was a touch of destiny in how we were brought together. One Saturday night my mother and my father and I were downtown shopping, as was our custom, for the stores stayed open well into the evening then. On our way back to where the car was parked, somewhere along busy Miami Avenue, mother and I made one last sweep through Cromer-Cassell's department store. There in the basement we came upon one of the rhythm bands, so-called, which were a feature of that era, like Tom Thumb weddings and street-corner evangelists. This band was just finishing up a performance; it could not have been long before closing time. Perhaps a dozen small children, all wearing jaunty overseas caps and blue-and-white shoulder-length capes, stood huddled together as they tapped and banged away at snare drums and wood blocks and triangles or shook their tambourines and castanets and tiny handbells, which were held up at ear level to be jiggled. We paused, my mother and I, and stood listening and looking up at the little platform where they struggled with the beat, following a sort of wand waved by the plump fairy godmother of a woman who seemed to lead them. This proved to be Mrs. Snow. I think my mother took my hand, seeing my enthrallment. I was not quite six years old, and I had never seen a musical group of any kind up close.

My wish to join must have been perfectly apparent to my mother, and before long I had a snare drum and cape of my own. (The drum was my sixth-birthday present, and the receipt for it is pasted in a scrapbook: Cromer-Cassell's, $6.50.) But very soon the drum gave way to lessons on the piano. And none too soon for me, for the sounds of the piano, in all their sonorities and relations, were a sort of heaven to me compared to the single, pitchless, snarly note of the snare. Just how this improved state of affairs came to pass I no longer recall, and there is no one now living who can tell me.

But it is possible that this was all according to plan, for Mrs. Snow was not only leader of the band but also gave piano lessons. Indeed, that was her profession, and the rhythm band was a sideline, mostly for show, for at heart she was a serious musician. She had recently come south from Massachusetts. Her Northern name evoked the whiteness of her hair and something also in her character that over the years was to remain remote and otherworldly, but she could be soft and melting too, motherly and enfolding to a child my age. How well the name suited her she realized, often commenting on it, with a little laugh. Snow itself was of course unknown to us in Miami, and even New Englanders were rare. Most people from the North had moved down to what we called the tropics for reasons of health, or so we assumed. Probably that was the case with Mrs. Snow herself, for she never looked truly well, now that I think of it. I remember still the thick white hose she had sometimes to wear over her swollen and empurpled legs. She saw no doctors, being a Christian Scientist. To stand at all then must have been painful, but to stand for long periods conducting a dozen children with noisemakers would have been an impractical torment. On these occasions, stoic though she was, she would allow herself a high stool, upon which she could sit back, with not much loss of dignity, keeping time with her baton.

As a teacher, Mrs. Snow believed in method and exactness, even for one just starting school, like me. Along with her older pupils I was required to take down during the first part of each lesson a simple sort of musical dictation. Upon the staves of student music pads bearing the Baconian motto "Writing makes the exact man" we would set down our key signatures, notes, rests, scales, and, under guidance, a few harmonic progressions. Before long we were being encouraged to compose our own simple melodies. Each week to our looseleaf notebooks was added a page containing the picture of a famous composer, which resembled in style the small busts commanding the mantelpiece and the shelves and even the sills of the Snow cottage. For Christmas that year—it was 1931—I received from my teacher a T. Presser card, sentimentally tinted: the face of the young Mozart superimposed upon a photograph of his "Gebursthaus." How foreign it all seemed to me! Somewhere beyond Miami and the South of my family lay faraway New England, and beyond that Europe, and in Europe the very Germany and Austria across whose territories I could picture, as on a map, the birthplaces of the great composers strewn like dots.

Every Wednesday afternoon—I think it was Wednesday—my mother would pick me up after school in the old Essex she had learned to drive for this very purpose. The first thing I would do then was open the lunch pail into which she would have packed a sandwich and perhaps a few cookies for the drive, which was in reality a rather short one, no more than four or five miles each way. And soon I would be feeling again the same sense of adventure and expectation that always accompanied these drives. All day in my first-grade classroom I would have been aware of what day it was and of what the afternoon held in store. By the time we were crossing the Seventeenth Avenue bridge over the Miami River—not far from where the Orange Bowl now stands, and which at that time was an especially picturesque residential area, with masses of red-green-yellow crotons and a scattering of traveler's palms along the approaches to the bridge, as well as two or three small caves hidden in the rocks below—the sense of adventure would be rising in me. On those days—but on those days only, for on other days the crossing of the bridge lost some of its charm and power as a symbol—I might imagine that we were crossing a sort of frontier into a different world, and one I wished, as in a fairy tale, to enter.

My mother and I were soon members of a circle which, at its widest, may well have included every child in the city taking music lessons of any description whatever and, of course, their mothers. I wonder now what the grand building could have been, in which the musical galas and banquets of those long-ago seasons took place, and where it could possibly have stood. It may just conceivably have been Miami High School, from which I was to graduate a decade or so later, but if it was, the connection never crossed my mind while I was attending classes there. In any case, there was somewhere a great labyrinthine building, of unusual intricacy, just the sort of building which makes an ideal setting for dreams, with numerous arches and arcades and courtyards—or so in retrospect it has become. I remember one performance there in which I took part. It was a pantomime enacting the story of Jonah and the Whale, one of several numbers during the course of a musical evening. I was small enough for Jonah, and a large young man played the Whale; somehow I was to struggle free from our joint costume during the performance. I don't think I have actually dreamed about this since, but the memory does seem to carry with it something of the phantasmagoric character of dreams. What it had to do with music escapes me now.

The little I knew of social and class distinctions I must have learned from these affairs. And yet at them the near poor, like us, did mingle quite democratically with the wealthy few. What there was of glamour for me would have come more from the newness and strangeness of it all than from any hints and glimmerings of wealth and fame. One or two retired coloraturas, whose names grew familiar through repeated appearances as sponsors on a succession of printed programs, represented the sum total of the local famous, musically. In 1932, when Paderewski appeared in concert, it was at the enormous Methodist church downtown known as the White Temple, from one of whose balconies my mother and I, like hundreds of others, gazed down at a small man foreshortened by distance. Now and then, invited to some recital or other, we did glimpse the sumptuous interior of some splendid house. And there would be occasional holiday parties, usually outdoors, behind massive vine-covered mortared walls, under tall palms. We children were often got up in costume for these, like juveniles attached to a touring stage company. All these years I have kept an impression of sparkling perfect teeth flashed by the seven- and eight-year-old beauties of those houses as they smiled vaguely in my direction. And once, on a raised outdoor terrace, upon a glass-topped table the like of which I had never seen, appeared a plate of tiny blue sandwiches, cut into triangles. I wondered immediately how blue would taste. No one seemed to be looking. I closed my fist over one or two of the tiny sandwiches, gently, as over a catch of butterflies, and made my way quickly down into the yard and around a corner to sample these unprecedented delights.

Our parents must have seen—how could they have failed to see?—that nothing at all practical could come from any of this. The half-dollar each week was like a coin paid the gypsy for her improbable prophesyings or slipped into the collection plate at Sunday morning services, with a silent prayer. The giving and taking of such lessons goes on even now, I know, and for much the same reasons as always, but during the Depression there seems to have been a special desperation about the process. Perhaps for us those lessons were supposed to be a way out, the moral equivalent of boxing for the successive waves of immigrants — Irish, Jewish, Italian — who had hung around gyms with the hope of becoming champions. More than one of the little girls I knew, their mothers fallen under the spell of Shirley Temple, wore their hair in tight curls back then and studied tap dancing. Tap was the ballet of the poor, and at the end of a school day you could hear a confusion of shoe-taps clattering off down the sunny corridors of Allapattah Elementary. As for me, my Georgia aunts and uncles, during our summer round of visits, never failed to ask what I wanted to be when I grew up. Usually I had an answer ready — accountant, aviator, first-baseman — but such answers were polite fictions. It would not be for a long while yet that I would want to be anything in particular. Music was for years what I liked more than anything else, but I never for a moment envisioned myself in the long tails and streaming hair of a Paderewski, taking bows. All the same, I can see now that, with my first lesson, just as my parents may have wished, I had begun to escape the lives we knew then — their life — whether I knew it or not. Whether I even wished for it.

Even so, after two or three years, my lessons with Mrs. Snow came to an end. No more "Marche Militaire" at the Snow recitals for me, no more after-school drives, no more blue sandwiches. It may be that Mrs. Snow had become too old and frail to meet the demands she put on herself. Perhaps she died or went back to New England. I wish I knew now; I think very kindly of her. She taught me the language of music, how to read and write it, and her training left me very quick at sight-reading, a knack which has enabled me all these years to read through much of the literature for the piano, not without mistakes, but without hard work either, and with all the conscienceless pleasure of the amateur.

Another possibility is that, for a year or two, my parents simply could not afford the cost of the lessons, although the family version, probably accurate, is that breaking off the lessons was my own idea. There were days I am sure when, instead of practicing, I would rather have been out-of-doors with the other boys, playing ball. Music was coming to seem a soft and feminine world to me by then, and the practice hour was *very* solitary. I can remember moments of impatience, the faint squeaking of the piano stool beneath me twisting in quarter-turns from side to side, and all the while the voices of friends at play in the vacant lot directly across from our house. But now when I try to think back to that time I wonder if stopping the lessons may not have had something to do with the death about that time of my best friend, a bright and cheerful boy from just down the street, as skinny and full of nerves as I was, who lingered on for months before his rheumatic fever finally killed him. His death terrified us that late spring when I was nine, all of us about his age who, dressed at our neatest, acted as pallbearers one sad afternoon. I was to weep off and on all summer, grievously. Some time during that period, I know, I was no longer taking piano lessons; that is all I can say for sure now. Before the summer was out I had fallen ill myself, with osteomyelitis, and during the long recuperation, which lasted through the winter and most of the next spring, there could be no question of resuming lessons.

Our piano—the same upright, I believe, on which my mother had practiced her own lessons—never stayed in tune for long. I wish I could remember the name of its maker, but all I know is that it was not a Steinway, not a Baldwin, not a Chickering. It did, however, have a loud, bright, rather brassy sound which I had prized from the start. On it pianissimo was far more difficult to manage than fortissimo, but in any case I preferred fortissimo. The music I produced was made to be heard! Once I was no longer taking lessons the piano tuner no longer had to come around, a saving, but the seasons of neglect took their toll. This precious instrument, with its darkening and chipped ivories, one or two of them glued back on slightly askew, went on sliding slowly downward out of tune, always downward, flatter and flatter, but unevenly flat from note to note. Some of the resulting combinations, different from month to month, used to fascinate me. Idly I would strike some favorite dissonance repeatedly, thrilled a little by its oddness. How far its pitch had sunk overall I realized only when friends from school bands, visiting, had to make ever more dramatic adjustments to their horns to bring them into tune with our upright's B-flat. Finally, it seemed to have settled into being almost precisely half a tone flat, resisting all efforts to make it hold a truer pitch, like some elderly person no longer willing to dress up for the world at large. I can still remember the unique plangency of its B just below middle C (actually B-flat). The resonance of that note remains in my ear as a prototype of all future resonances.

It was my friend Coney who encouraged me to ask for lessons again. He loved music, loved picking out tunes and harmonies at our odd-sounding piano, and had somehow taught himself to read music, perhaps with a clue or two from me. About my age, twelve or so, he needed lessons of his own, from a real teacher, but was shy about getting started and wanted company. We began lessons about the same time from Mrs. L, a neighbor, who wore long colorful skirts and seemed almost to belong to the same generation as her own daughter. Thought to be separated from her husband, she augmented her doubtful income by offering lessons in dance as well, both ballroom and tap. Her daughter danced with fire and spirit and could play the piano with a certain brave flair, a living advertisement for the range of her mother's skills. Coney lived a couple of blocks farther than I did from our teacher's house, and along the way had to pass a small grocery. On lesson afternoons he would sometimes be seen hurrying down Nineteenth Avenue, late as usual, a large paper sack bulging with soft-drink bottles clutched to his chest. These Coney would turn in at the grocery for the two-cents deposit on each. The family who ran the grocery must have hated to see him coming, but the proceeds enabled him to pay for the week's lesson with Mrs. L.

I like to think now that our experience was not unusual. Among the hundred thousand or so people in the Miami of the thirties there would have been six or seven other teachers like Mrs. L, if not more. And, in the nation at large, who can guess how many? There must often have been a man, ghostlike in the background, whose chief stay and support the teacher was. And during one of those moments in lessons when the eye begins to wander, the pupil might catch a glimpse of this mysterious figure, as I did once, though not at Mrs. L's. Outdoors he sat, ensconced in a sort of deck chair, under the shade of fruit trees, staring out across an ocean of half-mown grass at nothing, nothing at all. Did they drink, these lost men? Were they the victims of shell shock, of tuberculosis? Mrs. L's husband was none of these, but wrapped in a deeper mystery still. We saw little of him, for he was Hispanic and lived, as we pieced the story together, in Cuba. His visits were always brief, always unexpected. Suddenly he would be stepping off the bus that stopped at our corner. He was a small, fragile-looking person who carried himself stiffly and dressed in a black that seemed unnatural in that climate. The effort to recall this ghostly personage turns up a cane for him as well. Past one interested porch after another he would proceed, touching the tip of his cane delicately to the sidewalk before him, like someone experimenting with the idea of blindness. A diplomat of sorts, or so we had been allowed to gather. Where the notion had come from that he showed up only to demand money from Mrs. L I am not sure. Perhaps at some point she complained of this weakness to my mother. At any rate, we always suspected the worst of him, this courtly-looking little man who came and went like something in a dream.

Before long Coney and I found ourselves beyond Mrs. L's scope as a teacher. She must have known this time would come, and she remained sympathetic, interested in our futures. Mrs. K followed as my teacher. I used to ride my bicycle to her house, a mile or so distant. The greater distance I had to cover seemed for a while like a measure of progress. I would pedal through the sultry afternoons, working up to a furious speed and then coasting, no hands, music books safe in the wire basket clipped to the handlebars. Mrs. K herself could take me only so far into the piano literature — somewhere among the black keys of Chopin — but this proved to be just about as far as I really wanted to go at the time. The moods of the nocturnes and the ballades, dreamy and bittersweet, as they seemed then to me, were exactly right for someone just beginning to drift through the lovely-dark passages of adolescence. Sometimes I would move over on the piano bench while Mrs. K demonstrated how to handle a certain passage. And the few bars might extend themselves all the way to the end of the piece, for at such times Mrs. K was capable of forgetting herself. Transported, she would become another person. As the passionate notes of one or the other of the nineteenth-century Romantics, her specialty, sprang to life beneath her suddenly invigorated fingers, she seemed to rise briefly into some sphere of romance herself. And then her tensed hands would rebound upwards from the keys, to quiver suspended above the final echoing chord there, while she turned her head towards me and smiled, as if we shared a secret. But even as I returned the smile, she would be subsiding back into her ordinary self. This was not an illusion of mine. Clearly she felt something of it too, and this must have cast over her life a thin shadow of regret, the sort of mild discontent which adds a touch of mysterious interest to the characters of otherwise unexceptional persons. In the case of Mrs. K the effect was purely transitory. Only when she was, so to speak, inspired by the miraculously rapid and precise movements of her own fingers, as if she herself did not quite understand how it was happening, did this second Mrs. K bob to the surface, and then only for a few seconds at a time.

There seemed to be no one in Miami who could teach me what I really wanted to learn, which was to compose music. Already, without knowing nearly enough, I was composing what I could, obsessively. So was my friend Coney. We bought score-paper at Amidon's Music Store downtown and filled it with thousands of notes, a form of magic. At fifteen I wrote a long piece grandly entitled "Myth" and intended for an orchestra larger than any I had ever heard. But when finally, after weeks of procrastination, I inquired of Mrs. K whom I could study composition with, she had no idea. She lent me her harmony textbook from the conservatory. That was all very well, but limited, and I was looking by then for something far vaster, more challenging. Sometimes I felt that no one had confidence in me but myself. There was my mother, but she would have believed in me without cause or reason. A few years later—and, as I sometimes feel, too late, after the critical moment had passed—I was to meet the composer Carl Ruggles, Ives' friend, who wintered in Miami, and he very willingly took me on as a free pupil. Then, amply, the confidence which can be so important to the young was given me, and in it I beamed and I basked, proud, happy, a little in awe of the future. Had I met Ruggles at thirteen or fourteen I wonder if I might not now be writing music, and very happily, whether in Hollywood (as I secretly imagine) or in some academy or conservatory.

For several years I felt not exactly lost but suspended in a sort of vacuum. I had the sense of trying in vain to make headway against some unseen obstacle, as in anxiety dreams. Meanwhile I read the books available in the public library. Teaching myself to read orchestral scores, I read through what there was of Haydn, Mozart, Beethoven—nothing in the library then so new as Debussy. It may be hard for anyone now to grasp how difficult recordings were to come by, and especially of new music. I remember listening for the first time—and with what shocked delight—to Stravinsky's *Firebird*, an orchestral commonplace now. But the sudden explosion of the great drum at the start of "King Katschei's Dance" that afternoon! My face flushed with excitement as I heard that, there in the isolation of a listening booth on the mezzanine of the same department store where mother and I had first encountered Mrs. Snow's rhythm band. (The name of the store had been changed to Richards' by then.) There too I first heard the other

Stravinsky ballets and an early recording of Schoenberg's *Pierrot Lunaire*, featuring Erika Mann, Auden's proxy bride. The recording could not have been made long after she arrived in this country, fleeing Europe. Only the summer just past I had read her father's *The Magic Mountain*. Things seemed to come together somehow.

And who in all of Miami could have purchased the single copy of that album which was to stand for weeks unclaimed on the shelf? I could not afford to buy it myself, but I returned to it. I never really came to the point of believing that it had been shipped to Miami for me alone, but I did think that no one else in the city — in the whole state of Florida, for that matter — could have appreciated it just then quite so keenly. It was almost as if the recording had been undertaken for just that moment of revelation when I had first touched the needle to the groove in one of the listening booths at Richards'. Such are the grandiosities of adolescence.

W.S. Merwin as The Lice

John Sokol © *1981*

W. S. Merwin

The Skyline

This time I could almost have walked past it, looking for it, in the bright sunlight of late October. The afternoon shining everywhere. Yellow in the leaves; the telephone wires motionless.

What is it, after all, that I thought to recognize?

Over and over again we are told, and then discover, that when you go back it is all smaller. But each time there appears to have been a mistake. There is nothing to measure by, and whoever might know is not there.

And only five years this time, since I last came here, looking. No trace of that visit except this one. There is the place now, when I was still thinking it was a little farther — perhaps the width of one house, or half a house, farther. I suppose I had expected the shrinking to — what? Stop?

And this is all there is. The narrow lot between the long side of the apartment house and the one-story industrial structure whose purpose no one could ever explain to me, long ago, so that I have never known. It was described as "some kind of warehouse," and it appears to have changed least of anything here: a building never quite in use, always between uses. Both buildings were here when my father's yellow brick church stood on the site between them, in the days of streetcars and rumble seats. I was nine when we moved away, and the church building, with its steeple sometimes called a spire, and its cross full of light bulbs, like a sign advertising something else, was sold a few years later, and torn down not long after that.

I cannot see how that stolid yellow facade with its rose window dull as a box, seen from the outside, its twin front doors approached by a pair of cement walks and two flights of cement steps, and another walk, around to the side, to iron stairs down to the basement, could ever have fitted into this patch overgrown with the few species that return here, specifically here, remembering, whatever has happened to the place. I look to see whether sections have not been sold off, on one side or the other, but no, that is not possible: the lot takes up the whole space between those neighboring buildings. But then, only the site has grown smaller. The church itself never shrank at all. It vanished.

Like the size it assumed once in my father's eyes, when he first saw it, a year or so before I was born. A man of thirty, and it looked real enough to him, at some point, to be an object of ambition. What had he heard, from whom, that brought him to look up at it, here? Right here. Who met him, chosen by the elders? They stepped in off the street, talking. A few fragments of the cement walk lead into the tall autumn weeds. He stood there, someplace in the air, and preached. And the congregation sat in rows, above the place where the bushes have grown thick and the hardy asters are blooming, and listened. Over some section of the weeds they conferred, and found that a majority of them approved. Who urged? Who was persuaded? They elected to extend the call, as my father would say, to the younger man. Younger, I learned, did not mean younger than somebody else, nor than something else. Just younger. He was younger then. As I never saw him.

His first congregations had been small rural pastorates in western Pennsylvania where the roads were still dirt. He saw the church on Palisade Avenue as a step up in the world. He called it, for a time, a challenge. He would have denied that he found it, ever, frightening — subtly and sleeplessly vertiginous. Beyond where it stood, framed by the surviving buildings, is the famous view: the New York skyline, rising from the river, gray, keen, elegant, glittering. Massive and silent, over the water. Larger and closer than I had remembered.

I do not know whether my mother was with him, on that visit, nor what part she had in the decision to accept the call, when it came. In the mail. She believed in the duties of a minister's wife, and she never spared herself. As I understand the chronology, they moved to Union City — in the new Buick — only a few weeks before I was born. I was brought here, the first time, in my mother's womb. The First Presbyterian Church of Union City, New Jersey — though there was no second. They were informed that the neighborhood had changed considerably, before they came. So many foreigners moving in. Mostly Italians. People had moved away. Many members of the congregation had a long way to come now, on Sundays. That was part of the challenge.

Another was the condition of the building itself. My father pointed out run-down details with a sectarian satisfaction, clucking his tongue, shaking his head, poking the evidence with a slow, thick finger. Square yellow brick columns topped with cement flanked the twin entrances from the sidewalk. Cracks in the cement. The walks themselves needing attention. The patch of front yard neglected, between the walks, where my father already planned to install a glassed-in bulletin board facing the street: a flat box with a Gothic roof, the wood painted black every year. His pride. An innovation that he would bring to his congregation, right from the start. Besides announcements of church events he would fill it with posters, referred to half seriously as "signs of the times." Changed once a week, but recurring. One more frequently than the rest: the top section of a globe, with a huge figure of Christ looming over it, arms outstretched, bright yellow radiating from him into the space around him and down onto the dark topography of the curve below him, the unidentifiable dream continents. "I Am The Light Of The World," the poster said. The principal color was blue, which faded faster than the rest. I was disappointed, one day when I had been allowed to be present as my father opened a mailing tube and I learned that the posters came in series, including perhaps, the phrase "signs of the times" and, I think, a new copy each time of "I Am The Light Of The World." The colors were fresh and dark once more — a source of pleasure and encouragement to my father, in his shirt sleeves, as he unrolled it and held it flat. He said, to no one, that it was a lovely thing.

For a reason I do not know, it is the steps to the left-hand door that they climb at the beginning, my father brisk and charged with inexpressible office my mother moving more slowly on her small feet — the pace of a quiet stranger being led. In those days she dressed in long cotton jerseys reaching below the waist. Tans and pinks. And light shawls, all to disguise the pregnancy. She carried a folded white handkerchief, and looked up, with a distant smile. Both of my parents were short. The wide-brimmed gray fedoras that my father wore then made him look still more so. He had a way of shooting out his chin repeatedly, to pull the skin of his throat up through his shirt collar, and then giving his hat-brim an abrupt tug (origin, I believed, of the term "snap-brim") before stepping, with a bounce, into the street he was about to cross. The sound of his feet on the church steps was a deliberate announcement, and with another bounce, and a long stride, he swung the door open as a gesture, removing his hat with the other hand and waving her past him. Of course the doors too would need some work. The hinges were hoarse, the brass was green and mottled, the varnish was like thawing ice. But the heavy doors themselves, which were noticed only in passing—what power, what unguessed reserves, unbroken antiquity, silent presence they embodied! It made no difference to the doors whether they were locked or stood open. The smell of the wood, on the outside, was an unknown name. And on the inside it was the unfading echo of the marine interior darkness. On both sides the resinous taste was forbidden, bitter, heady.

Green carpet, musty cloud, met them in the shadows inside the door. The light muffled, filtered, refracted through small panes of leaded glass in double doors to the side, which led into the room between the entrances that was used for elders' and trustees' meetings, advanced Sunday School classes, and midweek prayer meetings, and for kissing the bride after weddings. In kindergarten and first grade I wondered whether I could have three brides at once, since I liked them all, and kiss them in that room with nobody seeing. But that would be hard, because the room was full of yellowish light from a row of stained-glass windows facing the street, and besides the glazed doors at either end, it had a row of clear glass windows into the main church, where people came and went and could see everything: the upright piano and its stool, the ranks of chairs, the bulletins piled on the tables. I realized that I would have to do the kissing somewhere else, and if possible without a wedding.

Inside the front doors, where the trees have grown up, steep dark wooden stairs, intricately made, went down to the basement. And up, on the left side to the organ loft, and on the right to the room under the steeple, where the rope hung that rang the bell on Sunday mornings. Only those authorized to do so were allowed to go up into either sanctum, and their comings and goings to the loft and the steeple were invisible. I knew those dignitaries at other times, in other places—even in other parts of the church. But the organist appeared (though I was told not to turn around and look to see if he was there) or the top of his head bobbed up behind the music rack of the organ, and the bell rang, proving the presence of the bell-ringer in the room under the steeple, without my having been able to catch a glimpse of either of them emerging from somewhere and climbing the stairs. At the beginning I could not understand how the organist got up there, and when I asked I was told to hush. It seemed to be a secret that he came and went at all, and I wondered whether we were supposed to believe that he was up there all the time. Once in the middle of a week I—I myself—was allowed up to the organ loft with my father. He, distracted and vexed, looking for something. Tiers of plain choir benches, under the rose window. Stacks of old hymnals with the bindings falling off. Choir music, folded flags, everything deep in gray dust. The closed organ, like a rounded crate, standing in the middle. Don't touch anything— very emphatically. My father bending down, peering into boxes, dusting his fingers, puffing. Just stand right there and don't touch anything. Seeing the familiar church from that new height, it felt as though the organ loft were floating like a cloud, or as though I had suddenly grown out of the top of my head and were flying over the pews below. My father didn't seem to find what he was looking for up there. When I asked him he didn't hear, leading the way down the dusty stairs.

The green-carpeted floor of the church auditorium sloped down to the brass rail and green velvet curtain in front of the communion table (nothing so "Roman" as an altar). Four aisles, and they were steep enough so that when four ushers had taken up the collection—better to say "the offering"—on Sundays, and had assembled in the back of the church under the polished balcony of the organ loft, and my father in his black gown had raised his arms and we had all stood up, and the ushers marched down front with the collection, to the rail, their pace accelerated and their tread grew heavier, thundered, as they reached the bottom and drew up short, to bow their heads over the wooden plates full of change and bills and folded envelopes, and wait for the benediction. While it was being pronounced the windows and the room still echoed. And then the organ took over, and "Praise God from Whom all blessing flow/Praise Him all creatures here below . . ." In the middle of it my mother's voice, not round but resolute, from up under the short veil of her hat.

In the pause before the sermon, during that low wave of rustling and settling that whispered through the pews and was gone, she produced from her purse two small pads of paper and two pencils and handed them, fragrant from her gloves, to my sister on one side of her, and to me on the other. So that we could draw pictures during the sermon, and keep ourselves quiet. Hold them down on your knee, not up to show. And don't use the eraser, or make a noise tearing the pages or turning them. Some of the congregation—she told her friends, in reference to the practice—some of the older members in particular, might not altogether approve. The young minister's wife, with ideas of her own. But others agreed that it was a very sensible solution; it was too much to expect the children to sit still and listen to the whole sermon, which was over their heads. What was over our heads? I asked, occasionally. But there it stayed, as I was content that it should. I was glad to be allowed to draw. My father pretended not to know that we drew during his sermons. My mother said to just not say anything about it. Each time it came to his notice he acted surprised to learn it, shook his head, but continued to let it pass. I listened to the sermons anyway, parts of them. What were called the illustrations. They were stories. The King of England sending a battleship to rescue one of his subjects. The child Teddy Roosevelt afraid to go to church because of The Zeal. The Zeal of Thy house hath eaten me up — he had heard that in a psalm. Which produced a murmur of knowing amusement that was over my head as well, but made me realize that grown-ups did not consider The Zeal to be frightening, though my father suggested that perhaps they should be more frightened of it than they were. Thinking it over, and looking around carefully, I concluded that our church probably had no Zeal at all. It was something from a long time ago, like a dragon. Where would a Zeal live, in my father's church? I tried to imagine one, hiding up in a big crack in the wall between the tall windows, or disguising itself as a huge stain on the stain-colored wallpaper, but I could never get it real enough to frighten me, on Sunday mornings. I knew that nothing so historic was likely to appear there.

On the other hand, those stains, shaped like great animals, shadows, clouds — I realized eventually that they were individual manifestations of The Damp that my father frowned and glowered about so often at supper. At such times the church was referred to as "The plant." It was The House of the Lord even so. "Couldn't the Lord stop the stains?" I asked. "Never mind," I was told, and the subject was washed over. A palimpsest. The congregation failed to raise enough money to repair the plant adequately. Faithful members of the church, when they were talking with my father, shook their heads about the others — half-hearted and unreliable — and sighed. The church, they agreed, could only be what the spirit of its members made it. Nodding of hats. As for me, I never could really see the stains on the wall as symptoms of the failing spirit of the congregation. The stains were themselves. They were always themselves. When they changed I leaped in my body. They were *appearing*. Their lives were unknown to everybody. I had no doubt of their power. To me they represented a different plane from the one on which adults of the congregation droned and agreed, so that direct conflict between the stains and the church officers was hard to imagine. But if the conflict was real, as it was repeatedly said to be—a ceaseless struggle with The Damp—I was certain of the outcome. The stains were patient and silent. They might be hidden, but they would survive and return, and with no effort on their part they would prevail in the long run. I felt respect for them; awe. But I was never afraid of the malevolence which my father and the church officers clearly attributed to them. I regarded them as remote, august spirits, who might even be friends.

They loomed most powerfully, and were discussed most often (though it was some years before I observed it) in the autumn and winter, when I had colds one after the other, and sat through the prayers with my nose stuffed up, and was supposed to try to wait until the hymns before blowing it, if I possibly could. Our pew was near the front, and I was not allowed to turn around and stare at anything, but during prayers, when our heads, supposedly, were bowed, I could tilt my face up to the side and roll my eyes to watch them, until my mother noticed. And on the way in and out I could look up at them, though I did not want it to be obvious that I was paying attention to them. In summer they withdrew into themselves and I would wonder where they were, and miss them. The sun came through the long yellow windows on the south, over the side aisle, at that season, and tapering bands of sunlight moved across the pews, the heads, the fluttering print dresses, the cotton suits, the fans (my mother said fanning yourself only made you hotter, and though there were cardboard fans in the hymnal racks, we were not permitted to remove them) and over the green carpet between the front pew and the low green velvet curtain hanging from brass rings on its brass rod. The sunlight whitened them all. I watched it change position in the course of the sermon, and between the beginning and end of a prayer. I saw it climb a brass post, the leg of the communion table. I saw it move. That bit of floor up in front of the church by the rail—how empty it remained, through the sermon! My father's voice flew over it, but the sunlight on the green pattern was untouched. There was the spot where I had been held up when I was a few weeks old, and baptized, one Sunday morning in autumn, by a friend of my father's named Andy. Andy Richards. Referred to as though he were a close friend of mine, though I think I never saw him after that day. But later I had such a clear image of being held up in an arm, and the green of the carpet, that I believed I really remembered that moment. I was told that it was impossible for me to have remembered something from that age, and the sunlight on the carpet — when in fact the baptism took place in the autumn — also makes it unlikely that the image is an actual memory, but it remains clear, and whether it comes from a dream or from suggestions or from a glimpse of the occasion itself I cannot now be sure. But the place — that was the place. I was told that I did not cry, as babies often do during that ceremony, but looked around, and at the touch of the water laughed.

On the same spot, near the baptismal font, sometimes on Sunday mornings in summer a folding chair stood empty, and when the service was drawing breath a guest performer would be announced. Then there would be a rustling of bulletins, in search of the name there. A melancholy old man in a gray shirt sat down in the chair once, gray hair plastered straight across his forehead, and without looking at anybody, in total silence, he opened a chewed wooden violin case and took out a saw and a violin bow, set the saw handle carefully between his high-buttoned black shoes with turned-up toes, pulled his pants tight around his legs, and still without looking at anybody began to draw the bow over the back of the saw, teasing tremulous water sounds out of the blade. Hairs of the bow broke and waved back and forth in a light of their own. He stopped after a while and started again, without a word. "Come Thou Almighty King." The notes wavered and emerged slowly, rising to a surface and evaporating from it. Several times he stopped, tore off the hairs, and started again, with sequences of notes that I did not recognize and followed blindly. Then he got up and bowed, put back the saw and bow, and took them past us up the aisle. Nobody seemed to know him. In whispers someone asked whether he was Italian, and someone said he was a carpenter. Another time a lady in velvet played a harp there, and my father, who habitually said that he loved music but couldn't carry a tune in a bucket, and who whistled the first six notes of "The Old Rugged Cross," and nothing further, over and over, all his life, to my mother's hopeless irritation, announced that we were fortunate to have been able to hear her, and everyone said afterwards what a beautiful instrument the harp was, and how long it took to learn to play it. Once a tall girl sat there and played a clarinet, accompanied by soft notes on the organ. I never saw any of those people again.

There in front of the rail my tool box was brought, for a bride to kneel on during her wedding at night. I was told about it afterwards — a laughing secret. I didn't see the wedding itself because it took place after my sister's and my bedtime, and because we were then considered too young to go to weddings. An evening wedding in any case (but it was *night*, I thought) was heralded by a special wave of whispers and consultations in lowered voices. It was more than a rarity. No one could remember whether there had ever been one at the church. My father had probably never performed one. It was spoken of as something modern, and a bit fast. Everyone involved seemed to feel that they were doing something racy, and to be slightly surprised to find themselves getting away with it. But Mandy, the bride — they kept telling each other — had very definite ideas. She was a character. She kept people waiting. My father said she was a clip. The stages in the making of her wedding gown provided news, on the sidewalk after church, for weeks before the event. There were several rehearsals of the ceremony, but it was not until the night itself, after I was in bed and supposed to be asleep, that my father came up to the house with two of the ushers and fetched the tool box. Mandy had decided that she wanted it to be a kneeling wedding, which was another daring notion in a Presbyterian service. People liked her, and said afterwards that it had been a beautiful idea, but you could tell that they would not have wanted it to become a custom.

No one was supposed to know that it had been my tool box, under the cushion she was kneeling on, unless my parents told them. I couldn't see why the use of the tool box shouldn't be mentioned in the ordinary way, but that was one of the many unexplained and perhaps inexplicable injunctions. The fact that they had used it, that it had occurred to someone (my father in his ministerial role) as the fitting centerpiece and support for a grown-up ceremony at the church, gave me a feeling of importance — mine, but remote. Not to be claimed, grasped, or acknowledged, and yet closer and more real than my sense of the box itself, which was mine in name only. It didn't look like a tool box, people said, admiringly, when my father showed it to them. You'd never know it was a tool box, they said. I didn't know what a tool box was expected to look like, and I would have preferred for it to look like one, even though they said it was better this way. There were real tools in it, which added to their surprise — and why should they be surprised, even though the tools were not used? The ushers never thought to take the tools out, and heard them clink as they carried the box down Fourth Street under the poplar trees and the street lights to the church, that night. The sound, and the memory of it, made them laugh. I knew each of those tools, its feel, its smell, and its name which I had been taught when the box was given to me at Christmas — my fourth Christmas, I think. Santa Claus had brought it, but it was my father who made the presentation, guiding everyone's attention to it with the promise of something momentous, and raised eyebrows and forefinger. Though it might be a little too old for me, yet. I would learn to appreciate it as I grew older. The box was not wrapped, but simply concealed under some paper and other presents, and tied shut with a wide, dark red ribbon in a bow, which was untied as I watched, and the ribbon folded and put away. My father's revelation of the box was preceded by a cloud of cautions: "Just a minute. Are you sure your hands are clean? Now be careful." What I saw was — a box. Or a chest. "It's a beautiful thing," my father said, shaking his head and clucking his tongue. It looked like a piece of furniture. Polished dark wood, which we were told was mahogany, with a scalloped edge around the lid — a yard long and a foot wide — and with antiqued bronze-finish handles on either end, though they were never to be used to lift it by, because they might not be strong enough. I must be careful not to scratch it, which meant not coming too near it. I was told that I might open it now, since someone else was with me, but as I started to, my father said, "Wait. Just a minute, now," and took hold of the heavy lid. "You'll have to be careful not to drop it," he told me.

A rich, forbidding smell rose from the dark interior. I realized later that it was compounded of the wood stains — one for the hardwood of the box, and another, that left an oily surface, for the softer wood of the small drawer and the runners it rested on — and from shellac and machine oil protecting the new steel of tools. It was the word of the box — magic, suggestive, enticing, treacherous, and oppressive. I was told that I must never open the box unless my father was present. And the tools were not to be used now, of course, but later, when I was older and had learned how. I would only scratch the box with them and cut myself and damage the tools, which were very fine, if I tried to use them right away. But one by one they were taken out and given to me to hold. Each time I was told to be careful, and taught the name. Hammer: blond, bright, cold. Be careful not to drop it on your toe. Other people, watching, echoed that wisdom. A plane, painted gray, with a red wheel on it. Full of potential damages. My father demonstrated how the blade came out, and put it back, and showed me how a carpenter planed wood, in the air. A tape measure, a screwdriver, a used stone chisel, a brace and bit. A square, the blue of whose blade impressed me, and its responsibility for squareness, pure squareness: its official possession of a universal form, which was all it was and all that it did—as a tool.

The flashiest of them all, the most solemnly prohibited, and the one that my father most admired and praised, was a hatchet, all of one piece of steel, as he showed me. He allowed me to hold it for a moment and then took it back to point out the notch for drawing nails, the round hammerhead, the handle made of rings of leather which I would never have thought were leather, the thinness of the blade, the way it rang when my father flicked it with a finger. He told stories about the sharpening of hatchets, and he put it away carefully at the bottom of the box, where I was never to touch it until I grew up. (My father explained that the collection of tools was far from complete, and that others might be added later on, now that I had a real box for them. As long as I behaved myself.) But the tool that appeared to me as the hope and eye of the whole assembly, the indication that the existence of these particular objects extended beyond their circumstances, the one with which I felt immediate friendship and a shared joke, was the small wooden level (I was not told, then, that it was called a "spirit level"—simply a "level"). Block of deceptively light wood, easily damaged, and on the top, under the brass plate, the glass tube, breakable, in which the bubble moved back and forth in its iridescent green fluid. That was the tool I believed in.

My mother stood aside, through all this, and watched. Unconvinced, but perhaps not aware of that; certainly not sure of it. Removed.

When I was told, in time, of Mandy's wedding, I imagined watching it from the organ loft. Everyone agreed that the box had looked beautiful surrounded by flowers and covered with a satin cushion. Later, reading of Pandora's box, I supposed it looked like the tool box.

But the more secular church events, the suppers and socials, as well as the Sunday School services and the children's Sunday School classes, took place in the basement. One surprising thing about the site is the way the basement hollow too has vanished, and all signs of where it was. A building can be removed, but a hole? They must have filled it in with rubble, and then roots groped through it in the dark again, as though for the first time. A few small pieces of crushed mortar look recent — added much later than the demolition, when the growth was already there and the lot had long since been "waste." The basement was probably not very deep after all. There were windows on all sides — far up the walls, it is true, but perhaps not quite as high as I remember them from the viewpoint of a child. They looked out into underground recesses with iron grilles across the tops. On the north side, toward the apartment building, they let in a poor, dirty light, but on the side to the west, facing the street, the light was clear and promising. On the south, toward the factory-warehouse, a flight of iron steps led down from outside, under a frosted glass roof, to a side door, and when there was some event in the basement, and the church, above, was not being used, that door was the main entrance. I remember it chiefly in winter, perhaps because on winter Sundays, when the turnout was small, especially during the increasingly frequent ailments of the furnace and boiler, services were held in the basement, which was easier and cheaper to heat, although the sounds of the boiler and radiators hissing and clanking sometimes racketed dramatically above my father's voice. Once, down there, during winter, I blew my nose during a prayer, because suddenly I had to, and a fat woman gave a little shriek — she thought the boiler was bursting. When the actual services were held downstairs the front doors of the church would be locked and after we were seated on folding chairs we could see the feet and legs of latecomers descending the black stairs outside the white window. They usually stamped, as though no one could hear them, at the bottom, in the cemented cubicle outside the door: when we had services down there it was often raining or snowing or sleeting outside, and after the closing benediction the few who had showed up congratulated each other and themselves on having come, even if they had got there late and had entered, embarrassed, in the middle of a prayer or of the sermon itself.

The basement ceiling was supported by iron pillars, which I found mysterious and admirable. Just like that they held up the whole thing, with no sign of strain. I would lay my hand on them to touch that utter ability. They were always cool, and if I set my ear against them I could hear that they rang. However quiet or far away it was, that note was always there. The iron pillars were a people to themselves. In my earliest recollections they are painted a somber red, and I think the whole basement then was old reds and browns. There was talk of how dark it was, and one year, after a drive for funds for the job, the basement was repainted: the back room toward the street, which was a step higher than the main room; the main room itself; and at least part of the kitchen, beyond, with its big coffee urns and zinc tubs under the grimy windows, and its slatted floor — an area totally forbidden to me, so that my knowledge of it is mostly shadows. The new color was pistachio green, though that was not what it was called. With a stenciled Gothic trellis design on it, repeated around the walls, in chocolate brown. Everyone was proud of the result. And the paint was not dry, the first gathering to celebrate it had not taken place, when the rains, which had been abnormally heavy that season, blocked the sewer and gutter on Palisade Avenue in front of the church, filled the avenue, and the black public water backed up and flooded the basement four feet deep, and the rain kept on falling for days. Roasting dishes and coffee pots, it was said, floated in the kitchen, and the slats of the floor bumped around like rafts. The furnace and boiler were left for dead, for a while. The walls dried out and were repainted, but the floor, they all agreed, would never be the same.

I see it was all turning green even then, though no one thought of it that way, no doubt. The pale mat green of the basement joining the water greens of the church above: carpet greens fading under sunbeams in the aisles, worn gray near the doors, looking newest and oldest in the corners, where the nap (a word I weighed and relished) stayed dark and untrodden, like velvet. And the deep green of the velvet curtains up front by the communion table, above which the brass of the rail, the gold of a cross on the table (my father's daring touch: staunch Presbyterians might think it Romish, he said, but he didn't see that the Catholics should have a monopoly on the cross), gilded vine patterns traced on the wall above the choir stalls, and the dull gilt of the organ pipes, stood out, shone, even when the church was unlit. But apart from their gleaming I can find no memory of any color in that part of the church that was the dim, removed focus of it all, into which the few members of the choir sailed at the beginning of services, in their black gowns, sank down, and melted into the shadow, and in which my father sat during anthems, out of sight, hidden by the wide lectern, from the pew where we were sitting. Out of that darkness, after a moment of silence, or in the middle of what the bulletin announced as an organ meditation, he would suddenly emerge with his arms raised, the sleeves of his gown hanging like those in the poster facing the street, and say dramatically, "Let us pray." During prayers I did not dare to raise my head and look at him for long, but through other parts of the service if I fixed my eyes on him I found that an aura of light came and went around him. It was a trick of the eyes, and I knew it, and knew that it would not be encouraged if I spoke of it, so I never mentioned it, but I learned to make that luminous phantom grow larger, more intense, spread out like rays in water, while my father's voice rose and fell, coming through it from somewhere else. The name for that part of the church was the sanctuary. It was holy, and forbidden to everyone except those taking part in a service. I stood up there once or twice, and filed across, at some Sunday School ceremonial. But then my attention was on the occasion more than on the place. I was aware of the strangeness of being on the platform, how high it felt, as though I were standing on glass, dazzled. Otherwise, that part of the church, as I remember it, is distinct but not defined. The faces of the waiting choir members are dim, or they fade out altogether. My father appears and announces, or he subsides from the pulpit in silence after a sermon. I was told that there was something up there in that place, which nobody could see, and that it was always there. It was in the pulpit, and near the communion table and my father's chair. It was not an "it." When the place was empty I would turn my eyes suddenly to look, though I knew I would not surprise what was there.

And the green continued, with the same carpet pattern, in the rooms on either side of the sanctuary. The choir room, on the north side, in the shade of the apartment building, where the light was cool as bare plaster, and the tops of the long, varnished cupboards in which the choir robes hung during the week were piled with boxes and brown paper rolls, and a door opened onto a narrow, steep, spiral staircase, lightless. On it pale green flower vases risen from the dead stood in tiers. It led, I learned, to an unmapped, scarcely known region behind the organ pipes. Up there were other organ pipes — real ones. Those stairs were totally forbidden, and I regarded with awe the few men of the congregation known to have climbed them.

And the green carpeted the vestry, on the south side of the sanctuary, into which the sun shone through the same yellow stained glass as that in the main church, but more intimately, since the room was much smaller. Again, in there, were cupboards for robes, but the room was grander and in better order than the choir room, just as there were bands of black velvet on my father's preaching robe and none on the choir robes. The room smelled of large books bound in leather, and the varnish in the sunlight. On the walls were two extremely large photographs, framed, under glass, of battleships, one of them the *Utah*. The brass plate below the picture said that it had twelve Babcock and Wilcox boilers. I have forgotten its maximum speed. If you looked closely you could see sailors, somewhat retouched, up above the smoke, in the round cage towers that were there so that the lookouts could see better and tell the people below where to aim the guns. In this room my father seemed to be continually mumbling important things to himself, leafing through papers. He sometimes said that he was running over his sermon in his mind. And here too a door opened onto a narrow staircase, a straight one. I imagined that it was secret. It climbed toward a window outside an upstairs study.

A few times, but very few, my father took me up to that study, which he used, off and on, during the first years in Union City. Two desks, side by side, made one long one standing in the middle of the floor — an arrangement that he repeated later in his life. Filing cabinets, wooden chests of drawers piled with folders, glass-fronted bookcases, shelves of registers and huge tomes, flags leaning in a corner, everything rich with dust. Nothing was to be touched. My father especially admired, praised, and told me particularly not to touch a revolving bookcase full of dust and small wrapped boxes, and a dictionary on the desk beside it, an immense volume whose merit was one with its fragility. On the farther desk the big Underwood typewriter, already old, accompanied him all his life, bulked under its black shroud. On the walls, photographs, portraits of former pastors of the church, and of unknown ancients; a picture of a beautiful woman standing and raising a flag — a commemoration of some phase of my father's brother Sam's World War career in the marines; class pictures, one of my father's own class at seminary, and others of classes he had never seen and knew nothing about. And that was enough questions, I was told. If I was to be allowed up there I must be completely quiet, or else my father would have to take me home. Did I think I could be quiet? I thought I could. My father turned me to the window just inside the door, looking out across Hoboken and the river. With a window seat, and a velvet cushion on it — green. There, my father said: I could get up there and look out the window and be as quiet as I could be. I could watch the boats coming and going and not say anything. And it was true. They plied upstream, downstream, in a silence I could watch, through the clear afternoon light of autumn, just as it is: the river blue and gray, the black hulls, orange hulls, gray hulls, the bow waves and the wakes. There were more of them then, as I remember. Liners, tugs, barges freighted with whole railroad trains. And ferries, yawning and turning to and from the dark arches in the green arcades of ferry barns on the far side. Smoke rose, utterly out of reach, unaware of being watched. White steam leaped from hooters, and long afterwards the sound arrived. And behind me the typewriter clattered and thumped, and my father muttered to himself. Once he pushed back his chair and took me downstairs into the church and had me sit in a pew — any pew! — prickly with responsibility, to listen to a passage of sermon. For him to go over it, for his own purpose, and to see (he added) whether I was old enough to understand. Since I was the only one in the pews, and had been charged with this extraordinary and wholly unexpected office, I imagined that the rhetorical questions were addressed to me personally, and tried to answer them, which was a bad mistake. After that I became invisible, and a while later was summoned to follow my father upstairs again, to the window seat. He spoke well of how quiet I could be, there, but said he could see that the sermon was still too old for me.

How often I was allowed up there, while he worked, I have no idea. Not many times, certainly, and they have run together. It may indeed have been only once. In our later years in Union City, after I had started school, he used that study less. But both of us came to speak of my going there to watch the river from the window, while he worked, as though it were a regular and cherished custom. Both preferred to think of it that way. He wanted to believe that he was companionable to me. My being there in that study represented a passing moment of expansiveness which he liked to think was the usual, the normal — though necessarily preoccupied — characteristic of his way with me. He hoped to be able to take it for granted. And for me, being there, even having been there, was a mark of his favor, a privilege and — as he himself said — a "surprise." I was told that I loved to watch the river, and it was so; and I was still far from beginning to distinguish the one (being told) from the other (it being so). Being allowed to watch the river was prized even more in retrospect, the feeling about it intensified by the rarity of the permission and the uncertainty of its ever being repeated. At the time and afterwards, that watching was a held breath. Which had its effect on the way it is remembered with a completeness that I could not have foreseen at the time. My father's own separateness is there deepening around him, and his fear of being wherever he imagined he was: the cockiness faltering, the rhetoric hardening over—they were all in that room at that moment. I was aware of them without knowing, and long afterwards I would be able to discover them and see that they had been there the whole time.

He sat at the desk in his shirt sleeves, thumping, pausing, muttering a muted version of the pulpit intonation and enunciation that were over my head. The sounds addressed no one I could imagine, and they arose from a person who was a mystery to me: my father The Minister, impressive and unknowable, as he was meant to be. It was a role concocted from the whole of his life, from ministers and local dignitaries whom his mother, and friends of her generation, had admired back on the Allegheny, in western Pennsylvania, before the present century. He had been born in a village on the river bank. Rimerton: a row of houses between the water and the railroad track. His own father had worked on the river in various capacities, was given to drink, and seldom at home. The seven children were brought up by their mother, a woman of powerful will, a fundamentalist, a Methodist, a Puritan. He was the youngest to survive. When he was eleven the family moved into town: Kittanning, where he got a job as a clerk in a hardware store. He had had so little schooling that the store owner had to teach him to add and subtract. He did other jobs around town, as well, and endeared himself to a local minister, who managed to get him a scholarship to Maryville College in Tennessee, to begin studies with a view to entering the ministry. It was a Presbyterian institution, and led inevitably to the Presbyterian Church—a deviation to which his mother was never wholly reconciled, even by the fact of having a son who had gone to college and become a minister. His academic background—or lack of it—and the hours of manual work entailed by his scholarship provided excellent reasons for overlooking the inadequacies in his schoolwork, and he got by. A few years later, with the help of recommendations from established ministers, he was admitted to Western Seminary, in Pittsburgh, and while there got a job, first as chauffeur to Dr. Shelton, the pastor of a large Pittsburgh church, and then as Dr. Shelton's assistant minister. It was at that church that he met my mother, and married her, and they went together to the first of the small country churches. In his mother's mind, in his sisters' minds, in the mind with which he had grown up, the minister was the great man, and there he was. An unquestioning Republican by upbringing, he had arrived within sight of Manhattan on the eve of the great depression.

The whole side of the apartment building catches the sunlight, as it has done for most of three decades. Curtains blow from the windows. People have grown up in those rooms, with no building next door. Trees on the site, of the kind we were told might be locusts, are several times taller than I am. Doves, mockingbirds, even a sparrow hawk, know the tops of them. I never saw those when I was a child. And there through the leaves, emanating its startling silence that is like an echo, is the same glittering city. I can almost see, over there, the place where I have been living for years.

R.K. Narayan as The Vendor of Sweets

John Sokol © 1981

R. K. Narayan

Los Angeles

Los Angeles at six p.m. Arrive at San Carlos. Find the room rather small — and I am not able to find a grocery store nearby. Eat sandwich for dinner and stroll down Broadway.

By bus to Venice to see Mrs. Dorothy Jones. A critic and serious writer on filmatic values, especially valuable is her study of Hollywood's treatment of foreign themes, which she did under the auspices of the Massachusetts Institute. More than all, her helpful nature and knowledge of film studios and personalities made it easy for me to visit the film world. Met her at six o' clock in the evening at her house in that far-off place. Over an hour's journey by bus right through the heart of Los Angeles. The magnitude of Los Angeles could be realized only in such a journey. The word "sprawling" is uttered the moment anyone thinks of Los Angeles, and one could understand the epithet now. Venice is nearly at the other end of the town, and searching for Glyndon Avenue on foot proved an interesting way of familiarizing oneself with this vast city. The types of faces one encountered were all different from anything one saw in other parts of the country, starting with the gallery of old men at Pershing Square; and the Bible lecturer haranguing them ". . . I can have all the wealth in the world. But I don't want it . . . I know God gives me what I want . . ." and so on. "I'll tell you about the Holy Ghost . . . Recently the wise men of California said that if a certain oil company should cease, the town would become a ghost of itself. . . . But this holy ghost is not a ghost like this threatened oil town . . ." He was clearly going off the rails, nobody in the least minding it. They paid no more attention to his lecture than they did to the pigeons hovering around and cooing. . . .

Tomorrow I'm going to make notes on the road of the bearded and other extraordinary personalities one comes across on the road. Women of tremendous beauty pass along in the crowds — and the men all look suspiciously like film toughs, and deliberately cultivated picturesque characters. A newspaper vendor near my hotel looks like W. G. Grace the old English cricketer with his beard and peaked cap. . . . He has begun to call today's evening edition, already stale, "Thursday morning edition," and recommends while I pass him, "Read it; you will be well-informed if you read tomorrow's morning edition, that's what it is actually!" It is about nine in the evening. Tomorrow is still far off. Is news printed ahead of occurrence? I wonder!

I must definitely give Milton Singer's camera back to him because I'll never photograph anything. The very idea of photography detracts my mind from watching any scene or situation with a free mind (as a writer). I start worrying how it will look in the view-finder, and am seized with the regret that, as usual, I've left the camera behind, or that I've carried it when there is no sun and so forth. It's all a useless preoccupation. Everyplace sells picture postcards, and that should be sufficient for my record, and the photographs are so much more competently taken!

First time in my life purchased a clock at the corner drug store. Bought a big one for one dollar odd, kept it on my table for five minutes, went down again and returned it, and bought a smarter one costing a couple of dollars more. "For an extra dollar, sure you get extra value, sir," moralized the store assistant. I bought this just by way of precaution against unpunctuality with regard to various engagements ahead. At Carlton (Berkeley), I could peep out and read the time on the Campanile tower, but here I could see nothing but dark, sooty walls when I looked out; and the view was always better curtained off.

By virtue of possessing the timepiece got up early, arranged my affairs tidily so that I had cooked, dishwashed, and was ready to meet Mrs. Dorothy Jones at eleven-thirty. She was very helpful. She drew up a list of persons for me to see at Hollywood, and sat at the telephone and filled up my programme book with the address and telephone number of each person. When she saw that I had a tendency to note my engagements on loose paper she presented me with a small pocket diary, and for a start put down all my engagements in it, and handed it back to me with, "Don't forget to look into it, first thing each day." Drove me to Hollywood, searched far and wide, and fixed a room for me in a motel on the Sunset Boulevard as a first practical step, as my downtown life at the hotel did not have her approval. After this a drive-in lunch and we went to the United Artists Corporation. Met Sidney Harmon (Security Productions), said to be a sensitive playwright and highbrow producer. He asked me a number of questions about India—from geology, population, down to individual daily life, and asked what exactly was the difference between Indians and Americans. But I have grown used to questions and never rack my head to find an answer, as from experience I find that most persons (like the Jesting Pilate) don't wait for an answer. He asked me suddenly what he could do for me at Hollywood, and when I told him I'd like to meet a producer interested in an Indian subject, he went on to dilate on the quicksand economics of the film, listed all the good films that proved a failure since the beginning, and finally talked himself into the conclusion that it would never, never pay, and nothing would ever pay in films. He quoted enormous statistics and spoke, he said, as a businessman. The recent success of *Giant* seemed to have brought a lot of confusion and rethinking in all production plans. One would think a big success would make everyone feel more encouraged but I've noticed film producers are afflicted with mixed emotions when they see any picture become an abnormal success. They call a halt to all their own plans, telling each other, "One can't survive unless one gives the public another *Giant*." For a moment I was oblivious of my surroundings not really knowing whether I was listening to any of our own movie moguls in Madras, Coimbatore or Bombay. They have all the same idiom, eloquence, and monologous tendency. They will set aside everything else to be driving home a point with "You know what I mean . . ." "You see what I mean . . ." with brief (and sometimes prolonged) interludes into the telephone. I liked Sidney Harmon and he promised to take me to the sets tomorrow. Dorothy suddenly remembered that she had to get back to her children and started off at four-thirty. I found my way back downtown by bus. Returned to my hotel and started out again to buy food-stuff. Found as usual all the grocery shops closing. This was the third evening in succession that grocery was unavailable. Returned to my hotel to find a call from Dorothy, who gave me for my diary-noting a number of engagements for tomorrow. I've to pack up and be ready to leave at noon tomorrow. Dread the prospect of packing again. Anyway time to leave this hotel — the traffic noise is getting on my nerves, and my room is so dark that I don't know whether it's night or day.

Dorothy phoned to say she would come at one in the afternoon. Frantic packing and cooking — two activities for which I am, by nature, unfitted, but which are on me all the time. For a brief half hour went out to visit the library on Fifth Street. It's a magnificent place on several floors with millions of books in every language in the world. At the information hall on the second floor (first floor in our reckoning), the lady pointed out to me the huge murals on the walls — showing the discovery of the coast and the founding of Los Angeles. Here and there on the niche were kept Egyptian relics of thousands of years gifted by a local collector. Went through the fiction department and saw *The Financial Expert* and *Grateful to Life* — the copies looked well thumbed and their issue cards were crammed with entries.

HOLLYWOOD

Afternoon occupy the motel on Sunset Boulevard according to plan. I'm now right in the heart of Hollywood. Call on Mr. Geoffrey Shurlock, Vice-President of the Motion Picture Academy who has taken over the functions of the old Hays Office, and applies the Production Code to new pictures; he is concerned with the censoring of scripts and reels. He flourishes on his desk The New York Times Book Section as a thing he studiously follows and claims that he is familiar at least with the reviews of my books. He asks about Indian films and I mention *Avvaiyar*. We have many other topics coming up but at four-thirty Dorothy remembers her duty to her children — Kelley must be picked up and then her husband at his office and we leave Shurlock. She puts me down at the library of Motion Picture Academy, which attempts to collect all literature and documents concerning films, a very thorough, comprehensive library, where one may read the accounts of films of half a century ago and all the press cuttings connected with them. I glance through an album presented by Richard Barthelmess (of Little Lord Fauntleroy) of old days, containing press-cuttings of his performances; including a letter of congratulations from Mary Pickford on the day of his marriage, in her own hand, with envelope preserved intact. A waft of history; the dust of time has settled down on many things here. Hollywood is already building up a past, creating a tradition, and, I think, rightly too considering the shattering impact of television at home and the trade restrictions abroad, and the general economic morass, in which, I'm assured by everybody, the trade is grounded at the moment.

ALDOUS HUXLEY

"Take the bus No. 89 at Hollywood and Highland and come along to the very end of the line — Beachwood Drive, I'll come and take you in my car," Mrs. Huxley had phoned last night. At Hollywood Boulevard, I got into the bus 89. I asked the driver, "I want to drive to the end of the line, what's the ticket?"

"Where do you want to go, Pal?" he asked.

I showed him Huxley's address.

"H'm. We go all the way down Hollywood Hill. Whatever is beyond is yours to manage, O.K.?"

He took me in with resignation — a cheerful soul, more talkative than anyone else of his kind I've seen. He told a lady who had failed to get off at the right "transfer" point, "Learn to know bus, honey." He also spoke to girls adopting a thin piping voice: with all this entertainment, I did not notice the passage of time and felt sorry to part when he stopped at a place and said turning to me, "Well, this is all, Pal; I go back now."

It was the beginning of a hill road with a drug store and laundry, and a postbox. A number of cars were arriving, driven by women, myself always wondering which of them might be Mrs. Huxley. As I sat there in a bench outside the store, a tall, handsome, old man, looking like Francis Ford of the old days came up and sat beside me and started talking. He said, pointing at the granite bastion at the entrance to the hill road, "There used to be guards posted in those days to keep off peddlers and others whom we didn't want here . . ." History again within fifty years! When he learnt I was from India, he said,

"Your country! A great job it's doing to keep the peace of the world. But it's a mad world — people don't want to live and let live, that's all. . . . How Britain exploited India and other countries! I'm a Canadian. Canada is the only country in which Britain's tricks did not work, although in World War I and World War II they made us the front line in every battle! . . . I suppose they did the same thing with India too! Sixty years ago I fought. . . ."

I had to leave him. "Excuse me!" I said and abruptly went off to look for Mrs. Huxley, who, I feared, might be looking for me. Very soon a small car came up—Huxley recognized me and brought the car down to my kerb. He got out of the car asking, "Have we kept you waiting?" Recognition was mutual and instantaneous.

His house was on the hill. As we entered his gate, there was another car standing, and he said, "I've asked Alan White of Asiatic Studies at San Francisco to lunch. He is an Oriental scholar, you'll like him."

At the drawing room, the furnishing and upholstery was all white, with glass windows bringing in light—(I suppose in order to help Huxley move around without difficulty on account of his sight). He took me to his patio and pointed out the magnificent valley ahead. He pointed out to a pot of foliage: "It's just sweet potato—which has just burst out in such foliage isn't it amazing! . . ." At lunch I knew he had to divide his talk between the other guest and me. They had terse references to works on Mahayana and Hinayana Buddhism, and he was rather surprised at the revival of Buddhism everywhere—and wondered if it was partly a political strategy. We spoke of Gandhi (Otto Preminger had once consulted him for a possible film of Gandhi); industrialism, and he asked many questions about India. Mescaline and the opening of the doors of perception were of course extremely recurring subjects. After the other guest left, he took me into his study—full of books and letters, and an uncovered typewriter.

"Perhaps you may want to rest?" I asked.

"Oh, no, I don't rest in the afternoon. Stay on, I may go down later and let us go together, if you do not mind it." I had mentioned *Gayatri Dhyana Sloka* earlier in the day in connection with his own thesis on colour perception as an aid to yoga. He wanted me to say more about it. I explained *Gayatri Dhyana Sloka* and the *Mantra* step by step, and suggested he might find more of it in Arthur Avalon's writing. He took down several of Avalon's books from his shelf and wanted me to show him the exact place where reference to Gayatri could be found. I couldn't find it anywhere just then, but I promised to write to him later about it.

"What books are now being published in India on Tantra? Are the theatres very active? How is the younger generation? Are they conscious of their cultural traditions? No? What a pity! When two nations get together they get the worst of each other—rope-trick and such things from your country and gadgets and mere technology from the West! Isn't it extraordinary! A most fantastic piece of history. Britain's one hundred years' association with India—a company going and settling down and creating all kinds of problems at that distance! Under Mescaline, a single bar of music lasts a whole eternity. I'm not a born novelist. It does not come easily to me. I've to struggle and work hard to get it out—not like Balzac for instance through whom it just flowed;—the novel form is wonderful if you can achieve it. As we grow in years, it becomes more difficult to write a mere novel—all meditation technique is just to open up our own layers of consciousness and experience—to feel the richness of awareness and not for any particular achievement or results. . . ." He quoted Blake.

"Yes . . . the Perennial Philosophy helped me a great deal in understanding. I'm glad I wrote it."

Calm, gracefully slow, and careful in movement, lean and very tall, with a crop of hair which younger people might envy, perfectly shaped nose and lips—it's a delight to watch his profile: his hands and the long tapering fingers; a check jacket and corduroy trousers and the hand-knit tie gave him a distinguished appearance. I sat talking in his study till he said he was ready to go out. Before starting he brought out his new volume of essays, "Perhaps you'd like to see this—well, the first two essays are good, I think." He drove me downhill with a promise to telephone me again. "We must get together again before you leave," he said.

Spent the Sunday in Dorothy's home at Glyndon Avenue, Venice. Kim, Kelly, and David the youngsters were wonderfully active. Jack, Dorothy's husband, was relaxed in an absolutely Sunday mood. They put the chairs, rough wooden ones, out in the yard. They showed me their guinea pigs, the fat cat, their parakeets. They thanked me one by one for a box of candies I had brought them. Jack, not a very talkative man, told me that his association with India was when he passed Madras coast at a distance of 30 miles during the War and saw a ball of fire shooting across the horizon—to this day this phenomenon remains unexplained to him; and at Colombo they got down and searched for beefsteak, a guide promising to help them took them to a restaurant where they palmed off lamb as beef!

Afternoon they became quite active building up a fire for barbecue—father and boys running hither and thither and setting it up. Sally Simmons—Dorothy's friend—dropped in; she was full of knowledge, observation, and curiosity. Her hobby was watching crowds and characters. She knew Hollywood (of normal life and people not of films) inside out. She declared that Hollywood was no longer what it was reported to be—it had ceased to be anything different from a normal town. It was a centre of oil business, aeronautic construction, and electronics, rather than of mere films; all the studios had moved outside Hollywood proper. We sat round talking, eating, drinking, and watching television, and it was eight-thirty p.m. when Dorothy drove me back to Hollywood. Before I left, little David brought me his file of stories—he wanted to be a writer. I blessed him and hoped he would be a writer with a Book-of-the-Month honour one day, much to the delight of his dad, Jack.

Visit to Sam Goldwyn studios, arranged by Dorothy with Sidney Harmon. At three o'clock I was there. The routine phone-up from the reception desk and so forth before the portals could open. Since I was a little earlier, I waited in his office. Harmon's Secretary, a smiling, cheerful creature, offered me coffee without sugar or cream. She explained, "It's really very good coffee, you know," endorsed by another visitor waiting with a portfolio under his arm. It encouraged the girl to explain, "You know, why it's so good? I make my own blend and kiss every grain. . . ."

"Well, in that event, I think I'll try it even without cream, you seem to have given it the right treatment," I said, and tried to enjoy the decoction.

"Are you hungry?" she asked next.

"No," I said.

"I have a packet of salmon sandwich which I can give you."

"Why don't you eat it yourself?" I asked.

"I'm dieting. I don't want to grow fat."

I did not ask what made her carry around sandwiches which she didn't intend to consume. I just said, "You don't look the kind that'll grow fat, but if you are destined to grow fat, no power on earth or in heaven can help you."

"We Americans eat too much," said the other visitor, and demonstrated it by offering to help the girl out of her salmon sandwich load.

Meanwhile the room was getting crowded with sleek men, and elegant women, all of whom nodded and said to me, "How do you do?"

I am too experienced in the film world to take too much notice of anyone or offer my seat. It's a free-and-easy world where there is a lot of relaxed, mutual indifference, and the courtesies of the humdrum world are neither missed nor noticed. I carried on the same technique when Sidney Harmon, whom I was waiting to see, who had been so warm and communicative two days before and had said I was to ask him for anything I needed in Hollywood, came out of the room. I just continued to sit and look away at a pretty girl who had emerged also from his room, a few minutes before. We might have been total strangers for all it mattered. He threw a brief glance at me and muttered a word to someone, and passed out of the room. I never saw him again. A new person (Public Relations?) came on to me with a fresh smile.

"Please come with me. Let us go down to the studio."

"What about Mr. Harmon?" I said, suddenly feeling that Harmon was slipping out of my ken.

"Yes, sure. He will meet us later. Shall we go down?"

"Sure!" I said catching the spirit of the hour.

We were presently passing on to a stage crowded with people. The moment the door was shut behind me, I might, for all it mattered, be in Gemini Studios — the same groups of people — half of them too tense and half too relaxed. Suddenly my guide put his finger to his lips and cautioned. It was as if we had stepped into a cave where a tiger was asleep. The tiger here was a temperamental director of whom everyone seemed afraid. . . . At a corner of the studio they were shooting a scene with Burt Lancaster and Miss Simmons. The cameraman was pointed out to me in respectful, nervous whispers as an academy winner — a Chinaman, with his thick glasses and five-foot height who looked so much like Ramnoth (of Gemini Studios at Madras) and moved about like him. It made me regret for a while about Ramnoth, a good friend and a film-associate for years, of whose death I had learnt from a newspaper which I opened in the plane while leaving India.

The man who guided me slipped away after handing me over to another, who spoke to me for a while, and slipped away in his turn, with a "Make yourself comfortable." I watched the endless rehearsals and preparations for the shot and found it was all the same the world over. The director was high-strung and kept saying, "Silence, gentlemen, someone is talking . . ." like a class teacher, and everyone giggled at the fuss he made and tried not to creak their shoes. I noticed on the set a property which intrigued me — Nataraja in bronze . . . ubiquitous God whom they pick up and carry about like some savage visiting a city and picking up an electric lamp (without current or wiring) for a display in his jungle home. To see Nataraja, the Shiva of India, included in the setting for a Chinese story being made in Hollywood seemed to me a grotesque but perfect international mixture. I slipped out in my turn and went back to my hotel without a chance to say thanks or good-bye to anyone.

Evening dinner with Sally Simmons, and then a drive, which she had arranged with an automobile-owning friend of hers. We went up the hill to the planetarium and saw half this country stretched out below, and then here and there nearly fifty miles of driving looking around Los Angeles. We ended up at a famous ice-cream café in the university village which offered seventy different ice-creams. The menu card displayed a list of all the film and literary celebrities who had tasted the ice-cream. While leaving, I saw at the doorway a niche in the wall and a very large Ganesha in white marble kept in it. Where did they get it from, the god from a distant land, blessing this ice-cream bar with prosperity! I told the manager, "Wherever you may have got it from, he is a god, Ganesha the Elephant-faced (because, oh, that's a big story in our mythology), who is the remover of impediments, and giver of prosperity; you probably owe your popularity to His kindness — apart from the quality of your own service."

UNLOVED

Visit the famous Universal International Studios. Lunch with William Gordon — head of the international section, who feels disturbed by the attitude of Indian Government, who were understood to be hostile to Hollywood in general. Nothing disturbs film folk so much as the thought that they are not loved and admired. India Government somehow averse to Hollywood. Mr. Gordon projected for me Bengal Brigade, which was refused a certificate in India. No use attempting to find a reason for the refusal since the Government itself had not given any. The producer had gone carefully through the script changing all words likely to offend the Indian sentiment — such as "caste." "Get out, you low caste" was changed to "Get out, you low class," but it had sounded to my ears "caste" until it was explained to me; in any case, it didn't matter materially since the word caste is by no means a tabooed expression. Why, why was the Government of India so inimical to Hollywood? I couldn't say. He took out huge files and showed me all the correspondence. The picture was not certified by Trinidad, Indonesia, and Hong Kong, countries which somehow accepted India's leadership in such matters. The nations of the world seemed to be marshalled against Hollywood. It was nice sitting in that well-furnished office and listening to all these problems. In no other walk of life do people arrange their office equipment so stylishly — the poorest film producer will have at least four coloured telephones and all kinds of table equipment which the President of a nation might envy. Mr. Gordon proved that India was a loser in the long run as every film producer interested in India would bring in at least two million dollars into this dollar-starved subcontinent. It was all high economics which I didn't quite follow. Ultimately Mr. Gordon hinted that if the Government continued its unfriendly acts, Hollywood would be driven to making pictures of India uninhibited, faking all the background in Hollywood, stories wildly misinterpreting India, which would certainly create box office records all over the world. I said, "Why not??" instead of worrying over Delhi attitudes.

Visit to Macgowan, head of the Theatre Art at the University of California. At first he mistook me for a visitor from Pakistan whom he had been expecting. He looked confused and bewildered by this slip. Personally I didn't mind. I see nothing wrong in being thought of as a Pakistani as long as I am not questioned on politics. He phoned his next-in-command to come up and join us. Before ten minutes were over I had collected an armful of departmental literature. The next man came up and kept the conversation going. He took me round to see the departments, handed me over to the director of cinema-teaching, and disappeared. This man, Richard Hawkins, proved a valuable friend. A deep friendliness abiding for three hours. I have lost all value for the duration of friendship, as long as it is good while it lasts. He showed me his film department; and then said that as he had particularly nothing to do at the moment, he would like to drive me around in his car. He took me up the hills all the way, and down to the ocean, and along Will Rogers Avenue, across the city, and all the way around and finally insisted upon driving me back to my hotel. He had been driving for over three hours continuously, a quiet, gentle soul, full of sensitive film values. Thanks to him I saw the entire Bel-Air area, more aristocratic than Beverly Hills, Santa Monica, Will Rogers Beach, and some of the hill locations of old-time movie chases on horseback.

At two o'clock Walt Disney studio with Dorothy and her son Kim. A guide met us at the Reception, and for the next two hours he explained everything in that fifty-six-acre ground, with its twenty-six buildings and one thousand five hundred employees working to entertain, amuse, and make money. Television, movies, magazine publications (eight million total sales in various places of the world) articles of amusement for Disneyland. How many things! How many! What co-ordination! It took six years to make a picture; one million drawings made for a feature. Shot frame by frame through a stop camera. Fundamentally, it depends upon a single individual, on the creative work of an artist. The animator actually draws pictures for every stage of movement, arranges them one under another, and flicks them with his fingers muttering the dialogue and syllables in order to synchronize sound and picture. To help them in this work all the dialogue is completely recorded first, and played back. The colour store, fantastic combination and numbers — made by Du Pont (seventy-odd primary colours made into two thousand by combination), the "Cel" painters, girls with their own radios and earphones to while away the tedium when their hands colour-copy. A place where genius, creative play on a large scale, toy-makers' spirit on a large scale, expert organization, technology, business, specialized engineering all combine. It's so crowded and so much organized that it made me wonder if there was space for Disney himself to do anything in. Our guide assured us that his spirit pervaded the place — when he passed with a nod or a word, he set his stamp. He was unseen, but like God he was pervasive. I wanted to ask which God ever possessed such a business acumen. I was told that Disney's brother managed all the business. The odium of commerce is on the other Disney, not on Walt.

Gef. Shurlock brought his car and took me to the Huntington Library and Picture Gallery at Pasadena — a most attractive place (Huntington was a railroad president) with its green lawns and parkland looking like an English countryside — names also, such as

Euston, Wembley, Oxford, and so forth. Huntington Library—where one saw Chaucer and Shakespeare first editions, Caxton's original, and ancient etchings, woodcuts, and illuminated manuscripts, and the art gallery with Gainsborough's *Blue Boy* and *Lady Turner* and various other pictures one has heard of all his life.

RESERVED

The famous cemetery, made famous by Evelyn Waugh's *Loved One*, Forest Lawn, was the next place of visit. A whole mountain converted into a burial ground by a big business organization. Flowers on picturesque tomb-plates, lordly avenues, churches, statuary and spacious lawns, meadows, and arbors—verily a place where one might live rather than be dead in. The speciality is that you could drive in and lay a wreath. I saw one or two mourners pulling up their motorcars beside their loved ones and laying flowers (supply of which is also a part of the business organization) on the horizontal tomb-plates. The tomb-plates do not stand out but lie flat along the sloping ground because they save space (which is the real sale-commodity here, selling the dead space to be dead in) and do not disturb the perspective. The plates are of metal with the names of the dead engraved on them with a nice cavity in each for sticking flowers as in a vase. Everything is provided for here. Under these Grand-Hotel-like perfection of arrangements there is no time to feel the pangs of bereavement. The sting of death is removed by business foresight. I noticed also schoolchildren picnicking in various corners of this attractive retreat. Ever since I entered California I had been seeing gigantic notices hitting one's eyes everywhere, ". . . 110 dollars assure a place in Forest Lawn," which I had taken to be some sort of Save-Our-Trees-and-Lawns campaign on a statewide scale. Now I understood that these were only advertisements of cemetery-space. The view of the city from the hills quite inspiring. At the massive iron gates, offices of life insurance companies too! Geoffrey wondered how these two businesses were compatible!

And then he drove me to the Hollywood Bowl, an open-air theatre which can accommodate twenty thousand at a time, on the mountain side, where concerts are held in certain seasons with parking space for twenty thousand cars. And back to his flat—stopping on the way to see the Tar-pits at a public park, where natural tar is oozing on the ground, where Indian cattle path lay, and where they have dug up an immense quantity of prehistoric fossils. Back to Shurlock's room on the eleventh floor looking over the entire city; where he made coffee for me, and we spoke of Indian castes, Gandhi, and Gita and so forth. He showed me a copy of Gita in translation which he has read for years. Dinner at a café. And then he took me up a mountain to show me the city view at night. We parted at eleven p.m. He must have driven me over one hundred and fifty miles today showing me the sights of Hollywood. He'd not let me thank him because he said he could not have seen Huntington Library but for me; he had been planning a visit to the Huntington Gallery and other places for about thirty years, and could achieve it only today. Great soul, silently suffering—having lost his wife three years ago; in his lovely flat on the eleventh floor, surrounded with music, books, memory, and a view of the city—he tries to forget himself in his work as a censor. He is one of the most lovable and popular men in Hollywood, although in his position he could easily make himself odious to everyone.

ALDOUS HUXLEY

Another afternoon with Aldous Huxley. As usual they came down to meet me at the bus terminal. Huxley took me for a walk to show a few places on the hills and a lake, an artificial one, which is supplying water to Hollywood, pumped up all the way from Colorado, nearly one thousand seven hundred feet up as he explained. He explained at length various statistics about water supply, his mind is really encyclopedic, storing up all sorts of facts and figures, as one notices in his latest book. I have left a copy of *The English Teacher* for him to read. I explained to him some of the psychic phenomena in it, and told him about the lesson Paul Brunton taught me years ago. He explained that he was trying almost a similar experiment, but would like to try the suggestions in my book too. He cheerfully takes up any mental experiment suggested to him. We talked of Forest Lawn and he said, thinking it over, that it's so colossal and detailed that it's past the stage of being laughed at, where there are chapels but no crucifixion, no cross, no suffering; only the Last Supper, but not beyond—a place where a discreet censorship is applied to death, so that no pain or suffering is indicated—these are not to be remembered; but death only as a happy holiday—even adding a sort of glamour to it, as a sort of inducement to book a space in Forest Lawn; chapel where recorded hymn goes on; and marriages take place immediately to be followed by a cremation. "In this country," Huxley said, "you come across fantastic things side by side. At one place you'll see a huge advertisement for Forest Lawn, next to it whisky, health food, and gambling at Las Vegas, probably also some religious activities, and something else. Well, consume whisky and ruin your health, or gamble and blow yourself out or think of God, but the end is the same in any case may be the underlying philosophy in all this. You found things rather jumbled up, in this country."

Mrs. Huxley said when we returned home, "*Grateful to Life and Death* is a beautiful title."

"It's the last line of my book—" I was rather surprised to hear her approval, as apart from Lyle Blair who changed *English Teacher* to *Grateful to Life and Death*, I've not met anyone to approve of the change.

During tea, which was very welcome after the walk, we were joined by—(name not clear at the moment) and his extraordinarily beautiful wife. This man continued the talk on Forest Lawn. It was rather careless of me not to have listened attentively when the visitor's name was mentioned, but I gathered from the talk that was going on that he had come to the States to direct an opera at the New York Metropolitan, that he had directed some outstanding pictures in England, and that he was eminent in the theatre world. I hoped for the best, thinking there would be an occasion for me to catch the sound of his name in due course. When we all rose to go Huxley told him that he could drop me on the way as they were going down the Sunset Boulevard and were in need of someone to show them the way. His wife drove the car, because the gentleman had found the gadget-ridden, left-drive, American car they had rented for the trip, as well as the traffic rules, beyond him. They stopped the car in front of my hotel on Sunset Boulevard. I thanked them and said, "You should come to India and make a picture."

"I would love to; it has always been my ambition to make a picture in India. Can't we discuss it sometime?"

"I'll be in London next month," I said.

"That will be wonderful. Why don't you give me a call when you are in London?"

"I will take down your number in a minute," I said; the engine was running as they were in a hurry to reach a party at eight o'clock. I felt awkward to hold them up. But I had to know where I could see him again. He seemed to be a worthwhile man, who knew my books, and also a friend of Graham Greene. I fumbled for my pocket book, which I had left behind, while holding a simultaneous conversation with him and his wife. And now suddenly drew up along the driver's window a police officer on a motorcycle. He wore a helmet and was grim-looking.

He held out his hand and said, "Your driving license and birth-date," to the lady.

"Why?"

"You are getting a ticket."

"What is that?" she asked.

He took out his book and started writing.

"Your birthday? Your name?"

The lady was distraught. She said, "What has happened?"

"You turned the wrong lane."

The gentleman tried to ask a question or two and said with resignation, "There is nothing I can do about it. Let her deal with him," and turned away from the whole thing to me at the other window, and said, "Please give me something on which I can write my address." At the other window the policeman was arguing with the lady. He seemed to derive a fiendish delight in tormenting this lovely person.

The lady was saying, "But I didn't know . . ."

"You should know the rules."

"What is a wrong lane?"

"You shouldn't have taken it," the officer said. He handed her a ticket. He was bawling at one window explaining to her the traffic regulations and also what was in store for her at the law court. She was angry and kept telling him that she was a visitor, a newcomer to the country, which only provoked the man to hold out more and more ter-rifying prospects for her. I felt a tremendous responsibility for the whole situation. If I had not asked them to stop at Highland Motel . . . I apologized aloud, through the window, to the lady on the other side, over the head of the gentleman. She kept asking something of the grim policeman, who wore a steel helmet and looked like a Martian just landed with a ray gun in hand out to disintegrate and atomize the citizens of this earth, and he was bawling something in reply. Her hus-band had completely detached himself from the whole proceeding. He snatched from my hand a journal I was carrying and wrote on it his name and London telephone number. It was a magazine Huxley had lent me to read a tough article on ESP by someone. I could not still decipher his name.

I told him, "Yes I will telephone, but perhaps you would be busy," wondering by what name to call him on the phone in London.

"Oh, I will be rehearsing . . . you will be welcome."

The lady: "This is ridiculous, we are returning to New York to-morrow early."

"Well, you will have to go later, that is all," the policeman said.

The motorcycle pattered out. In a quarter of an hour she could start her car again, mastering all its gadgets. They were so preoccupied that I had not the heart to say good-bye to them. On this confused note we parted.

I couldn't make out his name on the magazine cover. I telephoned to Aldous Huxley and learnt that he was none other than Peter Brook, the famous British stage director. Later when I went to London I tried to get in touch with him, but I learnt that he was busy at Stratford-on-Avon conducting the Shakespeare festival. His wife answered the telephone and said, "Oh, dear, I can't forget that awful evening. Wasn't it dreadful! I will never go to Los Angeles again."

Dr. Kaplan picks me up at twelve o'clock and takes me to Columbia Pictures to meet the writer-producer Michael Blankfort—fine, sharp, friendly man, who looks like a reincarnation of Arnold Bennett, with his moustache and chin. Lunch at Naples—a famous Hollywood restaurant and pub, full of atmosphere—low, head-scraping roof from which dangle hundreds of wine-baskets in miniature, autographed pictures of a million movie personalities, dim red light, smoke, and narrow sofa seats at the tables. I have learnt to manage these luncheons—having my own food (which I call heavy breakfast) earlier in the day and nibbling salad and stuff like that at the parties, the company itself being more important. Kaplan is a brilliant wit, scholar, and conversationalist; and Michael is equal to him. Michael is good enough to inscribe a copy of his novel and give it to me with the remark, "If I were a painter, I'd have given you a picture, but this is all I can offer."

Back to hotel, where Dorothy Jones comes to take me to the Twentieth Century-Fox. It's easily the biggest studio here. Our public relations takes us first to their chief cameraman, who explains at length their latest lens for use of wide screen and fifty-five-millimetre films; and good enough to show us some tests—amazing sweep the lens has without panning, which he demonstrates with sight boards arrayed ahead in a semicircle—the lens takes it all in one glance; and then close-shots also on the same principle, of any object at a distance of about seven hundred feet. He shows me several charts with enthusiasm.

"Any questions?" he asks.

"Oh, no. It's all so clear I've no questions." It's difficult for me, in spite of my vague, general interest in technicalities, to maintain an intelligent face while he is talking. He is a man completely submerged in his technicalities, and cannot think for a minute that there could be anything else in life worth thinking or talking about. Technicians are all-absorbed creatures. Moreover, through some initial error somewhere, I have been introduced as a novelist, screen-writer, and "Producer" from India, and it's too late for me to correct the error. It gives me a chance to observe closely technical matters. Next, in the sound department, they explain the changes that the advent of the magnetic tape has brought in. I'm taken through vast, complicated recording rooms.

"You must be familiar with the magnetic—"

"Yes, of course, naturally," I say. It's all very complex and impressive to me. Sound has always attracted me in a vague way, but I don't understand a thing about it. I manage to essay one intelligent query, suitable for the occasion.

"Are these compatible with fifty-five-millimetre frames?" The question, it's a cute one I think, passes the rounds, and they say, "Well, not exactly yet . . ."

And then we pass on to more theatres. I could probably appreciate it better if I saw something happen there. As it is, mere technicalities bore me; and then our guide takes me to see the "Lot"—"New York street," "Ocean and sky" "French village," "Egypt," "Blue sea and horizon," "A London street," all facades used for outdoor scenes, a symbol of "Maya," as Huxley said, permanently built on several acres of ground.

I'm soon out. I catch the bus on Santa Monica. The bus driver is very careless. First he shuts the door with me halfway through (some day an American is going to be cut longitudinally and only then will they alter the arrangement of doors in their buses) and next he crashes into a new Chevrolet. The cars are stopped. It's extremely calm. No police. Our driver distributes a card round to the bus passengers, "I'd appreciate, if you gentlemen will fill this," like a conjuror involving the audience in a trick. I look away. I don't want to be involved in anything. People get very busy writing down.

"Can you pull out your car — ?" he suggests to the man whose car has been rammed in.

"Yeah," he says and does so. If it were our country there'd be so much loud speech and action and recrimination, and comments from bystanders. Here no one bothers. No argument between the protagonists, no accusations or gesticulation. They exchange notes and papers — behave like real gentlemen in an ancient duel. And then the bus is on its way again, and the car is driven off. Only sign anything is amiss being a long piece of chromium-plated metal which is flung out of the Chevrolet. People are full of praise for the driver of our bus. They have silently, unconsciously become partisans. No one likes the man whose car has been rammed in — not even himself. They mutter, "It was a terrible piece of driving."

I feel irritated at having to go out again at eight p.m. I am on the brink of calling off the evening engagement. But Sally won't hear of it. She has fixed it with David So-and-so the writer. After a hurried meal, I'm out again meeting Sally in Hotel Roosevelt. We go by bus to David's home. Find the family quietly settled after dinner — with the daughter at her homework. David is a successful screen and television writer whose speciality is "Western." He is not a born writer. He does not like writing; does it only to make money — and hopes to retire, go on a holiday, and take to painting: he has adorned his walls with grotesque, obscure daubs in frames. He may be called the "Robot" writer. He is evidently very successful and in demand. Even while we were talking, producers were calling him on the phone. He looks on me, I don't know how. He views other literary work as mere prolific raw material for his screen version, I suppose. He even mentions that most book writers indulge in a vast quantity of unnecessary writing. However, I'm happy to talk shop with him. His wife evidently has great admiration for the profession and keeps saying that the percentage of human beings that could be called authors is ever so small, while there are doctors, barbers, etc., in any number.

The Metro-Goldwyn-Mayer visit. The same type of talk with the "International" man. Difficulties with India Government. *Bhowani Junction* was not shot in India because the Government did not give in writing any agreement that they'd make no demand on its world profits! Strange are the ways of Government and films. Lunch at the famous restaurant, watching the shooting for a while by the famous George

Cukor of *Les Girls*, more "Lot" inspection, New York, French village, Sea, and Forest. While crossing the lawns, a brief shake-hands meeting with George Murphy—an old-time actor, who says, "You are from Mysore? I have just met a convent sister from Mysore who is collecting funds for a high school. She and her companion: they were so charming, like a couple of birds alighting and flying away. I could not help giving a small donation because their appeal is so sincere. . . . You know about that school?"

"Name?"

"Christ the King . . ."

"Oh, that is where my daughter studied, it is next door to our house, what's the name of the sister?"

"Bernadine."

"She was my daughter's teacher." The world has shrunk suddenly. Who could imagine in these surroundings Bernadine, the kindest of teachers and the most despairing one for my daughter's arithmetic, who often came down to see me and say, "Oh, you must do something about Hema, the poor child needs special attention." There was nothing I could do about it, arithmetic being as much a terror to me. To hear Bernadine's name again after all these years! Human beings get knit up in all fantastic unbelievable ways, complex and unexpected links like the wiring at the back of a radio panel.

Visit Paramount Studio, which is just a repetition of other studio experiences. My guide, the grandson of Zukor, called Adolf Zukor the Second, slow, timid, shy, and very intelligent. He keeps saying, "I don't know what you can see here!" He crashes into a studio where a notice "Closed" is hung outside; they are shooting a scene with Lizabeth Scott and someone else.

Next engagement, visit to "Consolidated," a hectic place where I sit on a bench at the reception waiting for a man to appear and take me in. There is a spring door in front of me which is being pulled and pushed continuously—men and women chatting, preoccupied, and in a deadly hurry sweeping in and out. Those who wait at the reception are restless and fidgety, and those who move do so in a run; never was a spring door more agitated. It is a place where 16 mm. films are processed and sent off to various television studios, as it seems, exactly with a minute to go for the scheduled programmes. Finally a man turns up and takes me in to show a magnificent colour film on an Indian village made for the Ford Foundation. After the show, offers to drive me in his car to my hotel. An overactive man who wastes lot of my time by neither letting me go nor keeping me company, he makes me sit in his car and dashes in and out of various buildings on the way. So that I reach my hotel late in the evening.

A telephone call at my hotel.

"Is that Narayan?"

"Yes, speaking."

"*Namaste*, Narayanji." I was surprised.

"Who is speaking please?"

"Kenneth McEldowney." Another man whom I had lost sight of in Bombay seven years ago. Fantastic contacts really. He had seen my name in *Variety* the trade paper and had tracked me down. Years ago we should have made a picture called *Khedda* with the background of elephant-trapping in Mysore jungles, he had several reels of it taken in Technicolour and wanted me to write a story around the subject. We met in Bombay, discussed plans, and then kept writing to each other; a file developed, he became famous with his picture directed by Jean Renoir called *The River*, but the second picture never came to be done in spite of a very fat file of letters and cables growing out of it on my table. Ken McEldowney got into some contractual difficulties with the Government of Mysore, thought it best to abandon the project altogether, and the loser was myself since I had already worked on a number of possible stories for him. But it had an unexpected result. I had gone through so much research into elephant-catching in Mysore forests, where herds live and flourish and are rounded up through an elaborate system of drives, that I grew interested in the subject myself, and I may possibly deserve a doctorate in elephant affairs! . . . This man telephoned to me today and took me to his home in Bel-Air.

"VEDANTA PLAZA"

In search of Vedanta Society of Hollywood on Vine. The county authorities, having cut a freeway through a corner of the estates of the Ashram, have compensated by naming the area officially Vedanta Plaza. Hollywood is full of philosophy and yoga. At one end of the Sunset Boulevard we have the Self-Realisation centre with its own chapel, where I spent an evening listening to a sermon on "Reincarnation," where books by the late Yogananda, and mystic souvenirs, are sold. Young men and women were listening to the lecture on reincarnation. . . . They looked fashionable, modern, and young; one could not think they would be attracted by reincarnation, but there they were, voluntarily walking in and listening. The Self-Realisation centre incidentally has at its entrance one of the best vegetarian restaurants in the United States; the first step in self-realisation is good food, and that is provided for at the entrance, after which you could step in to hear a lecture or buy a book on *vedanta*. At the other terminus of the Sunset Boulevard four miles away I saw another signboard announcing yoga lessons by appointment. Here we have "Vedanta Plaza" officially included in the county registers — so that's where Indian philosophy stands at the present moment in Hollywood, which seems to me really a versatile place with its technology, television, aeronautics, world of illusions, and the world of enlightenment. . . .

Swami Prabhavananda, the head of this Society, is away at Santa Barbara. His next-in-command is a young person of the name of Swami Vandanananda, who left his family in Mysore when he was seventeen, about twenty years ago, spent over ten years in Almora at the mission's headquarters in the Himalayas. Like a true sanyasi, as one who has renounced the world, he had not thought of his home or written to any of his relations for over a decade. But talking to me in that hall brought back to his mind Mysore, his home in D. Subbiah Road, his aunt, uncles, and friends, and the Kannada and Tamil in which we spoke induced in him a slight homesickness, perhaps. I seem to have brought with me a waft of his old life for him. At six o'clock he left me and went to the chapel to conduct vespers. A number of inmates assembled and sat in silent meditation before a picture of Ramakrishna and the Holy Mother. Lamps were lit, flowers and incense. The prayer went on for a long time; in that stillness, I slipped out, when everyone sat with shut eyes, and wandered in the garden.

Later the swami joined me and took me to the dining hall. There are about sixty American men and women living in this ashram. They go through a course of studies and ascetic discipline; men and women are necessarily segregated — sometimes they change their minds and return to the mundane world; sometimes a romance develops and they wish to renounce the ascetic life and go out and marry; Swami Prabhavananda, the head of this institution, takes a very generous view of all such second-thoughts and never denies his disciples their freedom of action; some stay in the Ashram for ten years, become qualified to be called "Swami," learned and austere and carrying on the work of this mission in various parts of the world. . . .

With Aldous Huxley and Gerald Heard to the Loss Angeles Medical College where they address a group of medical men on Mescaline. They dwell on the deepening of consciousness as a means to helping the next phase of evolution, which must all be spiritual and mental, men having reached the peak in the material world. Mescaline, lysergic acid, are some of the drugs with which Huxley and Heard are experimenting. One memorable sentence of Huxley in the speech, I forget why he said it: "Alcohol is incompatible with automobile." At the end of the meeting my camera goes into action and I manage to take several group photographs with Huxley and Heard. After the meeting I stop off at Huxley's house for tea and talk. Later they drive me back downhill at the end of the day as usual. Huxley urges me to come back to the States. I dine at the Self-Realisation Centre Restaurant on the way and go back to my room for packing.

Checked out of my room at noon. I had grown rooted to this motel and felt sorry to leave it. The motel lady gave me a room till the evening train-time, free of cost. The whole day messed up by a hope of seeing Gerald Heard, and by the uncertain engagement with a young man I had met at the Huxley lecture, an underwater specialist. He was threatening to come any minute since seven a.m. to take me out in his car. I had to make Dorothy wait uncertainly at her telephone, although she called nine times to know when she should come for me. Finally the sub-aquatic man turned up at two-thirty in the afternoon, and drove straight to a television studio because he was under the impression that's what I wanted to do. He forgot that he had offered to take me to his house. I wriggled out of this mess; the only wise act for the day on my part being refusal to hand him my roll of exposed negatives, which he wanted to take charge of in order to help me get them developed. Dorothy arrived at three and immediately plunged into my travel and packing arrangements. Pack up and leave motel, seen off by the entire family who manage this motel. The old man said, "Give my respects to Nehru — he is a sound man."

Eduoard Roditi as The Delights of Turkey

John Sokol © *1981*

Edouard Roditi

Cruising with Hart Crane

The summer months of 1929 turned out to be the swan song of the so-called "gay twenties." These were remembered in the ensuing decades with nostalgia, at first by all those who suddenly found themselves deprived, after the shock of the Wall Street Crash in the fall, of the precarious carefree prosperity they had so recklessly enjoyed, then also, especially after 1960, by a much younger generation in whose eyes the era of the Charleston and of bathtub gin acquired the same kind of legendary glamour as the age of Nero or the Italian Renaissance. My own memories of that fateful summer remain strangely blurred and confused, perhaps because I was still under the illusion that nothing distinguished it particularly from previous summers and that it was still destined to be followed, year after year, by many a similar summer.

As in previous years, my family moved early in June to the country in Epernon on its annual hegira, before migrating in August to the seaside in Le Touquet too. I yet managed to stay on for a few weeks in Paris, with only one servant left in our vast and deserted apartment to keep house for me and my father, who occasionally stayed there overnight rather than commute daily by car from Epernon to his office in the Rue Ambroise Thomas, named after one of the most neurotic nineteenth-century French opera composers. Situated in a central section of Paris, close to the Folies Bergères, this street was in the very center of the French export trade, but close also to a number of historic and luxurious whorehouses, several of which had once been assiduously frequented by the painter Toulouse-Lautrec.

I was supposed at the time to be spending a few hours every day in my father's office, "learning the business" of the export trade, since my father planned to send me in the fall on my first visit to America, where I would of course meet many of his customers and business friends. But I soon found myself left by the busy office personnel to my own devices, with nothing to do of any use or interest. The employees of D. Roditi and Sons seemed almost to resent my presence, as if they feared that I might be spying on their zeal and honesty, and none of them had been detailed by my father to give me any special instruction. In addition, my cousin Charles, who had only recently become a junior partner in the family firm after the retirement of my flamboyant Uncle Victor, was distinctly hostile to my presence in the office. Whenever our paths crossed, he treated me as if I were a child still playing at being an adult. He seemed to make a point of ridiculing whatever futile occupation I managed to find and would laughingly ask me how much money I expected to earn for the firm that day. Sometimes he sent me out on some even more futile errand; on one such occasion, he deliberately sent me to the former address of a firm of manufacturers which had already been out of business for several years, instructing me to select there a sampling of their more attractive export lines of leather goods.

Within a few weeks, I therefore devised a routine of my own that seemed to satisfy everybody, if only because my presence in the office became less embarrassingly noticeable. Every morning, I either went to the office with my father, if he happened to have spent the night in Paris rather than Epernon, or else turned up "at work" by my own means ahead of him. If he suggested later that I lunch with him, we ate together in a nearby restaurant, Chez Boylesve, which was famous locally among businessmen for its gourmet food. Otherwise, I went surreptitiously home and lunched alone, solemnly served in our huge dining room by the only servant who still kept house for us. My afternoons were in both cases still officially devoted to "visiting manufacturers," but nobody ever asked me to report on my findings and observations, so that I actually spent most of my time at home, where I read or wrote poetry in solitary refinement, or else went out on a round of bookstores and art galleries that often ended, if I had enough money, in some Left Bank café. If my father planned not to dine in our Paris apartment but in Epernon with my mother, I refrained from returning to our apartment for a lonely evening meal and remained instead with friends in Montparnasse, many of whom were later destined to become famous artists or writers.

On one such occasion late in June or early in July, I thus decided, towards the end of the afternoon, to call on the American painter Eugene McCown in the very elegantly "Art Deco" duplex studio that he occupied in the Villa Seurat, off the Rue de la Tombe-Issoire, picturesquely named after a gigantic Saracen marauder. At the time of the Battle of Poiters where the Islamic invaders were defeated and Christendom was saved except from itself, Isoard or Issoire, as he is named in medieval French manuscripts, had managed to scout, ahead of the main body of Moorish troops, as far as these outskirts of Merovingian Paris and been killed and buried there.

This was a distant Left Bank section of Paris that was unfamiliar to me, inhabited mainly by the kind of people, Parisians of modest means or foreign artists, with whom my plutocratic family had no social contacts. Though I was destined to live not far from there nearly half a century later, it was still, in 1929, almost adventurous for me to go there, and it took me some time to find the Villa Seurat.

I had met Eugene only a few days earlier, I no long remember where or how, but most probably in the art gallery of the Librairie des Quatre Chemins, where I often browsed and bought books, and where several of Eugene's friends such as the painters Bérard, Berman and Tchelitchew, regularly exhibited their works. Wherever we may have met, Eugene had suggested that I drop by any afternoon to see some of his work in his studio. Dark-haired and blue-eyed, he had the clear complexion and the charm that the Irish race seems to develop more easily in America than on its ancestral isle, where poverty, a diet of lavishly administered carbohydrates and insanitary living conditions all too easily disfigure "peaches and cream" skin with pimples. From his native Kansas City, where he was born, according to his compatriot Virgil Thomson, "on the wrong side of the tracks," Eugene had drifted a couple of years earlier to Paris, where his facility as a painter, his ability to play gracefully on the piano the popular jazz of the age and, above all, his unabashed exploitation of his own charm soon assured him, in elegantly Bohemian circles, the popularity of a kind of human lapdog. He thus managed for a while to be engaged as pianist at the Boeuf sur le Toit, the fashionable nightclub named after a ballet of which Cocteau had provided the libretto and the title for Serge Diaghilev. Eugene was even reputed to have had a brief love affair with Cocteau, after which he very soon became one of those privileged young men who are invited everywhere without having to bear the expense of return invitations.

When I met him, Eugene was already, I believe, the lover of Nancy Cunard, who had recently been abandoned by the French Surrealist poet Louis Aragon, after Aragon had translated with her help and published, on her private press, a brilliant French version of *The Hunting of the Snark*. Completely dominated by his new love, the Russian-born Elsa Triolet who was suspected of being a Soviet spy if not also a real witch, Aragon was now well on his way towards becoming France's leading Communist novelist. As an apostate, he was excommunicated with bell and book by André Breton, the Surrealist Pope, and avoided like a leper by most of the orthodox Surrealists, but Aragon continued to exert by remote control a mysterious political influence on Nancy, who, a few years later, also embraced the Communist cause and drove an ambulance for the Loyalists during the Spanish Civil War. By that time, however, she had discarded Eugene, whom she began to suspect of spying on her on behalf of the American government. Nancy's last years, during and after the Second World War, then became, for her friends, a nightmare of *delirium tremens* and persecution mania. Because I had served in the Office of War Information and Eugene in the Office of Strategic Services, from which he was discharged as a psychiatric casualty, she accused us both, when I last saw her in London shortly before her truly pathetic death, of being secret Fascist agents. Actually, she had better reasons to distrust Eugene: shortly after the war, he had published in New York a somewhat autobiographical novel, *The Siege of Innocence*, in which he described himself, in a style derived from Ronald Firbank via Carl Van Vechten, as an innocent boy from the rural Middle West who was corrupted by, among others, an unmistakable fictional caricature of Nancy.

Be that all as it may, Eugene had already exhibited his paintings, on that summer afternoon of 1929 when I first dropped by to see him in his Paris studio, in a successful avant-garde gallery that also showed other young "neo-romantic" painters of promise who, in a reaction against Cubism, reverted to the somewhat dreamlike manner of Picasso's Blue and Pink periods. Eugene's own painting soon proved, however, to be very derivative. His compositions depicting ballet dancers or circus acrobats in tender pastel shades were then recognized as facile imitations, handled with much less power and feeling, of similar works painted by Tchelitchew in his earlier manner; to such an extent indeed that an unsigned work of Eugene's turned up in a London auction some four decades later and was mistaken for a while for an unsigned early Tchelitchew, until I was able to identify it, for the disappointed purchaser, as a painting that I had seen, that summer of 1929, in Eugene's Paris studio in the Villa Seurat.

However briefly, Eugene already belonged if only marginally to the "charmed circle" of Gertrude Stein, Natalie Barney and Harry and Caresse Crosby. Since Gertrude's recent estrangement from Ernest Hemingway, she seemed suddenly to resent, in the young men who formed her court, any professional success as artists or writers and, above all, any display of real virility. Eugene may thus have been expelled from her salon in the Rue de Fleurus at a very early date because of his relationship with Nancy Cunard, much as the American writer Bravig Imbs was also banished later, when he imported his bride Valeska from her feudal world on the shores of the Baltic Sea.

When I reached Eugene's studio on my first and only visit, I found him in the company of a rather shabbily dressed and seedy-looking man of uncertain age, whose expressionless, worn and gray face was ravaged by tics, and somehow reminded me of Buster Keaton, while his rumpled suit gave me the impression that he rarely undressed and simply collapsed at the end of each day on the nearest couch to sleep there fully dressed. When Eugene introduced this house guest to me, his very name, Hart Crane, left me speechless with awe. I had read *White Buildings* a couple of months earlier with enthusiasm, recognizing in its author a kindred spirit of a kind, in fact a pioneer visionary who strove, as I did too, to follow in English in the footsteps of Rimbaud. Even before my brief and cometlike 1928 appearance as a student at Oxford, I had also read occasional poems of Hart Crane in *transition* or elsewhere, and I even quoted him from memory in the English essay of my entrance examinations for admission to Balliol. Though I had meanwhile met both Archibald MacLeish and T. S. Eliot, recommended to each in turn by others of their age or of their circle, this was the first time that I chanced to meet, by surprise and without any preparation, a major American poet whose poems I had read in a collected volume and not merely as occasional contributions to some little magazine. In addition, Hart Crane seemed to know me by name and to remember reading the little that I had already published in *transition*.

Crane's appearance and manner nevertheless put me ill at ease. However shy and tongue-tied I may have been on first meeting either MacLeish or Eliot, the good looks of the former and the diffident urbanity of the latter soon offered me, in either case, a certain facility for communication, but conversation with Crane proved very desultory. Both he and Eugene were already fairly drunk; besides, they were engaged in a cryptic argument about Harry and Caresse Crosby, who were out of town and whose house guest Crane had recently been until, it appeared, they quarreled, after which Crane moved to Eugene's studio. Whatever the details of this argument and the occasion of Crane's quarrel with the Crosbys, the significance of this whole situation escaped me. In any case, both Crane and Eugene were drunkenly garrulous, repeating themselves in long rigmaroles and referring again and again to others who were also involved in all this but whose given names meant nothing to me. Besides, I had never yet associated to any extent with American homosexuals, so that the kind of slang that Eugene and Crane were using and that later came to be known as "camp" sounded in my ears like a secret language that I was not even intended to understand. If I remember right, they referred repeatedly, as far as I understood, to Caresse Crosby's jealousy and her refusal to admit that Harry, though married, continued also to have homosexual relations. Was Crane involved in these, I wondered, and had this involvement been the cause of their quarrel?

While I listened in silence to their cryptic verbal postmortem, I spent most of my time examining Eugene's few paintings that adorned the walls of his studio. Suddenly, Eugene announced that he had a dinner date elsewhere and had to hurry away. Would I be free, he asked, to stay with Crane, who couldn't speak much French and, that evening, would otherwise be hard put to it to find his way around Paris alone? I agreed, and we all three left the Villa Seurat together. Eugene hailed a cab and went off to his date, but Crane and I soon found a neighborhood bistro where Crane drank far more than he ate and treated me while I ate to an interminable and very confused discourse on the psychology of French sailors.

After dinner, Crane wanted to go to a *bal musette* in the Rue de Lappe. I had already heard about the low-life dance halls of this street that is tucked away in a slum behind the Place de la Bastille. It had only recently become fashionable, in Boeuf sur le Toit circles, to go there and dance the java, a popular and very fast Parisian waltz, among the apache pimps and their girls. But I had never yet been there and still had no idea that the *bals musettes* of the Rue de Lappe were also frequented by homosexuals who were allowed to dance together.

We went to the Bastille by the underground metro, with which, like the legendary chauffeur-driven Marie-Chantal of a later Parisian generation's jokes about the idle rich of my native *Seizième arrondissement*, I was still relatively unfamiliar. At the Chatelet station we had to transfer to another line and nearly got lost in the labyrinth of underground passages that connect its various lines and platforms. Unable to find a toilet in this maze, Crane began to curse the French and to rant about the charms of the New York subway, where the stations provide facilities for drunks to relieve themselves. Finally, Crane staggered towards the wall of a crowded passage and calmly pissed against its ceramic tiles. Passersby began to protest indignantly, but were fortunately all in a hurry to reach their final destination, so that we were able to avoid what might have developed into an embarrassing fight as Crane responded in a vituperative tone that could not be misinterpreted, even if his American idiom remained incomprehensible.

Whether at home or in England, I had always led a very sheltered life that had taught me to be acutely aware of social and cultural differences between myself and most other people. Never had I yet found myself facing this kind of situation that might well develop into a "public scandal" with strangers. I was all the more shocked, in the present case, because the cause of my embarrassment was a poet whom I admired as an ideal ever since first reading his writings. Nor could I imagine ever finding myself in the same kind of predicament with either MacLeish or Eliot. It seemed to me scarcely credible that this nightmarish drunk, now pissing in public against the wall of a Paris metro station and insulting in coarse terms the passersby who objected to his behavior, could also be the author of *White Buildings*. I was discovering for the first time the clay feet of one of my idols.

When we emerged at last from the metro at the Bastille stop, I had no idea how to reach the nearby Rue de Lappe, nor had Hart Crane. As he spoke practically no French, I overcame my timidity and guilt feelings and asked our way of a traffic policeman. While directing us, he warned me in a somewhat paternal tone to be careful once I got there. We thus turned off the Rue de la Roquette into the narrower Rue de Lappe, where I experienced my first real impressions of slumming. The malodorous garbage bins overflowing onto the sidewalks by the dark open doors of tenements revealed to me an aspect of metropolitan life that I had never yet observed in my own section of Paris, where the garbage is concealed and collected in the backyards of apartment buildings and private homes. An ambivalently apprehensive tightening of my bowels and a sudden dizziness in my head were symptoms of the emotional shock of my first contact with this degraded world of poverty, prostitution and petty crime that I was soon destined to know far more intimately, though I was still unaware, at this time, of the attraction it would later exert on me.

But Crane was instinctively here in his true element. Somewhat unsteady on his feet after so much drink, he seemed to be feeling his way like my old friend the Abbé from Roubaix following his divining rod to find water. The apache types, men and women who loitered in the dimly lit street or hung around the garish glare of the entrance to the dance halls, all scared me. Ignoring the main *bals musettes* of the Rue de Lappe, Crane led me to an even darker and narrower side street that branched off to our left into a kind of yard where we found the notorious Trois Colonnes.

Busloads of wide-eyed tourists are now brought here night after night to gape at its carefully rehearsed scenes of apache violence, all intended to give them the impression of having witnessed, in the safety of an inexpensive guided tour of "Paris by night," the ultimate of the wicked city's sin and depravity. When I first went there with Crane, however, the Rue de Lappe had only recently been discovered by adventurous Paris snobs. We even appeared to be, that evening, the only outsiders to have come to witness the *Walpurgisnacht* of its natives. Instead of seeking an empty table among those that surrounded the crowded floor, Crane decided to stand at the bar, where he promptly ordered two brandies. As he sipped the first of a series of these, he began to survey the hall and the bar with a critical eye, until his gaze finally rested on a group of young men at the far end of the bar.

On the floor, most of the dancing couples were composed of men, either two pale-faced and fragile queens of the kind that can inspire wild passions in a prison, or else of a triumphant and adoring queen and a self-consciously virile tough. At the bar, groups of other toughs were gathered, surveying the whole scene in a provocative macho manner. Among them were a couple of relatively handsome young French sailors in uniform, wearing their caps, adorned with the traditional red pompon, jauntily set at a precarious angle. Crane concentrated his attention on them, at the far end of the bar, and ordered drinks for them, inviting them with a gesture to join us. But they came accompanied by two older civilian toughs who had been drinking with them and now made it plain to Crane that he would have to invite them too. Crane began to protest in English that he had no intention of allowing them to treat him as a sucker, but the four Frenchmen, of course, failed to understand him and I was then obliged to translate Crane's objections as best I could.

I failed, it seems, to find the most tactful French turn of phrase to convey the poet's protest. An increasingly violent altercation ensued. Suddenly, my courage failed me and I fled ignominiously, leaving my charge to face alone the consequences of his behavior.

I never found out how that night ended for Hart Crane. Quite understandably, I was too much ashamed of my own cowardice to call on Eugene again in the Villa Seurat. When I next met him some four years later in London, neither of us thought of mentioning Crane, nor did we ever mention him in the course of our many New York meetings during the war years and after the war. Some four decades later, however, I chanced to read Philp Horton's excellent biography of Crane. Only then did I discover that the drunken and disorderly poet, only a few days after our meeting, had again allowed himself to become involved in a fight, this time in a Montparnasse café. Crane then insulted and struck a French policeman, after which he was arrested and, a few days later, expelled from France as an undesirable and troublesome alien.

James Tate as Riven Doggeries

John Sokol © *1981*

James Tate

The Route As Briefed

I always expected to meet my father on the street, probably down-town, because I imagined him wandering lost in a daze for years across Europe, through Africa, up South America, across the States, and finally some day standing at a streetlight down at 10th and Magee wondering which way to go now. I knew we would stop and stare at each other, drawn by some deep instinct that was a father and his boy — no matter he'd only seen a picture of me one month old, and I a bunch of worn photographs of him taken before my lifetime. I knew he would be changed; the war and the years of wandering would have stolen his handsome youth. I was ready for that. I had aged him in my mind many times, preparing for the fated reunion.

For all the continuing adoration in our household, I knew almost nothing about him. I have no idea what his interests were: only that he was kind, gentle, strong. I don't know if he had any time for college or work between graduation from Paseo High School and enlistment in the Air Force. I knew he was Number One in his Flight School Class and achieved the rank of Lieutenant while pilot of a B-17 in the Eighth Air Force flying out of England. He was up for leave when the crush was on with the bombing of Germany. They extended the number of combat missions just as my father was preparing to come home for Easter and see his beloved wife and newborn son. That's when he was shot down, the next flight.

We were living with my Grandma and Grandpa Clinton. Grandpa Clinton worked for the Federal Reserve Bank longer than any man in their national history. He was a very mild, level-headed man who refused to go to church with the rest of the family. One night he sat up from his sleep and said to my grandmother, "Virgil has just been shot down over Germany!" He woke the whole family and told them. Then he sat up alone the rest of the night and waited for the telegram.

They never found him. The rest of the crew was accounted for. Some were wounded. Some were dead. And some were in prison camps.

Roy Weaver, my father's best friend and co-pilot, was in a prison camp. His wife, Mildred, was my mother's best friend. They had even been photographed together several times by the *Kansas City Star* as two typical heroic and beautiful young war brides. Mildred had a daughter, born about the same time as me, named Joy.

My mother waited every day for information. Nothing came. Sometimes another telegram assured her that they were looking everywhere; or perhaps he had now passed from one status to another more grave (we never understood or accepted these). There were constant phone calls to wives or to servicemen home on furlough.

And then the war was over. No one in our house knew how to celebrate the great victory for which everyone at home had pulled so selflessly. We didn't feel like we had won. But you had to act happy for those whose beloved men did come back in one piece or pretty near.

Roy Weaver made it back without a scratch. He seemed okay at first. My mother waited restlessly for the right moment to ask him about Virgil. Why didn't Roy bring it up? The need was so obvious as to baffle my mother at his awkward reticence. We visited the Weavers three or four times the first month he was back; Mildred seemed to accept the situation and didn't know what to say to my mother.

At her wit's end, one day my mother finally broke the idle chat and said, "What happened to Virgil, Roy?"

Roy moved the coffee cup away from his mouth and onto the saucer and said, swallowing, "Well, the plane was hit. It was hit bad. Half a wing was on fire. Nobody was hurt but we were going down. I said to Virgil, 'Let's ditch it.' He said to go on, he was going to hold it until we were gone and then follow. And that was it. I never saw him again. Mickey Spoletto, our gunner, was shot while he was coming down. Mark Janowicz was sent to a camp in Italy and got shot trying to escape. Hal Ober, the navigator, was with me in camp."

He avoided looking my mother in the eyes. He took another gulp of coffee, leaned back and said, rather distantly, "I always asked everyone new when they came in the camp if they had heard any news about Virgil."

We waited for him to go on. But he didn't. He sank into himself. Several minutes passed in silence when all present floated in their own rich war melancholy. Only now after so much singing was it beginning to seem real.

"What did they say?" asked my mother.

"Nothing," he said. "Never a word. They never even found the plane. . . ."

Mildred Weaver called my mother two weeks later and said that Roy had disappeared. He had gone out for a paper five days before and hadn't returned. My mother and I went over immediately and I played with Joy while Mildred wrung her hands and cried on my mother's shoulder, saying that he had been acting strange ever since he had gotten back. And that it had been getting worse. We spent a lot of time with Mildred and Joy over the next three weeks until the police called one day and said they had found him. He had written two thousand dollars worth of bad checks all across the Midwest and West. He was in jail in Seattle and it wasn't until someone finally thought to have him examined by a psychiatrist that they realized he was a victim of total amnesia. He knew not his name, his address, nor a single fact of his life.

They sent him back to Kansas City, where he was put in therapy at the state hospital for several months, and then continued as an outpatient for some time after that. He got a job at the Chevrolet plant and Mildred seemed to be herself again. We all went on picnics together to Swope Park or Fairyland.

Sometimes at home my mother would stop what she was doing, ironing or making cookies, and take my hand. We would walk out on the front porch and sit down on the swing. "This is the day your father and I were married," she would say. Or "This is your father's birthday." Or "This is the day your father was shot down, three years ago today, Tommy. You would have loved him. He was so . . . kind. So handsome! Everybody loved Virgil."

And it was true, everybody did love Virgil. Everyone in my mother's family worshiped him, and his loss was an enduring pain to them. His name was spoken so often at the dinner table it sometimes seemed to me, who had never met him, that he had just left the room. Nobody could believe he was dead.

Roy Weaver knew my mother didn't believe him. The friendship was strained because of this. There seemed to be a terrific struggle going on inside of Roy one day when we dropped by to see Mildred and Joy. We were surprised to find Roy home from work. He shrugged off the inquiry my mother made by saying, "Oh, I thought I felt a cold coming on." Mildred was in the next room taking her hair down. We sat down with him. He stood up and started pacing in front of us with his eyes straight ahead at the wall. "You know, Norma," he said, "Virgil almost made it."

"What are you talking about, Roy. . . .?"

"You see, I helped Virgil escape, the first night after they had registered us and stripped us at the camp. I was to start a ruckus with the guard and draw all the attention, risk getting shot right there on the spot. Then Virgil could make a break for it. I would probably get shot anyway when they made the connection that I had rigged it. As much as I loved my wife and Joy, whom I hadn't seen yet, I would have laid down my life to put Virgil back safely in your arms with little Tommy. I tried, Norma, honest I did. I called that guard every name in the book. The guard came toward me all right; the trouble was, instead of engaging in any kind of fight with me he just slammed me a good one with the butt of his rifle in the back of the head, here, just at the top of the neck. I went out cold. I remember trying to fight my way back to consciousness: I kept thinking, I've got to save Virgil, I can't just lay here like this, I've got to pull myself up and save Virgil!

"When I came to, I had the sensation that I had just closed my eyes for a second. I was in my cot in the sleeping room. Everybody was asleep. I couldn't believe it. Had the whole incident been a dream? I looked over at Virgil's cot and somebody was in it. At first I thought it was Virgil, but this guy was bigger. I leaned over to Hal Ober, who was sleeping beside me, and said, 'Where's Virgil?' Hal looked at me and said, 'He made it.' I was so happy I felt like screaming, 'Did you hear that, boys? Virgil made it!'"

"He made it?" my mother asked incredulously.

"That's what I thought all that night. I didn't even mind my throbbing headache; I thought I had helped Virgil escape that nightmare. The next day out in the yard the guard who had hit me in the head the night before swaggered up to me and said, 'Your friend, the lieutenant, almost made it: too bad.' Apparently our temporary camp was within a few miles of Allied-held territory and Virgil was shot by a sniper within yards of freedom."

My mother sobbed into her handkerchief. Mildred came into the room and could guess what they were talking about. My mother tried to pull herself together.

"Well then, why wasn't his body found. . . .?" She couldn't finish.

Roy suddenly seemed elsewhere. "I don't know," he said. "I don't know. That's a good question."

Roy disappeared again after that. It was the same story. Wandering here and there aimlessly, a string of bad checks through Illinois and Ohio, finally catching up with him in Albany, no idea who he was. We had to take care of Mildred and Joy during these times. Mildred herself always seemed close to a breakdown; her nerves were in shreds. She couldn't talk about the war. "Let's talk about something else, what do you say?" she would say anxiously to my mother if my mother happened to mention anything to do with it. That didn't leave too much to talk about, since both of their lives had been so thoroughly changed by it, by what had happened to their husbands.

Joy, with whom I silently played in the next room, didn't know where her father went when he was away for so long. My mother told me. I had some thoughts about Joy's father, Roy. I thought he probably forgot everything and went crazy because he knew where my father was or what had happened to him, and for some reason he couldn't tell us, and that was driving him crazy and making him forget who he was. I knew he must be suffering, but I thought it was cruel of him to not tell us the truth. My mother and I secretly feared that he wasn't telling us the truth because the truth was too awful.

After he had been brought back again and gone to the hospital for a while and had a new job and seemed to be acting like a normal person, a good husband and father, we started seeing them again. It always took us a little while to get back to visiting them right after Roy came back, because we knew it must be hard for them. Mildred was very nervous. Joy was getting old enough to see that her father changed a good deal. They could tell when he was going to go off, but they didn't know how to stop him, were afraid to try.

I spent a lot of time now going through boxes of old photographs of my mother and father as young lovers in high school, Virgil in a baggy gray flannel suit and a white shirt open at the neck, his arm around my mother. They appeared to be very happy, very much in love. Then there were worried tender photographs of train partings, my mother and his mother kissing him on each cheek for the picture Mr. Woods was taking, shaking on his wooden leg. Then many handsome photographs of Virgil in flight school, standing proud with his classmates; and later his flight crew, they looking at him with personal pride and respect. Virgil working late at night in his office on the base, serious paperwork, his leather jacket on, his hat, looking up. My mother had an album the service had given her, and she filled it with clippings and mementos: napkins from dances at the base when he was stationed in Oklahoma at first and my mother lived there with him, just pregnant with me; anything pertaining to their lives, even a grim list of his classmates on which she had written in small script the fate of each young man — dead, prison camp in Italy, prison camp in Germany, wounded, home safe. Out of helplessness more than bitterness she was comparing her fate to others. Was she the only one whose husband was lost . . . just not found? Had the War Machine cranked down, disassembled itself and transformed the demons of death into babyfood and fast cars without uncovering a trace of Lieutenant Michael Virgil Woods or his B-17? Had they been just swallowed up by the heavens; had the friction between death and desire erased him?

There were the love letters, too, including excited fatherly remarks about little Tommy, and how Easter was coming soon and he would be home at last. I tried to imagine his voice as I read these. When I stared at the pictures and read the letters at the same time I could see his mouth move. And I was confident he would find us, no matter if he was like Roy and had forgotten his name, had forgotten where we lived. He would stumble on and when he found us then it would all come back to him and we would tell him how long we had waited for this day.

The older I got, the more I was convinced Roy Weaver had the secret of my father's disappearance. By the time I was six I was determined to get it out of him myself. My mother had given up hope of ever getting Roy to talk sense. It wasn't fair to question him, anyway, because he was crazy and suffered terribly himself. We didn't see them as much now. They had moved to another house and it was on the other side of town. The parents made plans to get Joy and me together because we still thought of each other as friends.

I didn't know how to act around Roy. If I forgot he was sometimes crazy, then he did something to remind me and I was embarrassed. And I didn't think it was nice to treat him as if he were crazy, even if I had known how to treat a crazy person. And besides, you didn't notice it most of the time. He didn't seem *very* crazy, just unnatural in the way he would look at me sometimes, as if (I thought always) he wanted to say something.

One time he was looking at me so intently and yet not saying anything that I finally broke the silence and said with uncharacteristic bravery, "Go on, what were you going to say?" He shook his head and said, "Oh, I was just thinking how proud your father would be of you. You look quite a lot like him, you know."

"I might not now," I said enigmatically.

"What do you mean by that, Tommy?" he asked.

"I mean he might look much different now, he would be older."

"Yes." We sat there in silence for a few moments and then he said to me, "Do you think about him much, Tommy?"

"Yes," I said.

"What do you think?"

"I think I'll meet him downtown some day," I said.

My mother and Mildred came back from shopping and it was time for us to go home. That was the most I had ever talked to Roy. I was more convinced than ever that he was hiding something from us. I told my mother on the way home. I said, "Why don't you just make him tell you the truth? Can't you force him?" She said she couldn't because Roy was sick and wasn't responsible for what he said.

Roy called that night and said he was going to tell her the truth. The truth was awful and he had wanted to hide it from her. Virgil had made him promise that he would never tell. The truth was, he said, that Virgil had lost both arms and legs and was taken care of by an old farm woman someplace in France, he didn't remember where.

We didn't see the Weavers after that. A few years later they moved to Texas. Every now and then my mother would say, "Remember Mildred Weaver?" And I would say yes. "They say he's just as bad, poor Roy."

In 1950 my mother was twenty-seven and I was exactly twenty years younger. For the most part we lived those first seven years with my grandparents on 47th Street Terrace, between Woodland and Garfield, in the center of Kansas City. My three aunts, Connie, Irma, and Marty, and my Uncle Everett lived there, too, in various stages of maturity. We were a big happy family and loved one another equally; there were no power struggles, each had his own place.

My real father, Virgil, was reported missing on a bombing mission over Stuttgart in April of 1944, five months after I was born. His parents, Mr. and Mrs. Woods, who were caretakers at the Kansas City Zoo and lived in a shack on the premises there, both died of grief before the end of '44. We had lived with them there at first, I'm told.

After two years of lonesome mourning and waiting, my mother started to date a little. She dated a Catholic by the name of Bud Tie, dark-haired and handsome with rosy beer-warmed cheeks and a slightly devilish smile. They went out once a week for the next four years, and sometimes he would even come over and sit with us around the radio. It was generally assumed they would marry some day. They were engaged on and off.

My mother surprised us all one day by announcing at dinner that she had just married this guy by the name of Joe Quincy. We had barely met him! To our knowledge she had been out three or four times in the past two weeks with him and we knew nothing about him, except that he was three years younger than she, was quite handsome by the standards of the day, and was employed as a lineman for the Bell Telephone Company.

Then there was a lot of sudden hustle and bustle. Boxes were packed and runs were made up to the new house. The new house was a little four-room white-shingled green-shuttered bungalow about eight blocks away from where we were, over on 49th Street, near Prospect, on a steep hill.

My mother hadn't bothered to find out much about Joe Quincy before she married him. In that first couple of weeks Joe and I ended up alone in the house several nights when my mother worked late at the chrome fixture company. The first night I was alone on the floor of my room lining up a hundred lead soldiers in impeccable rows when Joe came in and knelt down beside me. He smiled warmly but tensely, and said, "Ever seen one of these before, Tommy?" I looked down and there was a gun in his hand. "It's a .38." he said. I didn't know what to say. "Here, go ahead, hold it," he said, putting it out next to my hand on my knee.

"Is it loaded?" I asked, stalling.

"Do you want it to be?" he said.

"No," I said.

It was loaded and now he took the bullets out and put them on the floor by my cannons.

"It's heavier than I thought," I said.

"Go ahead and pull the trigger," he said.

"At what?" I asked.

"At anything," he said. "Shoot your lamp out."

"All right," I said. And tried to hold the gun up with my one hand steady enough to take aim at my lamp.

"You would have missed it," he said.

"How come?"

"Because you were shaking. Use both hands this time. Hold it out in front of your chin. That's right."

I admit I thought it a bit peculiar to have my brand-new stepfather teaching me to shoot the light out of my room with a .38. Though it could have been easily explained. All the men I knew hunted, were proud of their rifles. Joe didn't leave much room for interpretation, though. He started telling me about crime and gangsters in Chicago. He didn't say exactly what he had done there, but it was strongly implied that he had used that pistol on more than one occasion and even that it was "not too safe" for him to be back there right now. There was a certain amount of pride in the way he related the picture.

I didn't tell my mother right away, but I was certainly curious to know if she was aware of this man's past, if she knew about the gun, if she approved. Then Joe and I were again alone for a few hours one evening and it was I who brought him around to this Chicago hood world. He seemed reluctant to talk about it again. I asked him if he belonged to the Mafia, and he said "No no no," very irritably. He kept opening beer bottles and pacing up and down the living room where I sat on a low green chair and stared up at him, trying to understand him.

Then we could hear my mother's high heels coming up the two flights of concrete steps, weary from late night work. Joe looked at me and said, "Go into your room," very brusquely. I had never seen him like this before, but then again they had only been married a few days short of a month.

I did as I was told, resentfully, for I wasn't used to this treatment in the old house. I stood my soldiers up all around me. They had me completely surrounded. I didn't stand a chance. So I closed my eyes, held my breath and flew in a spastic explosion, all four limbs in a mad destructive whirl.

There was yelling, a real vicious fight going on out there. He was yelling, "We're going!" And she was yelling, "We're not going!" over and over and I could imagine that he was giving her what I called "Indian rub-burns" because she was screaming, "Let go of me! Let go of me! You're hurting me!". And I was so nervous I didn't know what to do, so very quickly I set up all the soldiers around me again and instantly demolished all hundred of them with a crazed running somersault.

Then she screamed in horror and pain, "Tommy, come here!" and I scrambled to my feet and plunged through the door into the living room. Both of Joe's bare forearms were gushing blood all over his clothes and the divan and the coffee table, the throw rug and the hardwood floor. I had never seen so much blood. I thought he was a goner. Joe was standing there, shocked, holding his arms, but delighting in the disbelief and reverence and horror on both of our faces. I had to call the ambulance while my mother got some clean rags to tie around his arms so he wouldn't lose so much blood. Joe was sputtering to himself in a delirium of self-pity, neither resisting nor assisting my mother. He was taken off and sewn up and was in the hospital for a couple of days.

Before the ambulance came, my mother was sure to pick up the knife from the pool of blood on the floor where it was almost hidden. She hid it on the back porch just in time. There were questions, but I don't remember the story we finally agreed on. I stayed home and cleaned up the blood while she went to the hospital with him. I barely knew what was going on — that is to say, what had happened.

My mother came home around midnight and I was still up. I told her I couldn't sleep until she told me what had happened. She said Joe had tried to kill himself because he was mad at her. That seemed pretty extreme to me, so I inquired further. She said he wanted to move out of this house right away, like tomorrow. And that she didn't want to, she wanted to stay right there. She had her job and I had to go to school.

When Joe came home from the hospital he found out he had been fired from his job with Bell. Now he was mad, he was sulking all the time. I tried to stay out of the house as much as I could when I was not in school, until my mother came home at 6:30. And even then I dreaded it. They yelled all the time. I stayed in my room, trying to lose myself to the soldiers.

I knew my mother was afraid, but I also knew she didn't want to alarm me. Then one day Joe's parents arrived from Detroit to stay with us for two weeks. I'd never seen people like them before. They were completely dissipated by alcohol. When I sat down for my cereal at 7:15 they were both there at the breakfast table with a fifth of bourbon and several ashtrays overflowing with butts. Repulsing me with their foul breath, they'd pat me on the back and say, "What do you say there, little boy?"

Then at dinner table at night old Mr. Quincy, barely able to hold onto the bottom of his chair to keep from rocking out, would start up with, "Joe thinks you ought to come on back up with us to Detroit, Norma. Pretty nice town."

"Maybe later," my mother would answer vaguely, concentrating on her meal. I wasn't saying a thing. Joe was doing all he could to hold back his rage against the world.

My mother and I were tremendously relieved when Mr. and Mrs. Quincy finally drifted away. Nothing was real while they were there. The haze they were in suffused the whole house and our way of seeing everything. Joe was supposed to be looking for a job, but my mother didn't believe he was. He was up to something. Out all day, with his .45 or .38, depending on his mood. From the fights I overheard I don't think he was pulling jobs so much as making contacts — of some kind, for something. Several weeks went by and Joe was visibly changing before our eyes. They didn't seem married so much as mutually trapped.

Joe taught me how to clean both of his guns, and this was something I enjoyed. It was one of those exclusive joys, where I knew I was the only kid in my third-grade class who could disassemble and clean a .45 automatic. Now that was a heavy pistol; I *had* to use two hands to hold it up steady and pretend to blow out all the lights. Joe gave me a bullet for it which I could carry around in my pocket and fiddle with, my forbidden secret.

One night they were really going at it. It was late. I had had the lights off for two hours but couldn't sleep. I didn't want to miss anything; and besides I was afraid for all our lives. The voices rose to a more and more frantic pitch and finally there were four terrible explosions at split-second intervals. Joe had told me that gun would leave a hole in a man's back as big around as a half-gallon can of peaches.

I must have had a moment's thought before running out there.

"Get back in your room, Tommy!" my mother yelled at me, with her hands clutching at her own face in terror.

Our neighbors called the police, not because they were afraid someone might have been shot but because the noise bothered them.

They were old. Again there was this ridiculous attempt to hide the evidence quickly. Rugs were moved to cover up the holes blown into the floor. Somehow my mother lied herself out of this one, too, with her innocent endearing face. Joe hid in the basement.

The next day I was sent down to the hardware store on Prospect to buy some plastic wood in a tube, and I got to spend three or four hours that afternoon and evening filling up the holes. It was still pretty conspicuous when I got done, but at least you wouldn't stub your toe in one of the holes.

I don't know if my mother had told her family what was going on. Perhaps she had told Connie, the sister closest to her in age. They were very close and gave each other advice in difficult situations. Connie and my mother had gone to Acapulco on a spree for six weeks with the government money my mother got after they gave up looking for my father and declared him dead.

But I think now she was really afraid to involve anyone. Joe was a desperate man and had to be handled very cautiously lest he tear into you, himself, or the floor with one of his deadly weapons.

I heard them up talking almost all one night; I wasn't trying to stay awake and eavesdrop. I was tired and their voices were a constant whisper all night, no yelling this time. I got up drowsier than usual at seven and was about to brush my teeth when my mother came into the bathroom and said to me, "Tommy, you're not going to go to school today." I failed to delight in this announcement the way a respectable seven-year-old should have; I knew something was up, probably something big.

I was given a quick bowl of cereal and then told to make myself useful by loading the car, a 1949 black Ford. My mother stuffed clothes and even my soldiers and towels and sheets into the trunk in a hurry. We were on the road for Detroit by eight, without so much as a good-bye to my grandmother or anybody.

My mother did all the driving. I sat up front with her and read the maps while Joe lay on the floor in the back seat under a rug. Every time we saw one of those black and white 1950 Ford police cars on the highway my mother and I bit our lips and she hissed out of the side of her mouth, *"Stay down,"* to Joe in the back. We ate in little roadside drive-ins, dusty root beer stands in small-town central Iowa; then into

Wisconsin, which was more beautiful, and I remember almost thinking we were on vacation. It was hard to think that for long, because Joe was back there asking us if it was clear and where we were and how much longer till Detroit.

When we got to his folks' place in Detroit, Joe rushed out of the back seat and up the walk to the door. My mother and I sat in the car at his instruction and waited. He was back in a couple of minutes, looking panicked.

"We can't stay here," he said, getting back in the car. "The place is being watched." His parents came out on the porch and woozily waved at us, as though we were leaving after a long visit. We were all tired and dirty and the car was littered with potato chip bags and Dixie cups.

"What about Tommy?" my mother asked.

"He can stay here."

"I'm not staying here," I said meekly.

"All right," Joe said, "but we've got to get moving. I don't feel comfortable out front here, this is the first place they'll look when they hear I've hit town."

My mother started the car and we took off. Mr. Quincy was hanging onto the porch railing and wishing us well.

My mother and I were back in Kansas City three days later. At school my friends said, "You been sick?" "No," I said, "I've been on a vacation." "Where to?" they asked disbelievingly. "Detroit," I answered proudly.

My mother and I stayed in the new old house alone. I got a pet alligator and two birds from Japan. It was quiet now. I missed my old chums in the neighborhood down on 47th at my grandmother's, but I could walk the eight blocks several times a week when I got lonesome up on our hill where mostly old people lived.

Occasionally one of them would ask, "How's your new dad?" And I'd have to answer, "I don't know." I didn't really know what had happened to him. We were all hysterical for a couple of days hiding around at Joe's old hoodlum friends' in Detroit. Then they got him, the police, but I don't really remember how.

In fact, for many years I didn't even know what for. Then my mother's youngest sister, Marty, told me one night. Marty was only three years older than me, seventeen years younger than my mother. "What ever happened to Joe?" I asked her years later.

"He got the electric chair," she said matter-of-factly.

"What for?" I asked.

"Didn't you know, Tommy?" she said. "Joe killed his first wife."

My mother and I took pride in our little house on 49th. I started a vegetable garden in the backyard. I had five rabbits in a hutch. After a year my mother quit the chrome fixture company and took a job with Encyclopaedia Britannica as a secretary. She still had to work late several nights a week, after dark. She was my best friend, so I was glad when she came up the hill. I would walk or run down the hill to tell her something.

In the summers we went swimming every day we could at the huge Fairyland Park public pool—just take the bus straight out Prospect to 75th, the end of the city then. But it was crowded all the same. After the epidemic in 1952 and '53 it should have been rechristened Polio Public Pool. That never stopped us. We came early so my mother could find a place for her beach towel. We both would be barbecued by three, darker and darker as the summer rolled on. I in the water, she on her beach towel.

And when she got her week off in July we took the bus down to Lake Tannycomo in the Ozark regions of southern Missouri. We would rent a little cabin and spend every minute of sunshine on the beach or out on an inflatable raft, dozing and soaking up the scalding reflection off the water. One day my mother and I both fell asleep on our separate rafts and floated down the enormous lake ten miles before I woke and yelled to her. We laughed about that for a long time.

At night there was the Barefoot Club. That was a little cellar tavern with sawdust on the floor (to encourage bare feet) and a rocking good jukebox sending out "ABC Boogie" for the young happy people to dance to. I danced quite a bit myself. My mother sometimes met nice men and would sit there in a booth drinking a few beers. Connie came with us once and they both met men they liked, though I don't know how seriously. I do remember that both of their men persisted after everyone had returned to Kansas City. My mother and Connie would talk on the phone about them and say how disgusting they were and then laugh like crazy, and then double-date once in a while.

We lived on in that house for five years until I was twelve. One day I traded my sizable collection of lead soldiers for a cheap set of plastic spacemen and regretted it immediately.

I never did make too many friends in that neighborhood. The old lady next door who called the police when Joe shot off his .45 went crazy one night and carved up my five rabbits. I discovered them the next morning, parts hurled savagely all over the backyard. I knew she had done it, and though I was afraid of her I pulled in my chest, crossed my fingers, and rang her doorbell. She pretended not to know why I was there. I finally found my voice and just as I found it broke into tears, grumbling, ". . . You killed my rabbits . . . you killed my rabbits. . . ." I had her there, she couldn't lie in the face of such a passionate accusation as I delivered. Yes, she said, she had killed my rabbits in the night. They were getting into her garden and eating all her carrots. That was a lie: the smartest and strongest rabbit in the world couldn't have broken out of that hutch. She had killed those rabbits just because she thought they *might* some day break out and eat a carrot or so from her garden.

I saved my money, my allowance and the bits I made raking leaves or shoveling snow, and in a month I was able to descend upon a pet shop and purchase a dozen guppies, three black mollies, three zebras, three neons, one pencil fish and one hatchet fish.

I did poorly in school. My fourth-grade teacher suggested I might be mentally deficient. My mother had to take time off from work and pay many visits to her. I was always apprehensive about these meetings. They made me nervous. One time Mrs. Webb suggested to my mother and the principal that I be taken out of school and placed in a home for children like me. My mother was outraged and told the teacher off right there in front of Mr. Thomas, the principal, and me. I fainted, right onto the floor. My mother exploded all the more. From my coma I could hear her furiously yelling. "See what you've done to him! Why, you shouldn't be allowed to teach children!" The principal consulted my test scores and took our side against Mrs. Webb, suggesting that possibly she had "the poor child" so frightened he wasn't able to perform. But the real truth was, I wasn't interested in school. I wasn't a silent genius; I was just a daydreamer.

The move away from my grandmother's old neighborhood of 47th Street, where I had so many friends, had more and more effect on me as time went by. I began to see that I wouldn't make new friends as good as they had been. Our lives had been magical then; a dozen of us in a four-year age-span had lived together day and night in the streets and in the woods in back of our houses, through all the seasons of the year for seven years. I could go back, but it was different now: some of them were already in high school, some had moved. By habit, as much as anything, solitude became a state of mind.

We spent several nights a week down at Johnny's Bar and Bar-BQ, around the corner on Prospect. We knew Johnny and he looked after us. I became the house shuffleboard champion when I was nine. No one could beat me. And, consequently, I could drink free Cokes all night and play the jukebox a bit. My mother and I had many friends in there. Sometimes we would go down with one of her boyfriends, and sometimes we went down alone but always ended up meeting somebody she knew. We could eat a sandwich there as well—good thick Bar-BQ beef or ham sandwiches.

Jarvis Thornton, a nice man she went out with for a year, would sometimes take us out to Mary's Roadhouse, outside the city limits, where they had a very wild Western band. It was very loud and there were usually at least a couple of fights before we got out of there, but there was a lot to watch so I looked forward to it. Jarvis wanted to marry my mother, and my mother liked him quite a bit. She used to ask me how I would like to have Jarvis as a father. I could never really imagine what a father was supposed to be. I tried to give her an answer when she asked me what I thought of any of the men that came over to our house. It was easy to see through some of them, especially since they always thought the key to my mother's heart was me and would make fools of themselves trying to please me. One fool promised me a motorcycle for my tenth birthday; even I knew that was fantasy.

I liked Jarvis and I felt sorry for him when my mother said no to his proposals. Their relationship had arrived at the point when she was either going to have to marry him or they would have to break up. He was there every night, pleading with her, and sometimes he would even be asleep on the couch in the morning. I thought this was pretty funny. Jarvis was really in love with my mother, you could see it on his face when he slept. He was very large and the couch was very small.

He said to me on one of these mornings in the summer of 1953, "Tommy, how would you like to go to camp?" I said, "What camp?" And he said, "Well, it's called Rotary Camp. It's not too far from here, just out Highway 50 in Independence." "What do they do there?" I said. And he said, "Well, they've got a swimming pool, and I'm sure they have a baseball field, and plenty of woods to hike around in. And there will be lots of kids your age, and your mother and I thought you just might like it."

I thought for a minute, and then said, "When is it?"

"Well, your mother and I could drive you out there today and pick you up in two weeks. And we'll come out and visit you on Parents' Day."

It seemed kind of sudden to me. I don't think I had ever been away from home that long, certainly never without someone else in the family. I didn't even know what the Rotary Club was. But I got the picture. They wanted me to go. "All right," I said, "I'll go.

That afternoon they dropped me off at the place with my suitcase. It wasn't much to look at. It was just flat dry ground with some tents on it. Nobody seemed very excited to be there, including the counselors to whom my mother, Jarvis and I were introduced. Then Jarvis and my mother said good-bye, and I immediately felt forsaken. I was put in a tent with five other boys and told who my tent captain or whatever they called him would be. He didn't like me for some reason right off, probably thought I was laughably timid or something. I didn't like him, but only because of the teasing way he spoke to me and whispered my name at night as a joke.

We were led rigidly through certain sports and events each day. It was the rigidity that made me nervous. Just as I was beginning to enjoy the baseball game or the swim or whatever, there was a whistle in my ears telling me to quick throw that down and pick this up. This also made it difficult to make any friends: twenty minutes to the second for each meal, no talking after lights out. If the Army is a vacation, then I was in the Army.

In my spare minutes between the events of the day I began to take an interest in the tarantula and scorpion populations that thrived all over the campgrounds and in the surrounding woods. First we found them in our beds at night, both tarantulas and scorpions. Though the tarantulas presented a more powerfully hideous view to the eye, we were told the scorpions were the ones to really watch out for. A scorpion would be just as happy to sting you in your sleep, while the tarantula would either just cuddle up beside you or pass on by. I got to be known right away for my fearlessness with regard to tarantulas. I watched them and knew their ways, knew how to handle them and, indeed, was not in the least afraid after a while to let a perfectly virile tarantula fully fanged walk across my naked shoulders and down my arm into my hand where I would stroke his hair affectionately (and with caution).

A photograph still exists, somewhere in all the boxes, of me, naked to the waist, the skinny torso swarming with my entire tribe of tarantulas, twenty strong, and an idiotic beatific grin across my face. I would lure them out of their nests in the ground by waving a match inside the lip of the hole, or by sticking a straw down and teasing whomever was home. They'd come out, fangs like tiny mastodon tusks flashing angry threats at me. Of course they could jump (so can scorpions), so there was a small amount of danger. But I was armed with a pair of pincers made from a hanger, and I was quick to pick them up, gently always. Then I would put them in a cardboard box with chicken wire across the top, and keep them alive and happy with Welch's grape jelly. I lost my fondness for scorpions when I realized right away that I could never let them walk on me. You could clip the tips of the tarantulas' fangs in such a way as to not hurt them — as long as they were prisoners anyway and would be spoon-fed their Welch's grape jelly, which they all loved madly — but you couldn't clip the stinger of the scorpion without killing him; that's what I figured out for myself at the time, though I might have been wrong. And they were, if not deadly in Missouri, mighty painful — have you on your back for a week with a foot swollen up like a balloon. And they never seemed to adapt to the jelly diet. They were either listless or depressed; they all fell into these two categories.

One morning we were told in the breakfast speeches that it was Frank Buck Day and we should all go out there and really work hard catching snakes so that our tent would get the most points and win. They would give out awards that night after dinner around the swimming pool. They said our parents had been invited and many of them would be there. I must not have been listening because I didn't understand what was meant by Frank Buck Day, and therefore none of the rest of what was said made any sense to me. I was supposed to go out there and help my tent win, and then maybe my mother would be there at the swimming pool tonight.

I didn't want to ask anybody what we were supposed to do because I didn't want to appear stupid. And I would never have dared ask my tent captain or whatever he was because he would have certainly torn into me then with some wicked ridicule. After a while outside, I could tell that the thing to do was find a stick. Everybody was running all over trying to find a certain kind of stick, a snake stick. I heard two boys talking about the point system: ten points for a rattlesnake, nine points for a copperhead, eight points for a water moccasin. Five points for a bullhead or a blue racer. Three points for a blacksnake. One for garter snakes and ringnecks. And so on. I was beginning to see the picture. And it didn't take me long to realize I didn't want any part of it. I didn't even care about the tent. I didn't really like any of them, and I hated the tent captain. And most of all, I was frightened to death of poisonous snakes, which seemed to me — despite my predilection for tarantulas — to be just good sense.

Frank Buck Day, "bring-'em-back-alive," was a walking nightmare for me. There must have been fifty kids out there in the woods screaming louder and louder, "I got one!" "I got another copperhead!" I carried the stick and the gunnysack and was leaping on tiptoes in order to spend as little time as possible on the earth's surface with the deadly silent creatures menacing through the brush like liquid stilettos. I pretended to have very bad luck, mumbling disappointed sighs when I let a four-foot copperhead slither over my shoe without reaching down and grabbing him behind his head.

To my utter amazement no one got bitten that day. I was relieved. And when the count came in, our tent was last. They figured it all up before dinner. I didn't care very much. My tent mates, rightly, said I was no help at all. The other five guys averaged around 32 points — that's about three poisonous snakes each with maybe a blue racer thrown in. I had three ringnecks at a point each. And to make it worse, these ringnecks of mine were only about two inches each, incredibly nice to hold in your palm. Like kittenish worms. But not worth spit on your Frank Buck scale: that was made very clear to me by our tent captain, the taunter.

We had to sit at our regular tables in the dining hall. If our parents had come we wouldn't know until after dinner. Some kids were able to look around and catch sight of their parents across the hall eating with the counselors and exchange waves. I couldn't see my mother and was trying to accept the fact that maybe she hadn't been able to come: either she had to work late, or maybe Jarvis had taken her out dancing or to Mary's Roadhouse.

We filed outside to the pool area as soon as we had finished our Jell-o. The ones who were going to get the awards were excited. The rest of us just accepted this as another event. My tent captain, Allen, who played sports in high school, pulled me aside when I came out of the dining hall.

"Come here, Woods," he said. "We're going to dress you up." I didn't know what he was talking about, but I knew I wasn't going to like it.

"What for?" I asked.

"Because, Woods, old boy, you have been elected 'Queen of Frank Buck Day.' "

I didn't want to bring it up now, but I still wasn't sure I knew who Frank Buck was, and what was the idea behind this Frank Buck Day I had just — almost — gotten through. Allen and two other tent captains took me behind the gardener's shed and started dressing me up in makeshift girl's clothing and putting lipstick on my mouth and other things on my eyes and cheeks and a mop parted down the middle on my head. I saw nothing funny about it, but knew I was trapped. Now I hoped my mother and Jarvis weren't out there, though I had wanted to see them very badly before this new turn of events.

I could hear the leader of the camp announcing the tent awards and then the individual awards with his bullhorn over the pool. There was applause and laughter. ". . . And Charlie Paddock wins the first place award for the individual with the most poisonous snakes: Charlie brought back twelve copperheads, four water moccasins and one rattler!" It was amazing. I knew Charlie Paddock and he was just an ordinary guy. Why does he get first place and I end up "Queen of Frank Buck Day"?

Just when Allen and another guy had finished screwing a pair of dangling earrings on me, I heard the camp leader saying, "And now folks, there is one last award that we give each year, and that is to the camper that catches the *least* snakes in our Frank Buck Day 'Bring 'em Back Alive' snake-catching competition. We call that award our 'Queen of Frank Buck Day Award!'" There was tremendous laughter. Allen grabbed me roughly under my arm and dragged me into the lights around the diving board where the camp leader was standing with his bullhorn.

"And our 'Queen of Frank Buck Day' this year is . . . Miss Tommy Woods! who caught all by *herself* three itsy bitsy ringnecks, about this long . . ." (he held up his thumb and forefinger a fourth of an inch apart). The parents and the campers were really laughing very hard now.. The campers were yelling things. "Come on up here, Queen Tommy," the camp leader said, standing on the diving board. "You aren't afraid of water, too, are you?"

"No," I said.

"We have a prize for you; yes, we do," he said.

I had on high heels, so it was hard to walk. They were too big and I kept threatening to crash on either side with each step forward I took.

When I got up on the diving board with the camp leader I was in such a state of embarrassment and humiliation I was afraid to look at anyone, afraid to see if my mother and Jarvis had come. The camp leader was saying some funny things which I couldn't hear, and then someone came up behind me and handed him one end of the most enormous blacksnake I have ever seen. It was six feet long and twelve inches around in the middle. Allen and the camp leader stretched the snake out to its full length in front of the audience, which responded with appropriate sighs and gasps. Then the camp leader said something into the bullhorn I didn't hear and they began to wrap the snake — it was, I remember he said, the camp's mascot of many years — around my neck. When it was wrapped around several times Allen handed me its tail to hold in my right hand and the camp leader gave me its head to hold in the other. There was a burst of appreciation from the parents' gallery. And then Allen and the camp leader pushed me off the diving board into the deep end of the pool.

I expected the snake to strangle me, but apparently it had been through this enough times to be interested only in disentangling itself from my neck and saving itself. By the time I surfaced, white with fear, my makeup running and my mop-wig turned around sideways, everyone seemed to have forgotten about the Coronation ceremonies. They were standing in threes and fours discussing the wonderful opportunities the camp offered. The campers were giving their parents hotpads and lariats they made for them, and the parents had Kool-Aid packages and Fritos for their sons.

I just wanted to creep through them as inconspicuously as possible and get back to the tent to change into dry jeans and scrub the lipstick off my face.

I heard my name called. "Tommy." My mother came up through the crowd to me and I felt ashamed to be standing there in that outfit, pained that she had seen me made a fool of out there in front of everyone. I desperately didn't want her to make a joke about it.

"That was terrible," she said.

I couldn't say anything. I was holding back.

"Where's Jarvis?" I said.

"He couldn't come."

"Aren't you going to marry him?" I said.

My mother married Dick Murray, she said, because he was a young widower with a son (seven years younger than myself) and on his way up as a salesman for Monroe Matic Shock Absorbers; that gaudy blue and yellow company Ford, with frantic hype all over it, reminded me of him.

The boy, BillyBob, was emotionally retarded, and no wonder; Dick, the father, had no tolerance for anyone less powerful and perfect than himself. But he was a liar and fraud. He talked about the Army; it didn't take us long to find out he meant high school ROTC. His stardom in basketball, baseball and football, too—all lies, a sandlot fumbler unliked in high school. But now he was making it. How his first wife died, we didn't know. BillyBob was six months old; he cried one night, she got up—pretty twenty-two-year-old—and died. The cause of death was never determined.

My mother caught Dick, who traveled four or five days a week, in the oldest game, not even through the first year, with lipstick on his collar. That did it, she'd never trust him after that. She was cold. And I didn't like him already. At first I thought it would be fine to have someone to play ball with, but he played with an anger in him that I felt—a difference of 100 pounds between us. I was good at baseball and swimming and nothing else. Dick couldn't swim so I became a champion in the next couple years.

We moved from the house on 49th right away. I had never understood where the house came from, how we got it. Then I heard my mother and Dick talking one night: she wanted to keep the house and buy another; she said the house belonged to me, Mrs. Woods had left it to me. But it wouldn't be big enough, Dick said. They could pay me back later when I was grown and would need it.

I was in the middle of seventh grade and was sorry to leave my friends. In the new school I felt I was an entirely different person. People saw me differently, and I guess I encouraged it. I was frustrated with the new life and took my confusion out on shoplifting sprees and gambling at school. At home, too, I took up the terrible practice of shooting certain kinds of birds—the starlings and bluejays that preyed on the cardinals, bluebirds and doves.

I found as many excuses as I could to visit the old neighborhoods, my Grandmother Clinton's on 47th and friends on 49th. But it was different; I had always loved my family and suddenly the new life hadn't the same fun. My mother found herself pregnant and this brought on her resignation, as well as her contempt: she had no way out of a doomed marriage, she thought, and would hold on without love until she could manage. We dreaded when Dick wouldn't go on the road. The screaming in the house, the threat of violence at all times, made life grim. But I could get away now and then, and I did. I was developing an image of black leather jacket and motorcycle boots.

To avoid the tensions and fights of the living room I would sit in my room at nights throwing dice against the wall, trying to understand patterns.

Vacations were always to the Ozarks, one place or another on the huge man-made lake. In those days it was not what you could call commercialized. We stayed in barren little cabins that were infested with scorpions. BillyBob was stung one time on the foot as he got into bed. We thought he might die, but the swelling went down in a week and he could walk again. I enjoyed looking for arrowheads and had found over fifty down there on different trips. We fished, rented boats, cooked out. Dick directed every activity. He sipped beer from early morning, though I never really believed he cared about drinking. It was just the way he was with everything — the few friends he had in the business he didn't really care about, certainly not if it meant getting a deal away from them. And the money, that was hard to figure out: he'd kill for it but it seemed he only wanted it in the first place to intimidate others. I guess it was power, which he equated with class, that he wanted most. And it was class, of almost any conceivable kind, that he had none of. Standing out by the barbecue, turning the steaks or hamburgers, he looked absolutely alone sometimes, like what he was: a stranger to himself and to us.

Amy was born, a small frail baby with underdeveloped respiratory system. We worried about her the first year. More than once we found her turning blue, unable to breathe, and had to slap hell out of her. My mother had tried to love BillyBob, but she was bothered with his slowness — no one called him retarded then; he was a sad boy, often turned in on his own thoughts, slow to respond and clumsy. Dick would alternately brag that his son was going to be the greatest quarterback of the day and beat him mercilessly for dropping a piece of food from his plate. The boy jumped whenever his father tried to touch him.

Dick was three years younger than my mother. He was an only child. His father was a plumber in the old neighborhoods where we had lived. Mr. and Mrs. Murray were gentle, affable people who got by modestly, read the newspapers, and listened to the radio at night. They tacitly understood their son's quick talent for cruelty.

Dick's fortune as an automotive parts salesman varied greatly in the seven and a half years that the marriage survived. He was "Salesman of the Year" the first year; but later, for years, money was the source of many, many ear-bursting battles. He was always the bigshot even when his big Buicks and Pontiacs were in imminent danger of repossession. He arrogantly bought three and four expensive suits when we didn't have enough to eat. He had to have the best in his business, he said; image was everything. But he wasn't likable, finally, even to his own peers in shock absorbers or spark plugs.

The fights mounted in severity from year to year. My mother couldn't go out of the house for a week while she waited for the black eyes and swellings to disappear. Dick grew louder, more obnoxious. It was unpleasant to shop with him as he invariably started a shouting contest with a clerk or manager. We all dreaded holidays, knowing he would be home more than usual and that everything would be ruined by one of his arbitrary regimens, instant wrapping-paper pickup on Christmas while he drank beer and belched orders on his back on the couch. BillyBob always did something wrong; he broke his new toy or wasn't paying strict attention to instructions.

I certainly wasn't immune to blows. Dick sensed increasingly that I lacked feeling for him — not that he offered any himself. I felt sorry for him at times, thought how awful it would be to be him. I knew I would get away from it in a few years. But I worried about my mother and Amy and BillyBob. BillyBob was getting worse. Finally his teachers at the elementary school wouldn't allow him to continue in public school. By the time Amy was four she was beginning to reflect the constant tension in her home: she sat in a corner and pulled out her eyelashes and was starting on her hair. My mother was taking tranquilizers and drinking enough to calm her "nerves." Her three sisters, who still lived close by in Kansas City, listened at length to the horror stories she had to tell. She hadn't a cent to her name; Dick Murray didn't even have enough to support himself. Amy was too young to leave even if my mother could get a job. And nobody knew what would happen to Billy-Bob if a divorce did occur. He was getting torn apart, perhaps unbeknownst to himself: Dick didn't want him, wouldn't know what to do with him except give him back to his parents as he had done after his first wife's death. And my mother felt selfishly that Dick Murray had taken enough of a toll on her family: BillyBob, now under psychologists' care, was not hers.

She was afraid for her life; I also thought Dick was capable of killing her. His failings as a salesman were taken out on her in brutal beatings where it was obvious he no longer had control of what he was doing. He never showed remorse; his pride wouldn't allow that. When I tried to interfere I was given the same.

After some of these fights Dick wouldn't return for three or four weeks. He had girlfriends all over the four-state area he worked. In the last couple of years he was away twice for six-month periods. My mother would find ways to get money out of him and she took a job herself in a bank nearby after Amy was in school. I was more interested in girls and cars than I was in school and sports. I hung around the drive-ins every night with a gang called The Zoo Club.

When my mother and I talked about Dick it was with single-minded hatred. We had talked about murdering him; it was strange how natural the subject seemed. We knew neither of us would ever get a day in prison if caught. There were now dozens of friends and neighbors who could testify to his inhumanity. I had once pulled a gun on Dick, his own .25 automatic, in the midst of a particularly fierce lashing of my mother. I had stood there in the doorway of my room, watching the beating for what seemed like ten or fifteen minutes. I went to his dresser and got the gun, hesitated, and removed the clip; then walked down the stairs into the living room and pointed it a few inches from his temple: "Get out!" I shouted bravely with my equalizer.

The plan that seemed best involved his company car. He drove like a maniac on the highway, 95 or 100, and spoke with reverence — the only time he found that tone appropriate — of the martyrs, those brave traveling salesmen who gave their lives to bridge abutments, etc., in the line of duty. Over coffee in the morning my mother and I discussed the merits of loosening lug-nuts. Let him die for his cause; surely there was sympathy behind that conception. As for protection, we finally took out an injunction forbidding him to step foot on the property. It had been advised by everyone. But Dick wouldn't be stopped: he cut his way through the screens one night and managed to jimmy the new lock we had put on. My mother woke with a shudder at him standing over her bed in the dark; she screamed for me and Dick laughed, said he just wanted to say hello. He had thought I was away.

The divorce action seemed to last forever, during which time my mother's emotional disintegration culminated in a drunken, fiery crash at noon in downtown Kansas City. She was thought dead at first but was revived by a policeman.

One day in March when I was eighteen I was sitting in a graveyard in Pittsburg, Kansas, and realized that no one in my family had ever visited my father's grave in Belgium. I didn't even know *where* in Belgium.

The first assumption of his death had been in an article in the *Kansas City Star*, September 4, 1945, eighteen months after his disappearance. It said, "Lieut. M. Virgil Woods of the Army Air Force, who has been reported missing in action since April 11, 1944, has been presumed by the War Department to have been killed. Neither the wife nor the mother has given up hope that Woods will return." The decision to go to Belgium came from a combination of changes in my life, though I don't think I connected them consciously at that time, that afternoon. I had been in compulsory ROTC that year, my freshman year in college. The whole experience had been difficult for me, resulting in harsh punishment, sometimes of a violent nature. We viewed many war documentary films that depicted correct and incorrect maneuvers and procedures. My mother's marriage was breaking up back in Kansas City. And I had done something for which I felt guilt: I had legally changed my name from Woods to Murray. I had been called Murray since our move to Prairie Village, Kansas, a new suburb of Kansas City, in 1956. And so I rationalized that the legal act now was practical. My names had caused confusion for years. But I hated Dick Murray and loved the memory, the instilled memory, of my father. Also, I had started to write poetry that year, my freshman year in college, and somehow my father was more on my mind than he had been for several years. He was never far from my mind. I knew so absolutely precious little! The entire range of our family was dedicated to his memory, but facts, descriptions, never emerged — only a vague misty praise. "Your father was a wonderful man." "Your father would be so proud of you." "You look more like your father every day." My grandmother even absentmindedly called me Virgil occasionally.

I never felt that it was appropriate to ask for these "hard facts" that nagged me. Was he or was he not actually found? It was years later that anything of this sort came out.

The government was paying my way through college to the tune of $110 a month. That was enough in Pittsburg, Kansas. But I didn't have anything left over. I called my mother and told her that I wanted to go to Belgium in June. I had been told from childhood that I had a $6000 trust fund — I never really knew who had established it for me, my father or my father's mother. I wanted to see if I could get a small part of it now for this good cause. My mother agreed to look into it for me, contact the lawyer, the legal guardian of my inheritance.

The $6000 turned out to be slightly less than $600. Lawyers' fees. I could have it all now if I wanted. There was obviously something fishy but I had little sense of money and $600 was something, it was enough. I booked passage on the *S.S. Groote Bier*, sailing from Hoboken to Rotterdam.

The voyage was six days. I took a train to Paris and contacted a woman with whom I had corresponded at the American Battle Monuments Commission at 20 rue Quentin Bauchart. She was a quite elderly lady who was extremely warm and helpful. She was shocked and amused at the decrepitude of the hotel I had chosen to stay in. We took long walks through the city. On several occasions she brought me small sacks of groceries that I could get by on in my room.

I had around $200 left after the round-trip ticket. I decided to spend $65 of it on a Solex, a small motorbike especially common in France. I left Paris for Liege, Belgium, slept in a field one night, and was there the next evening. It was too late to call the cemetery, the Ardennes Cemetery, twelve miles from Liege in the village of Neuville-en-Condroz.

I sat in my hotel and looked over the literature I had on the cemetery.

"The cemetery, 50½ acres in extent, contains the graves of 5,250 of our military dead, many of whom died in the so-called 'Battle of the Bulge.' Their headstones are aligned in straight rows which take the form of a huge Greek cross on a lawn framed by masses of trees. Nearer the entrance, to the south of the burial area, is the memorial, a rectangular gray stone structure containing a small chapel, three large maps of inlaid marbles, 24 panels depicting combat and supply activities, and other ornamental features including the insignia of the major United States units in Northwest Europe. Two of the maps depict operations of the American Armed Forces, the third commemorates the Services of Supply in the European Theater. On the exterior is some large-scale sculpture. Along the sides, inscribed in granite slabs, are the names of 462 of the Missing who gave their lives in the service of their Country, but whose remains were never recovered or identified."

A man from the cemetery picked me up in the morning. I was suddenly afraid. I was intent, nervous, sad and grim, all at the same time, and even considered the possibility of backing out, asking to be let out of the car. I could find my way back to the hotel somehow. I could lie to my mother, say I had seen it. I was very distracted and had trouble chatting with my host.

In the memorial, he asked if I had any questions. Would I like to see the flight plan for the mission on which my father was killed? I had never thought about such a thing; it was too much "of this world." I didn't know, so I said yes, I guess so, when what was really preoccupying me was his actual grave; that is what I had traveled all this way to see. The man had prepared for my visit and had some very hardcore information. Eight aircraft were lost in the raid on Stettin, the largest loss yet sustained by the 92nd Bombardment Group; twenty aircraft returned safely of the twenty-eight dispatched. Six aircraft of the 325th Squadron that flew as low squadron to the high group were lost to savage and persistent fighter and flak attack. The entire mission was flown at an altitude of about 15,000 feet and required eleven hours to complete. Crew members described it as one of the "roughest" in memory. Enemy fighters outnumbered friendly ones, and the flak was accurate, varying from moderate to intense. Bombing results were good.

My father's aircraft was believed to have exploded about twelve miles north of Brunswick, an early victim of the high group in the fighter attack.

The evidence of his death suddenly seemed incontrovertible. Did my mother know this? Did everybody know it? I studied the maps in a haze.

The man asked me if I was ready to be led to the grave. I told him I would prefer to find it by myself.

"When would you like to be driven back to your hotel?" he inquired. I told him I would meet him back in the memorial building in three hours if that was agreeable.

Fifty acres of white symmetrical crosses: it seemed vast, "as far as the eye could see." Avenues of crisp white crosses, thousands of statistics and stories. I felt like a small insect crawling through a dream city; how perfectly trimmed, how beyond reproach, what a self-sufficient entity. There was perfect silence. It was a beautiful, clear day, not cold or warm. What was it Harry Truman had said in his letter of consolation? *He stands in the unbroken line of patriots who have dared to die that freedom might live, and grow, and increase its blessings. Freedom lives, and through it, he lives — in a way that humbles the undertakings of most men.* What did he mean? What *possible* excuse?

I was in no hurry to find my father here. Death had leveled the worth of all these. And, besides, I knew he wasn't there. It was just a government's way to keep the records straight.

Still, when I did find it, there was a tremendous rush of chemistry: I had never been this close, in some inexplicable way, to touching him. I wept and lay down on the grave, falling asleep there as the sun came out and deepened my dreams. I saw my father in his B-17 still flying there "at about 15,000 ft." And then I came into view in some kind of plane, gaining on my father until I passed him, as in a cartoon, with scarf and goggles, waving. Why was I so sad? Why did I suddenly feel so old? When I awoke I took a color snapshot of the cross which said *Michael V. Woods, 1 Llt 325 Bomb Sq. 92 Bomb GP (H) Missouri Apr 11 1944.* No birthdate.

When I returned to Kansas City my mother and I talked at length about the cemetery. I didn't mention what I learned from the man who escorted me at Neuville-en-Condroz. Instead, when I was alone, I sought out the old box of photos, letters, clippings. They always seemed new to me: there was a world there I could never finish understanding. But he was some letter writer, eight written to his bride in the last week of his life alone. The words were simple, striving for cheerfulness and optimism, and overflowing with declarations of love. In the last few hours of his life he wrote, "Gosh honey I'll be the happiest man in the world when this damn war is over and I get to come home to you and Tommy. So help me! I'm never going to have you out of my sight again."

erek Walcott as Another Life

John Sokol © 1981

Derek Walcott

Leaving School

*Sometimes an ancient and infinitesimal detail will come away like
a whole headland; and sometimes a complete layer of my past
will vanish without a trace.*

TRISTES TROPIQUES

Our climate has two seasons, heat and rain. Sometimes, in childhood, this rain was like a sadness entering the earth, penetrating me with longing for our father. Even now, approaching the island, there are steaming gray piles of cumuli, the colour of boiled laundry, heaped on its mountains. It looks impenetrable or abandoned. Brown, broken precipices with the tattered gray lace of ocean, the single, tilted flag of a canoe, while the noise of the engines carries the memory of rain, of cold, clean cataracts pitching through gulches of giant fern, and the smoky, sulphurous sound of "Sainte Lucie."

Yet, when I think of my own headland, Vigie, it is never in rain, but the colour of that epigraph, copied in brown ink; the colour of burnt seagrape leaves, and of roofs rusting in drought.

In elementary school we had been taught that Saint Lucia was "The Helen of the West" because she was fought for so often by the French and British. She had changed hands thirteen times. She had been regularly violated. In fact, her final capture by the British had the quality of a cuckold's surrender, since she remained faithful to her French colonial past. Her name was clouded with darkness and misfortune; Columbus had named her after the blind saint; her saint's day was December thirteenth. Even her natural history was tragic. I had seen enough in childhood to believe it: a landslide that swallowed a mountain village after heavy rains, the memory of Saint Pierre, and, the year after I left school, a fire that destroyed half of the town.

Now, when I stood on the long wooden verandah of St. Mary's College, I could see clear across the charred pasture of Castries to the

Vigie promontory. "The balcony" was a position I had earned as a prefect, but now, as an assistant master, I could loiter or strut there if I chose. It ran past the headmaster's study, and had been proscribed as sacred ground by our last Head, a choleric, absentminded English Catholic whose name was T. F. Fox-Hawes. Mr. Fox-Hawes had also defined the "alley" back of the college as out-of-bounds until five minutes before school, a decree which sent a schoolboy population in blue serge blazers and blancoed cork "bughouses" wandering through the town "before the bell." Bells obsessed the Head. He selected his bell-ringer carefully. It was a post more responsible than a prefect's. If a wind tilted the bell and the clapper rang lightly, the school shuddered, since Foxy would be out roaring, "Who rang the bell?" It had been the same with the school balcony. But now, Foxy's era was over. The Irish Brothers of the Presentation had taken over the college.

Despite his short-fused temper, we had worshiped Foxy, and hated to see him go. So did he. He hated displays of sentiment. So we hung back under the roof of the galvanized iron customs shed, by a rusty gate and waved when we were sure his ship was headed for England, turning between La Toc point and Vigie. Our last English headmaster, he had been a lonely man, devoted to parades, fond of sailing and Conrad's prose, proud of the benignity of his Empire. He left the names of battles drumming in us, Blenheim, Waterloo, Malplaquet, of heroes who had actually quartered here, Sir John Moore, victim of Corunna, Admirals Abercomby and Rodney and the graves of an Inskilling Regiment on the Morne, where there were barracks built by the Royal Engineers, with the same rational, Romanesque brickwork as those at Vigie. Apart from the Cathedral, they were our only "architecture."

The only important buildings left after the fire were in the two blocks on either side of the verandah: one was the convent and the Ave Maria Girls' School, the other was the presbytery with its French priests, and the Roman Catholic Boys' Primary School divided from the college by "the alley." Leaving school had meant half-circling the block. I had been editor of its weekly Wall magazine, of its first Annual, and a prefect. Little else.

I had given up sports early. In first or second form. Because I had been christened a prodigy, I couldn't endure failure, except it was so ridiculous that it looked like self-sacrifice. I had been considered a promising, conventional off-break bowler, but "conventional" had no promise in it. All those promises were a long way behind me, all those angry, urgent cries to leave the life of a young silverfish and get out in the sun, and in the swim.

"Walcott, man!" Man was the cry, whatever your age. "Get out there and give Abercomby a point, boy!" Once Walcott had tried. Pale, sallow, big-headed, the blue heart of his house blazoned on his singlet, the blue stripe of his house running down the seams of his shorts, flailing away towards the tape. Then how come fathead Simmons, who he was sure was bound to come last, put up a desperate burst for Abercomby (his own house) to save himself? Also, what was the point of being a wicketkeeper when some full toss, meant by an ambitious stylist to be swept to leg, just missed my Adam's apple by a gulp? I was so furious that I stretched out flat behind the stumps, playing dead until the team collected around me, then rose, threw off the gloves and left. Abercomby had to look elsewhere for points: in essays, and in conduct. In addition to the Black Book, where canings were noted, and the Detention Book for minor crimes, the Brothers had introduced the Alpha Book for academics. I concentrated on getting points for Abercomby there.

Behind me on the balcony, the classrooms were humming with a generation being introduced by the Brothers to the wonders of natural science. Above the remaining town were the thick green hills boiling all day with their broad-leaved, volcanic vegetation. That was the nature I had learned to love in childhood. The one road inland coiled out of Castries up Morne Fortune, where the graves of the Inskillings were, the harbour below wide and hazing rapidly between trees. It crested that view that took in the Martinique channel, and sinuated through a cane-green valley towards snake country. It climbed again across the spinal ridge of the island, then it fell into the wide, heartbreaking Atlantic coast with its dirty breakers, its gray, unpainted villages with their squat Norman-style cathedrals, to split on the clean, windy southern plain of Vieuxfort, with its runways and arrowing highway, where the Americans had built an air base. I had known that road by heart from boyhood, traveling on its brightly painted trucks loaded with passengers, creaking with freight, the names of its villages plaiting into each other like straw, Forestière. D'Ennery, Ravine Poisson (where the village was buried), Praslin, Micoud, D'Aubaignan, and the odours of its fruits, moubain, corrosol, gouyave, and the very strong odour of the sea.

In those days I would leave our house on Chaussée Road equipped for such pilgrimages with a small, brown cardboard suitcase of clothes and painting and writing materials. I would bid my mother good-bye, and the cook would see me down to the country bus terminus on the wharf. I was going off alone into the country, "*en betassion*," to write.

I spent those vacations at the large, wooden roadside hotel of a farmer-spinster who had been my father's friend, writing poems which I showed her; one or two a day, preparing myself for the life I had chosen. She treated me with amused respect, introduced me to the writings of Whitman, and at other times she would indulge in reminiscences of my father whom she had loved.

I had come from a genteel, self-denying Methodist poverty. My mother, who was headmistress of the Methodist Infant School, worked hard to keep us at college, even if my brother and I had both won scholarships, by taking in sewing. My mother's friends, those who had survived my father, had been members of an amateur dramatic group, some cultural club which had performed Shakespeare and given musical concerts, when my father was their "moving spirit." These friends included a violinist, an ex-merchant seaman, an inveterate reciter who had seen Barrymore's Hamlet, and a professional painter named Harold Simmons.

Their existence, since most of them were from a religious minority, Anglican Methodist or lapsed Catholic, had a defensive, doomed frailty in that steamy, narrow-minded climate. Perhaps because of this they believed in "the better things of life" with a defiant intensity, which drew them closely together. Their efforts, since the pattern would be repeated for my brother and me, must have been secretly victimized. Their presentations were known as "The Anglican Consette" (concert) or "The Methodist School" or "Teacher Alix Concert," with all the vague implications of damnation. My brother Roderick and I would go through the same purgation later.

All through adolescence I had experienced some of this mockery and persecution, even public damnation. The hell of others, of limbo and purgatory was something that, being an outsider, I learned to envy. I learnt early to accept that Methodists went to purgatory or hell, a Catholic hell, only after some strenuous dispensation. I was thus, in boyhood, estranged not only from another God, but from the common life of the island.

Perhaps it was this that made me find in the actual hell of the great fire a certain exultation, since it had destroyed that other life.

From then on Saint Lucians would refer to it as an historical phrase, as they had once of "*en temps cholera*"; all that year I lived in the traumatic wake of a heat wave. The air above the ruins, for months after, seemed to ripple like a washboard. There was a powerful sense of the unreal, the absurd. It was long after the shock of that destruction that the shapes of houses vibrated in memory and could be, in our imagination, placed rigidly into their foundations. This was a plain of blackened walls, ridiculous arches of doorways, of steps that marched in air.

The older life was unimaginable. The fire had humiliated the smug, repetitive lives of those Civil Servants, merchants and Creole professional men who had lived in rambling wooden houses with verandahs and mansards, attics for mongoloids, alcoholic uncles and half-cracked ageing aunts, that rigidly constructed French-colonial life of the petit-ponche and the evening stroll. Down to the wharf to look at the island schooners and back, always along the same streets. All that had disappeared in smoke.

Down by the wharf, past the coal dunes near my grandmother's house, I had watched during childhood the crossing friezes of erect, singing women carrying huge panniers of anthracite coal, each weighing a hundredweight, but the port was no longer a coaling station. That had gone too. What still remained was the rhythm of the Church's calendar year, its bannered, chanting processions, Les Enfants de Marie, Retreats, and Friendly Society parades. During such processions I would feel that the town was empty and belonged to me. Every dusk the Cathedral of the Immaculate Conception flamed palely for vespers, drawing your friends from games in Columbus Square. Now, all those people, and they were a large part of the town's population, who had their properties destroyed by this Act of God, had been moved to the Romanesque barracks on the Vigie headland, a cantonment of refugees and destitutes. In fact Vigie was temporarily the new town, and when evening came those of us whose houses had survived preferred to go out there than to stay on that depressing, scorched plain where most of the city had been.

Still, all of those refugees on Fire Relief, poor man and merchant, seemed happier during those chaotic months, sharing a common elation of having suffered. On moonlight nights, all around the barracks of the cantonment, from Married Women's Quarters to Officers' Mess, you could hear laughter, screams and singing across the broken water. The promontory had once been the green preserve of the Vigie Golf and Country Club, a haunt of retired white or near white Civil Servants and Army officers. The buildings on the crest of the hill still were occupied by them, but they too would be gradually invaded, besieged.

In fact, the topographical changes of that headland chart the social evolutions of the island. It is now an airfield, but in our house on Chaussée Road we still had a pale watercolour of my father's of "The Coconut Walk," an avenue that I could only vaguely remember now that I was eighteen, that showed what it had been like. Now, everyone that I loved lived out there. From the balcony I could make out the Army morgue which Harry Simmons, who was now Fire-Relief officer, had converted into a studio, and Barnard's Hill, where Dunstan St. Omer, Hedwig Henry, Claude Theobalds (the son of the amateur violinist) and I had studied painting.

This was a low hill shelved with white-walled, red-roofed villas that formed the thick end of the Vigie headland. We had been invited to study painting with Harry Simmons on Saturday mornings when he heard that we were interested in art, that St. Omer was a prodigious draughtsman for his age, that Henry and I wrote verse and painted, and that Theobalds, apart from being an athlete, was truly his father's son.

Wherever you grow up as a writer, even with the limitations of a colonial boyhood, you depend with filial piety on older intelligences that help to shape your mind. I had been very lucky. In addition to the intelligent indulgence of the farmer-spinster, my adolescence fed on the approval and faith of teachers, professional and instinctual, who had loved my father, and those who were amazed at my industry. These included one of the Brothers of the Presentation, a college master who gave me extra lessons in French poetry and who read my verse, a Dominican lawyer and that astigmatic, garrulous, and benevolent man who had been botanist, editor, anthropologist and painter.

Harold Simmons had been my father's friend. It was my father who had interested him in painting. My father had died in his thirties, when my twin brother and I were a year old, my sister three, but on the drawing-room walls of our house there were relics of his avocation: a copy of Millet's *The Gleaners*, a romantic original of seabirds and pluming breakers he had called *Riders of the Storm*, a miniature oil portrait of my mother, a self-portrait in watercolour, and an avenue of pale coconut palms. These objects had established my vocation, and made it as inevitable as that of any craftsman's son, for I felt that my father's work, however minor, was unfinished. Rummaging through stuffed, dark cupboards, I sometimes came across finely copied verses, evidence of a polite gracile talent, and once a sketchbook of excellent pencil studies. I treasured the books he had used: two small, blue-covered volumes on *The English Topographical Draughtsmen* and on *Albrecht Dürer*, and the thick-ridged, classical albums of John McCormack and, I think, Galli-Curci. It was this veneration that drew his friends to me.

They may have realized that I had no other ambition. Below where I stood on the balcony was a plaque on the fourth-form wall with a gilded list of Island Scholars who had become doctors and lawyers, or, infrequently, engineers. There was no writer or painter among them, and I had failed to win the Island Scholarship because of my poor mathematics. In Foxys' era it had been awarded biennially on achievement in the London Matriculation. I had failed the exam once, and I might have won the scholarship if, as happened under the Brothers, it had been awarded for special subjects, but by the time the Higher School Certificate was introduced I was seventeen and too old.

Those boys who knew the hopelessness of their one chance, for whom a "classical" education meant a rut for life in the Civil Service, grabbed at the opportunity to make money working in the oil refineries of Curaçao. By the time I had reached the Sixth, they had left in batches, their school life broken, their education incomplete. They left as frightened boys and returned hardened men. The life there was rough. It was tireless, materialistic, but you could not afford to break, because there was nothing to return to, you were indentured anyway, and sending part of what you made back home, or else, on that sterile, cactus-ridden boom-camp, where everyone spoke papiamento, you whored on Campo Allegre, or gambled, or tried at nights to educate yourself.

Until Curaçao, for every doctor or lawyer the Board numbered it destroyed the ambitions of his classmates. It even took its toll among the winners, some of whom collapsed from tension and the exhaustion of new studies in Edinburgh, Oxford, London or McGill. It was a grinding, merciless system. Those who surrendered hope and became Civil Servants went through accepted, brief periods of protest with idleness or drink, then settled desperately into what they had feared, early marriage, a large family, debt and heavy drinking. Some who had slid to the gutter preferred to stay there, or go mad. They had "missed it by one mark," or by being born a month too soon. But "The School" was what made or broke you. It was the only way out, and once every two years it let just one boy through.

These things are not written without pain, for their heroes still suffer the abrasions of that life; but since our apprentice days on Barnard's Hill Dunstan and I knew what our professions were. We would be what we could do, what we loved best. Mr. Simmons had set up that example. But now Dunstan had gone to Curaçao. I was not lonely, though. I was in love.

Here I imagine myself on that balcony, in an inherited, heavy brown sports jacket, gray flannel trousers, a tin of Country Life cigarettes in my pocket, waiting for late afternoon, when I would go across the harbour to her house.

A., who was still a schoolgirl at the convent, lived with her parents and innumerable sisters in a stone bungalow with a concrete landing stage below Harry's house. Every dusk now I would walk through the burnt-out town to the yacht basin and hire a rowboat and oarsman to take me across the still, dark-green harbour towards Vigie. Sitting there on the stern, with the town's cries fading, and the only noise the feathered oars creaking in the oarlocks, I felt suspended, as if the world around me were unreal, the white-pillared, gutted Government Offices and the Morne, and the brickwork, yellow cubes of the Barracks growing larger.

The trip cost only a shilling. The boatman, who would begin to cast off from the wharf as soon as he saw me coming, hardly spoke. To arrive after that still, twilit voyage and find A. playing with her sisters on the small pier, or waiting at the doorway, was even deeper peace. Years afterwards, when I had to study Dryden, I would think of his poem on the Great Fire of London and his "Annus Mirabilis" as one poem, since both blent in that year.

Love of that kind never returns. It contains, because of its innocence, its own extinction. It is so self-content, so assured of immortality that it irradiates not only the first-loved but her landscape with a profound benediction. I was content to spend hours in A.'s vicinity, not always in her physical presence. In fact, we must have had few moments alone. There were always others about: shrieking children, other schoolboys, or the guests of her father's club. Yet we were so happy that we could ignore each other. It is easy to dismiss all this as adolescent, to prove that at that age we love ourselves, that underneath such calm there are the first intuitions of loss and the ennoblings of sexual desire. Maybe. But A.'s presence was consummation enough. She gave off a nimbus whose quality was golden, the colour of the light itself, and it made her the generator of those canoes that returned at dusk, and of the stillness of the water. There was nothing frail about her. She had a firmness of sinew and purpose that sometimes made her petulant, quarrelsome, stubborn and coarse. She was graceful, gentle, resolute. I had surrendered my heart to her as wholly as I had surrendered my imagination to her landscape.

Luna Park, where A. lived, had been converted from an unprepossessing concrete shed into cramped family quarters to one side and a spacious restaurant-nightclub on the other. Her father, a little man given to the most fiercely ornate monologues, had great faith in me as "an artist, my boy," but none as a prospective son-in-law, whose only prospects seemed to be a lifetime's teaching at the college. He wanted better for his daughters, and it was to impress and placate him, as well as to be near A. that I offered to decorate the restaurant walls with "panels."

These were simply slabs of concrete bedded against the walls by a prison corporal who was a part-time mason. Their design was neo-Nicholson. Circular cement plaques horizontally cut by a narrow slab, and for real daring, a collage of torn newspaper, the outline of a fish etched in with the edge of the trowel, and other Cubist leftovers of bottles and guitars. For A.'s father, who had once prophesied that the name "Walcott would blaze like a meteor across the black midnight sky of Saint Lucia," the panels confirmed my talent but not my prospects. But he treated me courteously, cunningly, his bushy eyebrows and corrugated forehead fixed in perpetual amazement that a mind like mine, bent on higher things, should be another banal worshiper of his beautiful daugher. He would win in the end.

For me, though, everything was beginning, the culmination of a secretive childhood spent in reading, writing and playing with my brother for hours with stick-puppets in our backyard, elaborating our own cowboy and detective plots, into public poems, plays and paintings like those at Luna Park. Some months before, when I felt that I was ready to be "published," I had sat on the landing of the stairs and asked my mother, who was sewing at the window, for two hundred dollars to put out a booklet of poems. She did not have that kind of money, and that fact made her weep, but she found it, the book was printed, and I hawked it myself on street corners, a dollar a copy, and made the money back. It went into a "second edition." I was writing plays or sketches for the school and for a group we had formed, and I had already painted two huge backdrops for a convent concert that had taken me six months.

What made me feel more "professional" was that Harry would let me have the use of his studio on Saturdays and during vacations. This meant permission to play his classical records on the gray-metal, red-buttoned radiogram as loudly as I wanted, the use of his neat, battered Royal typewriter, his library and his liquor cabinet. I was drinking a lot, for I was now moving in a circle that included hard, talkative and intelligent drinkers: Simmons himself, and the Dominican lawyer, another lawyer who had won an Island Scholarship and had recently returned, an English architect and his painter wife.

What names, what objects do I remember from that time? The brown-covered *Penguin Series of Modern Painters*: Stanley Spencer, Frances Hodgkins, Paul Nash, Ben Nicholson; the pocket-sized Dent edition of Thomas's *Deaths and Entrances*, the Eliot recordings of *Four Quartets*, dropped names like Graham Sutherland, and Carola and Ben Fleming's and Harry's reminiscences of ICA student days, and Harry's self-belittling ancedote of how he had once heard that Augustus John was aboard a cruise ship and he had rushed up to see him with a pile of canvases and how John, agreeing to look at them, had glared back and said, "You can't paint a damn, but I admire your brass!," BIM magazine, Henry Swanzy's Caribbean Voices programme, Caribbean Quarterly, and the first West Indian novels, *New Day* and *A Morning at the Office*. Once Mittelholzer had sat in our drawing room and warned me to give up writing verse-tragedies, because "they" would never take them.

That year I was hardly ever at home. My life lay between A.'s house at Luna Park and along the path that wriggled up the hill to Harry's Morgue. At school, I now felt more sympathy with the Brothers. They were at least young and outspoken. Besides, I found in their accents and in their recollections of Irish events and places, in their admiration for Synge and Yeats, for Pearse, and even for Joyce, an atmosphere, fortified by those martial Irish tunes that the school choir was taught, by the morning and evening litany droned out by the assembled school under the galvanized iron roof of the college yard, an atmosphere that summoned that of my current hero, the blasphemous, arrogant Stephen Daedalus.

> "Help of the Sick,
> We are Sick of Help,
> Towers of Ivory,
> Pay for Us,

Comforter of the Afflicted
We are afflicted with Comfort . . ."

I was now consumed by poetry, whatever expression it took. I shared
with one of the Brothers, a flushed, tubercular-looking mathematician
who also wrote verse and had composed the new school song (did we
have one before?), a new cynicism for the Empire and a passion for
James Clarence Mangan's poem:

> O, my dark Rosaleen,
>   Do not sigh, do not weep!
> The priests are on the ocean green,
>   They march along the deep . . .

for Fergus and Cuchulain, and in the struggle and wrestling with my
mind to find out who I was, I was discovering the art of bitterness. I
had been tormented enough by the priests, and had even been savaged
in a review in the *Port of Spain Gazette* by the Catholic Archbishop. Like
Stephen, I had my nights of two-shilling whores, of "tackling in the
Alley," and silently howling remorse. Like him, I was a knot of para-
doxes: hating the Church and loving her rituals, learning to hate
England as I worshiped her language, sanctifying A. the more I
betrayed her, a Methodist-lecher, a near-Catholic-ascetic, loving the
island and wishing I could get the hell out of it.

My adolescence was over.

But nearly two more years of this life would go by before I left the
school, A., and the island. In those years Dunstan would return, fed up
with the materialism of Curaçao, dedicated to God and to a career,
right here in his own island, as a painter, while I was beginning to
acquire a little fame from abroad: kind reviews from Roy Fuller, a
recommendation to Longman's from Christopher Fry . . .

In those years my love for A. strengthened. When I was at last
given a Colonial Development and Welfare Scholarship, for which I
had mechanically applied, I felt that it was breaking up a settled, pur-
poseful life.

Yet, on that last morning at the Vigie airport, how cruel, selfish
and unsurprising was this exhilaration of departure! Of farewell to A.,
who arrived late and hung back shyly in the crowd, to Harry, to
Dunstan smiling wisely, and how merciless to hope that the island and
A. would preserve herself (since they were one) under some sacred,

inverted bell of glass, and that I was incapable of betrayal! All those island mothers, brothers and first-beloveds who had seen us go, they knew an older pain than ours. We felt a gentle pity for their familiar clouds, roads and customs. We imagined that their lives revolved around our future. We accepted as natural their selfless surrender.

Under the engines, as it did when you climbed the Morne, the promontory hazed and widened, until there were no more figures, only houses, roads, and a landscape narrowly receding into cloud.

Edmund White as Forgetting Elena

John Sokol © *1981*

Edmund White

A Boy's Own Story

An odd side effect of writing is clarity. Just putting things down gives them a greater clarity than they may possess in memory, where they are pungent but vague. Like a blind man's hands exploring a face, the memory lingers over an identifying or beloved feature but dismisses the rest as just a curve, a bump, an expanse. Only *this* feature — these lashes tickling the palm like a firefly or this breath pulsing hot on a knuckle or this vibrating Adam's apple — only this feature seems lovable, sexy. But in writing one draws in the rest, the forgotten parts. One even composes one's improvisations into a quite new face never glimpsed before, the likeness of an invention. Busoni once said he prized the most those empty passages composers make up to get from one "good part" to another. He said such workmanlike but minor transitions reveal more about a composer — the actual vernacular of his imagination — than the deliberately bravura moments. I say all this by way of hoping that the lies I've made up to get from one poor truth to another may mean something — may even mean something most particular to you, my eccentric, patient, scrupulous reader, willing to make so much of so little, more patient and more respectful of life, than the author you're allowing for a moment to exist yet again.

When I was eleven I started going to a bookshop every day after school. I was fascinated by a woman who worked there. She moved and talked and even sang as though she were on a big stage and not in a very small store. I had seen an overweight and coquettish diva portray Carmen, and this woman seemed just as ready for the role — a peasant blouse worn off the shoulders and so low as to reveal the top of large breasts; black hair drawn back into a ponytail that hopped almost of its own accord from her back up onto her shoulder, where it would perch like a pet as she nuzzled it with her cheek; a tiny waist sadistically cinched in by a stout black belt that laced up the front; ample hips in rolling, uncorseted motion under a long skirt that swirled in meticulously ironed pleats around her; and small flat feet with painted nails in sandals she remained true to even on snowy days. She bathed herself in a heavy, ruttish perfume that suggested neither a girl nor a matron but rather the overripe coquette, the sort of imposing beauty one could imagine a weak nineteenth-century king taking on as his mistress. This scent, as shameless as her half-naked body, billowed to conceal or shrank to disclose her other abiding odor, the smell of burning cigarettes. She could sit for hours on a high stool behind the counter with an open book and kick her pleated skirt with a dangling leg and stab out one cigarette after another into a small black ashtray from the Stork Club in New York. On television I'd seen Sherman Billingsley, the host of the Stork Club, introduce the viewing public to celebrities visiting his restaurant; some of this glamour now attended the woman's smoking. Each of her butts was lavishly smeared with blood-red lipstick; the growing mound of smoldering butts resembled an open grave, ghastly trough of quartered torsos. As she smoked she hummed throatily, then exhaled, coughed, paused; her eyebrows shot up, her trembling upper lip curled back on one side to reveal a big, red-flecked front tooth, her jaw dropped, her spine grew, her massive shoulders shook — and out came a high, high head tone. Then a snatch of nasal Gounod tossed off saucily, scales sung in muted vocalese ripped open here and there to full volume (dark sleeves slashed with crimson silk), then a bit of hey-nonny-nonny . . . She turned a page in the novel and blindly reached for the smoking ashtray. The low scabrous radiator that ran the length of the display window clanked and hissed. Someone came in as the bell rang out merrily. The cold air cut the angled, floating panels of blue smoke to ribbons. The woman put her book down and dashed lightly to greet the customer. Her body, which in repose appeared Levantine, in motion took on a balletic lightness. She cocked her head to one side and smiled. In the cold winter daylight sifting down through the high windows and reflected up from the banks of snow outside, I could see the thick layer of pancake makeup covering her face and neck but stopping short of her shoulders. The makeup was so evidently painted on and of such an unlikely hue that I gasped: this woman must be very old, I thought, to need such a disguise.

Everything about her intrigued me and I returned day after day just to be near her. I watched her so hard I forgot I existed; she provided me with a new, better life. For hours I stood in front of one bookcase or another reading as the dirty snow melted off my boots and left black tracks on the wood floor. First I'd remove the cap with earflaps and stuff it in a pocket; ten minutes later I'd unwind the maroon scarf. My mittens dangled from the elastics that clipped them to my cuffs; as my real hands, white and small and nervous, ferreted for a book on a high shelf, these bigger, darker, simpler hands hinged limply against my sleeve. The coat came off and fell in a heap on the floor; then a sweater threw its twisted body onto the coat: clumsy wrestlers. The woman hummed and placed a small nickel-coated pot on the hot plate. The upper third of each windowpane was steamy; as a result, a passing man was striated into blurred and clear zones, his neck detailed down to the stubble but his face an embryo's still streaming within the caul. Although it was only four the light was already dying; the world creaked from the cold and hugged itself hopelessly. Blue mounds of snow cast bluer shadows. But inside, everything was cheery and animated. The woman, whom the new customer called Marilyn, was laughing at his long, murmured story and her laugh was lovely.

By the third long afternoon I spent there I'd fallen into conversation with Marilyn. She made some comment or other on the book I'd been holding for half an hour as I kept stealing glances at her and eavesdropping on her snatches of song and remarks to customers. She said to me, "I noticed you're intrigued by that set of Balzac. It's a very good buy—the complete works for just forty dollars. That's about a dollar a volume. You can't beat that. And it's a handsome edition, the titles in gold stamped on leather, which may or may not be real. Turn-of-the-century."

I was not a fast reader. Months could go by before I'd finish a single book. The project of reading all of Balzac would obviously absorb the rest of my life. Was I prepared to make that commitment before I'd read even one of his novels?

"How interesting," I said, as I'd been trained to say to everything, even the grossest absurdity. "Who was Balzac?"

She smiled and said, to spare my pride, "Ah, now there's a good question. We'll wait till Fred comes. He can tell us both."

Fred, it turned out, owned the store. Whereas my teachers always went slowly, repeated everything, summarized frequently and assumed nothing, Fred tossed off his lessons as though he feared boring me. Here was a tall man with ragged red hair streaked prematurely gray and acne-pitted skin and workclothes that weren't quite clean and hundreds of scraps of odd knowledge he stored in his head just as he secreted (in the pockets of his faded blue shirt or his baggy chinos or the blue vest from one second-hand suit or the brown jacket from another) tiny slips of paper on which he jotted notes for his stories. The slips were of five different pastel shades; whether this variety followed a system or merely injected random color into cerebrations so exalted they would otherwise have been uniformly gray I have no way of knowing — certainly at that age I had no way of judging him, only of gazing at him with awe.

His eyes, grotesquely magnified by thick glasses, never met mine. When he spoke to me he scrutinized a point precisely a foot to the left of my head. His voice was so soft and low and expressionless that one might have ignored him had Marilyn not listened to him with such deference. Since everything she did was theatrical, "listening" also had to be pantomimed: she stood like a schoolgirl and her hands, pointing down, were pressed together in inverted prayer. Her mouth was pursed, her head lowered; at a certain moment in Fred's mutterings her head would start to bob wildly and those strange tones of assent that can only be transcribed as "Mmnn" would issue forth from her throat on a high, surprised note and then on lower, affirming ones — even, finally, on a very low grunt that bore the unintentionally rude message, "Of course. Everyone knows that. Get on with it." None of this was subtle. It was really quite ridiculously overdone — or would have been had Marilyn been concerned at all with the impression she was making on other people. As it happened, she wanted only to conform to a role she was simultaneously writing and reciting.

The exact dimensions of that role became clear as the years went by. She saw herself, I was to learn, as the grisette in a nineteenth-century opera — as Mimi or Violetta or Manon. Like them she was impulsive, warm-hearted, immoral and pious. Like them she must remain eternally young — hence her flamboyant clothes and gestures and hectic displays of energy (the middle-aged imagine the young are energetic).

Later, much later, when I was sixteen and eighteen and twenty I'd meet her downtown where she worked at a museum and we'd go off in the middle of a dim winter afternoon to a deserted bar and drink Manhattans (I remember because they were the first drinks I ever ordered). Another afternoon I attended a madrigal concert she sang in at the public library, something planned in conjunction with an exhibition of one page from the hand of that monster Gesualdo. There she was, breasts half-exposed and working, eyes turned inward, trembling upper lip rising on one side until it suddenly everted, her face painted an unlikely yellow and her hair dyed a brittle blue-black, her clothes still "youthful" but now so out-of-date that the few members of the audience under twenty-five would have had no idea what she was signifying. They might have thought that she was an emigrée wearing the national costume of Estonia and that these songs—these gliding transits, startling rhythms and suave, uncomfortable harmonies—were folk songs in need of a pitch pipe. One afternoon over Manhattans I confessed to Marilyn I was gay and she told me she was, too, and that she and Fred had known all along that I would be, even when I was eleven.

"And Fred? Was he gay?"

"Oh, yes. Didn't you know? I thought we all knew about each other," Marilyn said as she redrew her eyes in the compact mirror.

"Well, I knew you both liked me and that I felt good with you, better than with most grown-ups."

"Then why did you stop coming by the shop? Waiter, another round."

"Because my mother told me I couldn't see you any more. The old ladies in our hotel told my mother that you and Fred were Communists and living in sin."

Marilyn laughed and laughed. "Of course the truth is we're both Catholics and gay and never touched each other. Perhaps those ladies even knew the truth but"—shriek of laughter—"assumed that Communism and living in sin, that those two things together equaled being gay."

I was wearing a Brooks Brothers sack suit of black and brown twill that ran on the diagonal and a soft felt fedora from Paris and this getup, which seemed so stylish to me, cast our conservation into the light of an excited urbanity, as did the cocktails, no doubt. Elevated tracks ran outside above the bar and, whenever a train passed by, our table trembled under our elbows and the glasses, accidentally touching each other, registered the shock in a muted chime. The light in the bar was as murky as old water in an aquarium dimmed by storms of fish food beat up by lazy fins, but I could peer out through it at the stark black parallelepipeds stenciled by the el-track supports onto a sidewalk bright with mica chips and frost, the permanent glitter and the passing. A radio played a rhumba.

I asked her news of Fred and she said she'd lost touch with him, that the last time she had heard he was still living with an Indian tribe in the Yucatán, where he'd gone to write his stories. And I recalled that when I was thirteen I'd run into him at the public library after not seeing him for a year. But he was no longer contained in his blue vest and brown jacket with his hair tousled but cut—no, now he was a wild man, something strapped with hemp to his back, his hair and beard flowing red and gray over his shoulders, his calves wrapped up to the knees in orange and red rags, feet shod in boots with cleats, eyes still big and averted behind glasses now mended with black electrician's tape and his hands much redder and bigger and flatter somehow, as though he'd hammered each finger flat. I didn't recognize him, but he touched me on the shoulder; and when I looked up into those eyes peering a foot to one side of me and saw the acne scars above the sprouting whiskers and heard his dull, mechanical and very soft voice, the sound of a voice choking on its own phlegm — well, then I knew him but didn't want to, so drastically transformed was he. If he'd had an iguana on his shoulder he couldn't have been more exotic. He told me he'd been in Mexico for a few months and was heading back there soon, that he had no money but lived by doing odd jobs — that this precariousness was necessary to his art. Before, in the shop, his dull muttering and his magnified, frozen eyes had seemed pitiable signs of shyness, but such an interpretation had fitted him only in his scruffy bourgeois guise, had fitted the sound of the clanking radiator and the smell of reheated coffee. Now that he was released out of his confining shop and had turned himself into a gaudy fetish, into a hank of streaked hair and bright rags, now his gaze seemed paralyzed by grandeur and his voice remote only because it was the sound of divinity. As a little boy I'd recognized that my imaginary playmate, Tom, was free but only by virtue of enduring total isolation; now Fred (but was this huge, mumbling, godlike bum really Fred?), now this new Fred was telling me mendicancy was the price of making art. And what finally became of him and his stories? Was he absorbed one day into the Yucatán jungle? I've been told that in some Indian villages in Mexico homosexual men live in a separate compound where they take care of the tribe's children; is Fred still living as some ancient nanny respectably obscured by pure white veils of beard and hair, his glasses long since broken and abandoned, his constant murmur unheard below the squeal of warm, naked toddlers who clamber over him as though he were nothing but a weathered garden god half-sunk into the creepers and vines, his notebook of handwritten stories open to the elements to scatter its pages as the leaves of a calendar in old movies fly away to indicate the passage of years, even decades?

And Marilyn? The last time I saw her the color of her makeup had gone iodine, her lips had thinned, her hair had become a spiky black cap and her large, rolling eyes no longer seemed a coquette's but those of a virgin martyr, protuberant, cast up, the whites wept clean, the lower lids sooty with despair. She told me that for the last two years she'd been living in a boardinghouse in a room next to that of a young violinist whom she loved and who loved her fraternally but, alas, not passionately. He was planning to become a Benedictine and she thought she'd follow him into Holy Orders. "This is the great love of my life — not a woman as always before but a beautiful young man who doesn't want me. How ironic! We met through music. His beauty, his music, his indifference — don't you see?"

"Not exactly."

She smiled the hazardous, hard-won smile of the lover determined to have found a consolation: "He was sent to me to awaken in me an appetite only God can feed. I've been such a sinner — waiter, another round — but I never became coarse or jaded or thick-skinned. I was ready for God's gift." Her hair didn't satisfy her. She studied it in her compact mirror, shifting the small round glass from side to side, top to bottom; a macula of light searched her face intensely and dissected it inch by inch, swerving here, hovering there, highlighting the withered cheek, the crepey neck, the hard, jutting chin. It moved where the glance of the contemptuous beloved would go. She propped the compact up between the oil and vinegar cruets and her fingertips touched her hair with wonderful delicacy as the reflection glowed steadily in her right eye and even seemed to travel surgically through it. At last she blinked and snapped the glass shut. "I still feel like a young girl, as though everything is about to happen. And don't you see" — her dry, rough hand with the painted nails seized mine — "I *am* a sort of spiritual debutante."

Not long ago I had drinks with my twenty-year-old nephew and his girlfriend, whom he'd met at a literary salon his classmates conduct. She writes haiku and journal entries but aspires to fiction and she was wearing a black beret, black lipstick and a plum-colored cloth overcoat with very high shoulders, a cinched-in waist and a ratty old fox neckpiece, only one amber-glass eye still in place beside the moulting muzzle. As luck would have it these several decades later and just twenty blocks north of the bar where Marilyn and I used to meet, this child ordered a Manhattan and tossed it back in three stylish gulps. Under her arty guise and her talk of sex and self-expression she was a placid Midwestern girl, large and comfy and ruminative, someone you might find in a neighbor's kitchen at noon over a cold cup of coffee and a full ashtray, all rueful irony and tips about bargains. Perhaps Marilyn, when I first met her, was no older and I only ascribed a great age to her because of her makeup. Perhaps Marilyn, when I first met her, was just as new to her bohemianism as this child is to hers. In our imaginations the adults of our childhood remain extreme, essential — we might say radical since they are the roots that feed these luxuriant, later systems. Those first bohemians, for instance, stay operatic in memory even though were we to meet them today — well, what would we think, we who've elaborated our eccentricities with a patience, a professionalism they never knew?

Soon after I first met Fred and Marilyn they decided I must learn German in order to read the novels of Hermann Hesse, at that time still largely untranslated. Hesse's mix of suicide, mysticism and sexual ambiguity had launched them into a thrilling void; reading him, they said, was like being in an airplane above the breatheable stratosphere. He wasn't healthy. In fact, a smell of taint seeped off his pages. He wasn't right or even wise, but they never stopped to check his words against what they knew to be true since they adored him precisely as an exit out of experience and an entrance into the magic theater of sensations wholly invented. In place of the torpor of everyday life Hesse called them to a disciplined quest — even if the Grail he offered was vaporous and poisoned.

The teacher they'd selected for me was a part-time professor at the university. He lived in one room in a huge pile thrown up as faculty and graduate-student housing. He had a double bed that pulled down out of the wall; by day it hid behind two white doors with cut-glass doorknobs. When he greeted me for my first lesson I was overwhelmed by his size. He was six-foot-four and brawny and I looked up into chestnut hair sprouting from his nostrils; my hand was lost in his. He was at once formal and hearty and spoke with a strong German accent. Our lessons followed an exact system and began and ended at fixed times without interludes or chitchat. By the same token the professor bounded about in a shirt open to his navel; his sleeves rolled up above his massive biceps, and on his desk I saw a photograph of him in a swimsuit at the beach holding his girlfriend aloft with just one hand. Like many athletes he found it impossible to sit still and his grammatical points and pronunciation tips were underscored with a ceaseless tattoo. He slapped his knees. He rocked back and forth in his straight-backed chair. He shot his hand up in a menacing Sieg Heil — but only to reach back to scratch between his shoulder blades, a difficult feat for someone so musclebound. As I sat beside him (I almost said *within* him, so totally did he surround me) I became more and more feeble. He'd stride up and down the small room, kicking the baseboard of each wall when he reached it as if to protest the insult of such a small cage for such a mighty lion. Before I met him I could have imagined someone huge and stupid and taciturn; I could just as readily have pictured a brilliant tiny chatterbox, bald pate and soft curls fringing it, a midget dynamo who read everything and played the cello when depressed. But a giant with callouses on his palms at the base of each finger, someone who breathed in a conscious, voluntary, magisterial way as I tentatively recited my lesson and who stood and folded a huge paw over his jaw before delivering a judgment about my performance — such a man was so new to me that he confused me, he thrilled me.

One winter Friday afternoon at four he didn't answer his door. Desperation seized me. I hadn't realized how devoted to him I'd become. Our sessions didn't call for devotion. I'd simply show up, obey his commands and sink into a desire to please him that seen with any objectivity could only have been called devotion. But things didn't go that far, there wasn't the absence necessary for adoration until that afternoon when he didn't open his door. For some reason I was convinced that he was inside but in bed with his girlfriend, that lithe, tiny woman in the black swimsuit whom the Herr Professor had held so effortlessly aloft last summer, a simple smile on his face. He was in that bed which, when pulled down, no doubt filled his whole room and there he was heartily rolling on his tiny but acrobatically receptive partner. Soon enough it would be time to push the bed back behind its white doors, to gnaw on a sausage and quaff a beer and then, in his lordly way, open the door to his ridiculously young pupil. I didn't knock very loudly because I didn't want to break his concentration or rhythm; the only question was had I calibrated my knock so as to indicate my presence but not to annoy him?

And yet — what if he wasn't at home at all? What if he had forgotten our lesson? As long as I thought his closed door was barring me from those deep invasions of a fragile body, just so long was I content to stand in that shabby, windowless corridor. Waiting for my teacher was no burden to me (wasn't Hesse himself teaching me the value of a patient apprenticeship?). But what made me frantic was the fear that no one was behind the door. No bed, no lazily smiling German face, no huge hand stroking a pale, engorged pelvis—nothing, an unlit room devoid of everything but a ticking clock and a refrigerator that groans and goes dead, groans and goes dead.

And I was terrified someone would ask me what I was doing in the hall. A great deal of time had already gone by. People had begun to cook supper and the overheated corridor was filling with the smells of food. I had peeled off my coat, scarf and sweater. I sat on them and leaned against a wall. In the distance I could hear the elevator doors opening and closing. An old woman shouted into a telephone. Another woman was giving instructions to a child. This corridor was a sort of catch basin for the domesticity raining down around me. The smells. The irritations. The complicated lives of absolutely everyone. Since our own complications fill so much of the foreground, we prefer to reduce other people to stylized figures who always act contentedly and in character, but two hours in the corridor are a reminder that there are so many people—so many such fully developed and irritable people—that there's no oxygen left for a child to breathe; he'd be wise to press back into the shadows, to hold his breath, to look and listen but never, never to contend.

My professor didn't come that day. Of course he phoned the next with a reasonable excuse. Of course I should have anticipated just such a hitch and explanation, but my need, though usually held in check or released only on imaginary beings, could, if turned on someone real, devour him. I'd so seldom asked anything of anyone. The gods were my company; the lilac in flower embraced me; books did all the talking but only when I permitted the monologue to begin. They were transparent companions whose intentions were never in doubt. Gods, flowers, words—why, I could see right through them! Nor did they waver into or out of focus or leave even an inch of the surround blank. Whereas people batted thoughts and feelings like badminton birdies at you, a whirr that might take you by surprise, that you might not even see but that you were expected to return until the air began to go white with feathery travels, the gods made no such demands. They propped themselves up on gold elbows and lazily turned their wide, smiling faces down on you. When their glance locked with yours their eyebeams lit up. In an instant you were they, they you, gods mortal and mortals divine, the mutual regard a reflecting pool into which everything substantial would soon melt and flow.

The same year I began my German classes the boys I knew started playing a violent game called "Squirrel" ("Grab his nuts and run").

Guys who'd scarcely acknowledged me until now were suddenly thrashing, twisting muscles in my arms, their breath panting peanut butter right up into my face, my hands sliding over their silky skin just above the rough denim, and now his gleaming crotch buttons were pressing down on me as his knees burned into my biceps and I put off shouting "Uncle" one more second in order to inhale once again the terrible smell of his sweat.

Or the light was dying and piles of burning leaves streaked the air with the smoky breath of the very earth. My hands were raw with cold, my nose was running, I was late for supper, my shirt was torn, but still I called him back again and again by shouting, "I'm not sorry. I just said that. I'm not sorry, I'm—"

"Look, you little creep"—his voice was much lower, he was a year older, he came at me, really mad this time, I didn't want his anger, just his body on top of me and his arms around me.

Or the minister's son—that small, athletic blond with the pompadour preserved in hair lotion and the black mole on his full, hairless cheek, that boy who strutted when he walked, preferred his own company to everyone else's and who had a reputation among adults for being "considerate" that was directly contradicted by his cheerfully blind arrogance—he was someone with whom I could play Squirrel in the late afternoons after his trumpet practice (he shakes the silver flood of saliva out of the gold mouth and snaps open the black case to reveal its purple plush, worn-down here to a slick, reflecting whiteness, roughed-up there into à dark bruise, then he places the taut heroism of the instrument into that regal embrace and locks it shut: the case becomes the dull geode with the mystic heart).

Even in the winter, as winds blowing up off the lake cast nets of snow over us and the sun pulsed feebly like the aura of a migraine that doesn't develop, we lunged at each other, rolled in drifts, squirrels hungry for hard blue nuts in the frozen land. Suddenly fingers would be squirming and pulling, a wave of pain would shoot through me, his sapphire eye set in white faience would arc past and dip below the shadowy horizon of my nose, hot breaths would tear out of my lungs and cross his—at cross-purposes.

The summer I was twelve I was sent to a camp for boys. We lived in tents in rows on the grounds of a famous military academy. The massive, reddish-brown buildings with their green turrets and gables were closed for the season, but the adult staff—the captains and generals in perpetual uniform—stayed behind to run the camp and earn an extra income. The campers, though younger than the usual cadets, were nevertheless submitted to the same military discipline. In fact our camping activity, beyond nature hikes and swimming lessons in a chlorinated indoor pool, consisted of nothing but drill and inspection. We learned to make a bed with hospital corners and to stretch the rough flannel blanket so taut a coin would bounce on it. Everyone owned precisely the same gear, stowed away in precisely the same manner. Shoes were placed just under the cot, each pair four inches from the next, each shoe of a pair two inches from its mate. Trumpets awakened us and sent us to bed. We marched to the mess hall where we were served cold mashed potatoes and boiled cabbage; more horribly at breakfast we ate bacon in congealed grease and scrambled eggs floating on hot water. After breakfast we marched double time back to our tents, where we had an hour to prepare our quarters for white-glove inspection. Our captain saw everything and forgave nothing. He could find that single pair of knee socks at the bottom of a steamer trunk that wasn't properly rolled and he would hand out to the offender enough demerits to fill all his free time for the rest of the summer.

He was a small, wiry man with black eyebrows so full that if they weren't pressed or combed into place they would stick out in disconcerting clumps like brittle, badly-cared-for paint brushes or could droop down over an eye in a droll effect at odds with the command he was barking. His skin was a tan mask clapped over a face that always appeared seriously exhausted; the dark circles and drained, bloodless cheeks could be seen through the false health of his tan. I ascribed his weariness to irritation. In fact he was much older than the other instructors. He may even have been close to retirement age. He might have been ill and in pain and perhaps his irritation was due to his ailment.

After lights-out he became someone new. Although he was still in uniform his tie was loosened, his voice seemed to have dropped an octave and a decibel, he had bourbon mysteriously and pleasantly on his breath, and his regard had grown gentle beneath its thatch of drooping eyebrows. He stopped by each tent, sat on the edge of each cot and spoke to each boy in a tone so intimate that the roommate couldn't eavesdrop. My roommate was a tall, extremely shy and well-bred redhead from a small town in Iowa. Someone who seemed not at all eager to confide in me nor to seek my friendship or even comments, as though he recognized that this life at least was worth enduring only if it remained unexamined. And yet his silences did not guarantee that he was altogether without thought or feeling. At unexpected moments he'd blush or stutter or his mouth in mid-sentence would go dry—and I could never figure out what had prompted these symptoms of anxiety.

One night, after our captain had lingered longer than usual in his cloud of bourbon and then passed on to the next tent, I asked my roommate why the captain always stayed longer beside him than me.

"I don't know. He rubs me."

"What do you mean?"

"Doesn't he rub you?" the boy whispered.

"Sometimes," I lied.

"All over?"

"Like how?" I asked.

"Like all"—his voice went dry—"down your front?"

"That's not right," I said. "He shouldn't do that. He shouldn't. It's abnormal. I've read about it."

A few nights later I woke up with a fever. My throat was so sore I couldn't swallow. My sheets were wet and cold with sweat. Even when I lay still I could feel the blood running through my veins; a metronome was ticking loudly within me and with each tick an oar of sensation cut into the water and pulled against it. No, now I could detect a line of divers jumping off the prow to the right, the left, right, left—the columns of marching boys advanced across the floor of the chlorinated pool. I closed my eyes and felt my heartbeat pluck a string in the harp of my chest. Was the night really so cold? I had to get help, the infirmary, otherwise pneumonia. My roommate was propped up on his elbow speaking giddy nonsense to me ("I like, I like, I like the Lackawanna") until I opened my eyes and saw him serenely asleep, his face the cutting edge of the prow as it parted a sea of liquid mercury. The flow, clinging to itself, boiling but cold, had swept me overboard with a chipmunk who was singing snatches from the Top Ten through the painful red hole in his neck—I sat up, I could barely swallow, I whispered my roommate's name.

When he didn't respond I put on my regulation cotton robe and regulation black slippers and walked up and down the raw clay roads between the rows of tents. Was that the first streak of dawn or the lights of a town? Should I wait till reveille? Or should I awaken our captain now?

I walked and walked and watched the night sky phosphoresce like plankton in the August sea. Gold would glimmer at the horizon and then feed its way up through delicate glass circuits into the main switchboard, where it would short out in a white explosion that would settle into a fine jeweler's dust. Were those bats overhead? I'd heard that bats lived in the school towers. Here they were, supersonic, blind, carnivorous and getting closer, lacing their way from eye to eye up the tongue.

At last the captain heard my knock and came to the door. He had a whole tent to himself, I could see, and he was still awake with a mystery novel and a bottle of bourbon, although he appeared confused — at least he didn't know who I might be. When he'd unraveled my identity and figured out I was ill, he urged me to spend the rest of the night with him. We'd go to the infirmary first thing in the morning, he said to me. We'd go together. He'd take care of me. I had to insist over and over again on the urgency of my seeing a nurse now ("I'm really sick, sir, it can't wait") before he finally relented and led me to the infirmary. Even as I was pleading with him I was wondering what it would be like to live in this spacious tent with him. But why hadn't he noticed me before? Why hadn't he tried to rub me? Was I inferior to my roommate in some way? Less handsome? At least I wasn't abnormal, I said to myself, glancing over at his haggard unshaven face, at his profile with its shelf of eyebrows in the darkness bright with mercury.

The next summer I refused to go to camp until my mother lied and told me I'd be a junior counselor in charge of dramatics at a lovely place in the northern woods where practically no discipline existed and what there was would be waived in my case. I rode up north before the season began with the owner of the camp, who humored me ("Yes, well, you'll have to decide which plays you'll want to stage — you *are* the dramatics department"). After he said such things, he seemed to choke on his own generosity; his mouth would contract into an acidic kiss.

We were driving farther and farther north. I sat in the front seat with the owner of the camp and looked out at the tall pines, so blue they were almost black against the gray spring sky. The road was the same color as the sky. When we came to the top of a gentle rise and looked down, the road below seemed forlorn and distant, enchanted into the shadows. But as we sped through the valley, the road came close and brightened and the crowns of the blue-black trees slid over the car's polished metal hood. In the back seat behind me lolled a special camper my mother, upon the advice of the owner, had warned me to avoid ("Be polite, but don't let him get you alone"). She seemed reluctant to explain what the danger was, but when I pressed her she finally said, "He's oversexed. He's tried to take advantage of the younger boys." She then went on to assure me that I mustn't despise the poor boy; he was, after all, brain-damaged in some way, under medication, unable to read. If God had gifted me with a fine mind He'd done so only that I might serve my fellow man.

In this brief parting word of warning, my mother had managed to communicate to me her own fascination with the wild boy. The day had turned cool and the car windows were closed. The motor ran so smoothly that the ticking of the dashboard clock could be heard. When I cracked the vent open I heard volleys of birdsong but the birds themselves were hiding. In the valley below, empty of all signs of humanity except for the road, a mist was curling through the pines. I didn't really know the owner of the camp, and so I felt awkward beside him, ready to discuss whatever he chose but afraid of tiring him with my chatter. I sat half-rigid with expectation, a smile up my sleeve. And I felt the sex-crazed boy behind me who was half stretched out on the back seat, the sunlight from between the passing pines rhythmically stroking his body.

After it got dark we stopped for gas and a snack. Ralph, the special camper, said he was cold and wanted to sit up front with us just to keep warm. There was nothing affectionate or come-onnish in his manner to me in the coffee shop; I could tell desire and affection had not clasped hands across *his* heart. He was alone with his erection, which I could see through the thin fabric of his summer pants. It was something he carried around with him wherever he went, like a scar. Perhaps because I'd never yet ejaculated, I couldn't imagine lust as something satiable. In the dark interior of the car, brushed here and there by a dim, firefly glow from the panel, Ralph's leg pressed mine. I was forced to return the pressure lest I lean against the driver and cause comment. When I caught sight of Ralph's face in the magnesium explosion of passing headlights, he looked exhausted, mouth half-open, a thirsty animal whose eyes had turned inward with craving.

The camp, when we finally reached it at midnight, was a sad, cold, empty place. The owner had to unlock a thick rusted chain that stretched from tree to tree across the narrow dirt road. When we reached an open field our car waded slowly, slowly through grasses as tall as the roof and wet and heavy with dew. At the foot of the hill glimmered the lake through a mist—more a chill out of the ground than a lake, more an absence, as though this fitful, shifting dampness were the expression of what was left in the world after everything human had been subtracted from it. I was given a bunk in a cold cabin that smelled of mildewed canvas; Ralph was led off somewhere else. As I tried to fall asleep I thought of him. I pitied him, as my mother wanted me to. I pitied him for his dumb animal stare, for his helpless search after relief—for his burden. And I thought about the plays I would direct. In one them I'd be a dying king. In my trunk I'd brought some old 78s of *Boris Godunov*. Perhaps I'd die to those tolling bells, the Kremlin surrounded by the forces of the pretender, his face red and swollen with desire.

There was a week to go before the other campers were due to arrive. Some local men with scythes swept their way through the overgrown grasses. Someone else repaired the leaking roof in the main house. Stocks of canned food were delivered. The various cabins were opened and aired and swept out. A wasp's hive above the artesian well was bagged and burned. The docks were assembled and floated between newly implanted pylons. The big war canoes came out of winter storage and were seasoned in the cold lake. I worked from the first light to the last—part of my duty as a junior counselor. Ralph had no chores. He stayed in his cabin and came out, sleep-sand in his eyes, just for his meals, led wherever he trudged by the big implacable bulge with the wet tip in his trousers.

Every afternoon I was free to go off on my own. The chill still rose off the lake but at high noon the sun broke through its clouds like a monarch slipping free of his retinue. The path I took girdled the hills that rimmed the lake; at one point it dipped and crossed a bog that looked solid and dry, planted innocently in grasses, but that slurped voluptuously under my shoes. I'd race across and look back as my footprints filled with cold, clear water. A hidden bullfrog gives a low gulp and repeats the same sound but more softly each time under the steady high throb of spring peepers in full chorus. A gray chipmunk with a bright chestnut rump scurries past, his tail sticking straight up. Canoe birches higher up the hill shiver in a light breeze; their green and brown buds are emerging from warty, dark brown shoots. A hermit thrush, perched on a high branch, releases its beautiful song while slowly raising and lowering its tail.

I came to know every turn in the path and every plant along the way. One day, late in the summer, I pushed farther into the woods than I'd ever ventured before. I clambered through brambles and thick undergrowth until I reached a loggers' road sliced through the wilderness but now slowly healing over. I followed that road for several miles. I entered a broad field and then a smaller clearing surrounded by low trees, although high enough to cut off all breezes. The sun burned hotter and hotter, as though someone were holding a magnifying glass over me. I took off my tee shirt and felt the sweat flow down my sides to my stomach as I bent over to pick blueberries from low bushes. The ground was wet. Sweat stung my eyes. A huge bee hung buzzing, motionless, in the air. I was so happy alone and in the woods, away from the dangers posed by other people. At first I wanted to tell someone else how happy I was; I needed a witness. But as the great day revolved slowly above me, as the scarlet tanager flew overhead on his black wings to the distant high trees, as an owl, hidden and remote, sounded a hoot as melancholy as winter, as the leaves, ruffled by the wind, tossed the sun about as though they were princesses at play with a golden ball, as the smell of sweet clover, of bruised sassafras leaves, of the mulch of last year's duff flowed over me, as I crushed the hot, sweet blueberries between my teeth and then chewed on an astringent needle from a balsam, as I sensed the descent of the sun and the slow decline of summer—oh, then I was free and whole, safe from everyone, as happy as with my books. For I could thrive in the expressive, inhuman realm of nature or the expressive, human realm of books—both worlds so exalted, so guileless—but I felt imperiled by the hidden designs other people were drawing around me. The tender white bells of the flower by the rotting stump, the throbbing distillation of blue in the fringed gentian, the small, bright-green cone of the Scots pine—these were confidences nature placed in me, wordless but as trusting as a dog's eyes. Or the pure, always comprehensible and sharply delineated thoughts and emotions of characters in fiction—these, too, were signs I could read. But the vague menace of Ralph with his increasingly haggard face, this boy at once pitiable and dangerous, who had already been caught twice this summer attempting to "hypnotize" younger campers and was now in danger of expulsion, who studied me at meals not with curiosity, much less with sympathy but with crude speculation (Can I get him to do it? Can he relieve me?)—this menace was becoming more and more intense.

After the other campers appeared and the summer's activities had been under way for a week, I understood that I'd been betrayed. There wouldn't be any plays for me to put on, and I had exhausted myself for no good reason with all-night fantasies of the rehearsals, the performances, the triumphs. My mother's promises had just been a way of getting me out of the house for the summer. A few miles away my sister—shy to the point of invisibility in the winter, unpopular, pasty, overweight—had emerged once again into her estival beauty. She was

Captain of the Blues, bronzed and muscular, her hair a gold cap, her enthusiasm boundless, her manner tyrannical ("Get *going*, you guys"), as though all she needed to flower were the complete absence of men and the intense, sentimental companionship of other girls. Once my sister and I were out of the house our mother was free to pursue her amorous career; would she present us with a new stepfather on Labor Day, someone too young and handsome to seem quite respectable?

One afternoon, while the other boys were off on a canoe trip, my counselor showed me some "art photographs" he'd taken, all of a naked young man on a deserted beach. The cabin was quiet, the light dim as it filtered down through the old pines and the half-closed shutters, the blanket on Mr. Stone's bed rough under my bare legs as I sorted through the large, glossy prints. I'd never seen a naked adult man before; I became so absorbed into the pictures that the cabin vanished and I was there before the model on that clean white sand. My eyes were drawn again and again to his tanned back and narrow, intricate, toiling white hips as he ran away from me through a zone of full sunlight toward a black, stormy horizon. Where was this beach and who was this man, I wondered; as though I could find him there now, as though he were the only naked man in the world and I must find him if I were to feel again this pressure on my diaphragm, this sensation of sinking, these symptoms of shame and joy I fought to suppress lest Mr. Stone recoil from me in horror as it dawned on him my reactions were not artistic. Exactly how a photograph, especially one of such blatant physical beauty, *could* be artistic baffled me, for surely such a model would upstage any mode of rendering him. Or was my fascination with him abnormal?

Mr. Stone inched closer to me on the bed and asked me what I thought of his photographs. I could feel his breath on my shoulder and his hand on my knee. A thrill of pleasure rippled through me. I was alarmed. I stood, walked to the screen door, made a display of casualness as I stooped to scratch a chigger bite on my ankle. "They're neat, real neat, catch you later, Mr. Stone." I hoped he hadn't noticed my excitement.

At that age I had no idea that hair could be bleached, a tan nursed, teeth capped, muscles acquired; only a god was blond, brown, strong and had such a smile. Mr. Stone had shown me a god and called it "art." Until now, my notions of art had all been about power, not beauty, about the lonely splendors of possession, not the delicious, sinking helplessness of yearning to possess. That young man pacing the beach — with knees that seemed too small for such strong thighs, with long, elegant feet, with a blur of light for a smile, a streak of light for hair, white pools of light for eyes, as though he were being lit suddenly from within that delicately modeled head poised on a slender neck above shoulders so broad he'd have to grow into them — that young man came toward me with a beauty so unsettling I had to call it love, as though he loved me or I him. The drooling adult delectation over particular body parts (the large penis, the hairy chest, the rounded buttocks) is unknown to children; they resolve the parts into the whole and the physical into the emotional, so that desire quickly becomes love. In the same way love becomes desire — hadn't I desired Fred, Marilyn, my German professor?

I went running through the woods. The day was misty; someone had seen a bear eating blueberries and I turned every time I heard a branch snap. A thread of smoke emerged from a dense stand of pine trees across the lake. After I passed the rotting stump and the white flowers beside it I felt as though I'd pressed through a valve into my own preserve and I slowed down to a walk. I stopped to breathe and I heard a woodpecker far away, knocking softly, professionally, auscultating. The trees, interpreting the wind, swayed above me.

Where the path crossed the loggers' road, Ralph was sitting in a sort of natural hummock created by the exposed roots of an old elm. He had his pants down around his knees and was examining his erect penis with a disbelieving curiosity, a slightly stunned look emptying his face. He called me over and I joined him, as though to examine a curiosity of nature. He persuaded me to touch it and I did. He asked me to lick the red, sticky, unsheathed head and I hesitated. Was it dirty? I wondered. Would someone see us? Would I become ill? Would I become a queer and never, never be like other people?

To overcome my scruples, Ralph hypnotized me. He didn't have to intone the words long to send me into a deep trance. Once I was under his spell he told me I'd obey him, and I did. He also said that when I awakened I'd remember nothing, but he was wrong there. I have remembered everything.

C.K. Williams as With Ignorance

John Sokol © 1981

C. K. Williams

Combat

Ich hatte einst ein shönes Vaterland . . . Es war ein traum.

HEINRICH HEINE

I've been trying for hours to figure out who I was reminded of by the
    welterweight fighter
I saw on television this afternoon all but ruin his opponent with counter-
    punches and now I have it.
It was a girl I knew once, a woman: when he was being interviewed
    after the knockout, he was her exactly,
the same rigorous carriage, same facial structure — sharp cheekbones,
    very vivid eyebrows —
even the sheen of perspiration — that's how I'd remember her, of course
    . . . Moira was her name —
and the same quality in the expression of unabashed self-involvement,
    softened at once with a grave,
almost over-sensitive attentiveness to saying with absolute precision
    what was to be said.
Lovely Moira! Could I ever have forgotten you? No, not forgotten,
    only not had with me for a time
that dark, slow voice, those vulnerable eyes, those ankles finely ten-
    doned as a thoroughbred's.
We met I don't remember where — everything that mattered happened
    in her apartment, in the living room,
with her mother, who she lived with, watching us, and in Moira's bed-
    room down the book-lined corridor.
The mother, I remember, was so white, not all that old but white:
    everything, hair, skin, lips, was ash,
except her feet, which Moira would often hold on her lap to massage
    and which were a deep,
frightening yellow, the skin thickened and dense, horned with calluses
    and chains of coarse, dry bunions,

the nails deformed and brown, so deeply buried that they looked like
  chips of tortoiseshell.
Moira would rub the poor, sad things, twisting and kneading at them
  with her strong hands,
the mother's eyes would be closed, occasionally she'd mutter something
  under her breath in German.
That was their language — they were, Moira told me, refugees, but the
  word didn't do them justice.
They were well-off, very much so, their apartment was, in fact, the
  most splendid thing I'd ever seen.
There were lithographs and etchings — some Klees, I think; a Munch —
  a lot of those very flat oriental rugs,
voluptuous leather furniture and china so frail the molds were surely
  cast from butterflies.
I never found out how they'd brought it all with them: what Moira told
  was of displaced-person camps,
a pilgrimage on foot from Prussia and the Russians, then Frankfurt,
  Rotterdam, and here, "freedom."
The trip across the war was a complicated memory for her; she'd been
  very young, just in school,
what was most important to her at that age was her father, who she'd
  hardly known and who'd just died.
He was a general, she told me, the chief of staff or something of "the
  war against the Russians."
He'd been one of the conspirators against Hitler and when the plot
  failed he'd committed suicide,
all of which meant not very much to me, however good the story was
  (and I heard it often)
because people then were still trying to forget the war, it had been
  almost ignored, even in school,
and I had no context much beyond what my childhood comic books
  had given me to hang any of it on.
Moira was fascinated by it, though, and by their journey, and whenever she wanted to offer me something —
when I'd despair, for instance, of ever having from her what I had to
  have — it would be, again, that tale.
In some ways it was, I think, her most precious possession, and every
  time she'd unfold it
she'd seem to have forgotten having told me before: each time the
  images would be the same —

a body by the roadside, a child's — awful — her mother'd tried to hide
 her eyes but she'd jerked free;
a white ceramic cup of sweet, cold milk in the dingy railroad station of
 some forgotten city,
then the boat, the water, black, the webs of rushing foam she'd made
 up creatures for, who ran beneath the waves
and whose occupation was to snare the boat, to snarl it, then . . . she
 didn't know what then
and I'd be hardly listening anyway by then, one hand on a thigh, the
 other stroking,
with such compassion, such generous concern, such cunning twenty-
 one-year-old commiseration,
her hair, her perfect hair, then the corner of her mouth, then, so far
 away, the rich rim of a breast.
We'd touch that way — petting was the word then — like lovers, with the
 mother right there with us,
probably, I remember thinking, because we weren't lovers, not really,
 not *that* way (not yet, I'd think),
but beyond that there seemed something else, some complicity between
 them, some very adult undertaking
that I sensed but couldn't understand and that, as did almost everything about them, astonished me.
I never really liked the mother — I was never given anything to like —
 but I was awed by her.
If I was left alone with her — Moira on the phone, say — I stuttered, or
 was stricken mute.
It felt like I was sitting there with time itself: everything seemed somehow finished for her,
but there seemed, still, to be such depths, or such ascensions, to her
 unblinking brooding.
She was like a footnote to a text, she seemed to know it, suffer it, and,
 if I was wild with unease with her,
my eyes battering shyly in their chutes, it was my own lack, my own
 unworthiness that made it so.
Moira would come back, we'd talk again, I can't imagine what about
 except, again, obsessively, the father,
his dying, his estates, the stables, servants, all they'd given up for the
 madness of that creature Hitler.
I'd listen to it all again, and drift, looking in her eyes, and pine, pon-
 dering her lips.

I knew that I was dying of desire — down of cheek; subtle, alien scent —
that I'd never felt desire like this.
I was so distracted that I couldn't even get their name right: they'd kept
the real pronunciation,
I'd try to ape what I remembered of my grandmother's Polish Yiddish
but it still eluded me
and Moira's little joke before she'd let me take her clothes off was that
we'd have lessons, "Von C . . ." "No, Von *C* . . ."
Later, in my holocausting days, I found it again, the name, Von
C . . . , in Shirer's *Reich*:
it had, indeed, existed, and it had, yes, somewhere on the Eastern
front, blown its noble head off.
I wasn't very moved. I wasn't in that city anymore, I'd ceased long
before to ever see them,
and besides, I'd changed by then — I was more aware of history and was
beginning to realize,
however tardily, that one's moral structures tended to be air unless
you grounded them in real events.
Everything I did learn seemed to negate something else, everything
was more or less up for grabs,
but the war, the Germans, all I knew about that now — no, never: what
a complex triumph to have a nation,
all of it, beneath one, what a splendid culmination for the adolescence
of one's ethics!
As for Moira, as for her mother, what recompense for those awful
hours, those ecstatic unaccomplishments.
I reformulated her — them — forgave them, held them fondly, with a
heavy lick of condescension, in my system.
But for now, there we are, Moira and I, down that hall again, in her
room again, both with nothing on.
I can't say what she looked like. I remember that I thought her somewhat too robust, her chest too thick,
but I was young, and terrified, and quibbled everything: now, no
doubt, I'd find her perfect.
In my mind now, naked, she's almost too much so, too blond, too gold,
her pubic hair, her arm and leg fur,
all of it is brushed with light, so much glare she seems to singe the very
tissue of remembrance.
but there are — I can see them now and didn't then — promises of dim-
ness, vaults and hidden banks of coolness.

If I couldn't, though, appreciate the subtleties, it wasn't going to hold
    me back, no, it was *she* who held me back,
always, as we struggled on that narrow bed, twisted on each other,
    mauling one another like demented athletes.
So fierce it was, so strenuous, aggressive: my thigh *here*, my hand *here*,
    lips *here*, *here*,
and hers *here* and *here* but never *there* or *there* . . . before it ended, she'd
    have even gone into the sounds of love,
groans and whispered shrieks, glottal stops, gutturals I couldn't catch
    or understand,
and all this while *nothing would be happening*, nothing, that is, in the way
    I'd mean it now.
We'd lie back (this is where I see her sweating, gleaming with it, drenched)
    and she'd smile.
She is satisfied somehow. This is what she wanted somehow. Only
    this? Yes, only this,
and we'd be back, that quickly, in my recollection anyway, with the
    mother in the other room,
the three of us in place, the conversation that seemed sometimes like a
    ritual, eternally recurring.
How long we were to wait like this was never clear to me, my despera-
    tion, though, was slow in gathering.
I must have liked the role, or the pretense of the role, of beast, primed,
    about to pounce,
and besides, her hesitations, her fendings-off, were so warm and so
    bewildering,
I was so engrossed with them that when at last, once and for all, she let
    me go,
the dismissal was so adroitly managed that I never realized until per-
    haps right now
that what had happened wasn't my own coming to the conclusion that
    this wasn't worth the bother.
It's strange now, doing it again, the business of the camps and slaugh-
    ters, the quick flicker of outrage
that hardly does its work anymore, all the carnage, all our own omis-
    sions interposed,
then those two, in their chambers, correct, aristocratic, even with the
    old one's calcifying feet
and the younger one's intensities — those eyes that pierce me still from
    that far back with jolts of longing.

I frame the image: the two women, the young man, they, poised, gra-
cious, he smoldering with impatience,
and I realize I've never really asked myself what could she, or they,
possibly have wanted of me?
What am I doing in that room, a teacup trembling on my knee, that
odd, barbed name mangled in my mouth?
If she felt a real affinity or anything resembling it for me, it must have
been as something quaint —
young poet, brutish, or trying to be brutish — but no, I wasn't even
that, I was just a boy, harmless, awkward,
mildly appealing in some ways, I suppose, but certainly with not a thing
about me one could call compelling,
not compared to what, given her beauty and her means, she could have
had and very well may have, for all I knew.
What I come to now, running over it again, I think I want to keep as
undramatic as I can.
These revisions of the past are probably even more untrustworthy than
our random, everyday assemblages
and have most likely even more to do with present unknowables, so I
offer this almost in passing,
with nothing, no moral distillation, no headily pressing imperatives
meant to be lurking beneath it.
I wonder, putting it most simply, leaving out humiliation, anything
like that, if I might have been their Jew?
I wonder, I mean, if I might have been for them an implement, not of
atonement — I'd have nosed that out —
but of absolution, what they'd have used to get them shed of something
rankling — history, it would be:
they'd have wanted to be categorically and finally shriven of it, or of
that part of it at least
which so befouled the rest, which so acutely contradicted it with glory
and debasement.
The mother, what I felt from her, that bulk of silence, that withholding
that I read as sorrow:
might it have been instead the heroic containment of a probably reflex-
ive loathing of me?
How much, no matter what their good intensions (of which in her I had
no evidence at all)
and even with the liberal husband (although the generals' reasons
weren't that pure and came very late),

how much must they have inevitably absorbed, that Nazi generation,
   those Aryan epochs?
And if the mother shuddered, what would Moira have gone through
   with me spinning at her nipple,
her own juices and the inept emissions I'd splatter on her gluing her
   to me?
The purifying Jew. It's almost funny. She was taking just enough of me
   to lave her conscience,
and I, so earnest in my wants, blindly labored for her, dismantling
   guilt or racial squeamishness
or whatever it was the refined tablet of her consciousness deemed it
   needed to be stricken of.
All the indignities I let be perpetrated on me while I lolled in that luxurious detention:
could I really have believed they only had to do with virtue, maiden-
   hood, or even with, I remember thinking—
I came this close—some intricate attempt Moira might be making to
   redeem a slight on the part of the mother?
Or might inklings have arisen and might I, in my infatuation, have
   gone along with them anyway?
I knew something, surely: I'd have had to. What I really knew, of
   course, I'll never know again.
Beautiful memory, most precious and most treacherous sister: what
   temples must we build for you.
And even then, how belatedly you open to us; even then, with
   what exuberance you cross us.

Tennessee Williams as A Streetcar Named Desire

John Sokol © 1981

Tennessee Williams

The Man in the Overstuffed Chair

He always enters the house as though he were entering it with the intention of tearing it down from inside. That is how he always enters it except when it's after midnight and liquor has put out the fire in his nerves. Then he enters the house in a strikingly different manner, almost guiltily, coughing a little, sighing louder than he coughs, and sometimes talking to himself as someone talks to someone after a long, fierce argument has exhausted the anger between them but not settled the problem. He takes off his shoes in the living room before he goes upstairs where he has to go past my mother's closed door, but she never fails to let him know she hears him by clearing her throat very loudly or saying, "Ah, me, ah, me!" Sometimes I hear him say "Ah, me" in response as he goes on down the hall to where he sleeps, an alcove sunroom connected to the bedroom of my young brother, Dakin, who is at this time, the fall and winter of 1943, with the Air Force in Burma.

These months, the time of this story, enclose the end of the life of my mother's mother.

My father's behavior toward my maternal grandmother is scrupulously proper but his attitude toward my grandfather Dakin is so insulting that I don't think the elderly gentleman could have endured it without the insulation of deafness and near-blindness.

Although my grandmother is dying, she is still quite sound of sight and hearing, and when it is approaching the time for my father to return from his office to the house, my grandmother is always downstairs to warn her husband that Cornelius is about to storm in the front door. She hears the Studebaker charging up the drive and cries out to my grandfather, "*Walter, Cornelius is coming!*" She cries out this warning so loudly that Grandfather can't help but hear it. My grandfather staggers up from his chair by the radio and starts for the front stairs, but sometimes he doesn't make them in time and there is an awkward encounter in the downstairs hall. My grandfather says, "Good evening, Cornelius" and is lucky if he receives, in answer, a frigid "Hello, Mr. Dakin" instead of a red-eyed glare and a grunt.

It takes him, now that he's in his eighties with cataracts on both eyes, quite a while to get up the stairs, shepherded by his wife, and sometimes my father will come thundering up the steps behind them as if he intended to knock the old couple down. What is he after? A drink, of course, from a whiskey bottle under his bed in the sunroom, or the bathroom tub.

"Walter, watch out!"

"Excuse me, Mrs. Dakin," my father grunts breathlessly as he charges past them on the stairs.

They go to their bedroom, close the door. I don't hear just what they say to each other, but I know that "Grand" is outdone with Grandfather for lingering too long downstairs to avoid this humiliating encounter. Of course Grandfather finds the encounter distasteful, too, but he dearly loves to crouch by the downstairs radio at this hour when the news broadcasters come on, now that he can't read newsprint.

They are living with us because my grandmother's strength is so rapidly failing. She has been dying for ten years and her weight has dropped to eighty-six pounds. Any other person would be confined to bed, if not the terminal ward of a hospital, but my grandmother is resolved to remain on her feet, and actively helpful about the house. She is. She still does most of the laundry in the basement and insists on washing the dishes. My mother begs her to rest, but "Grand" is determined to show my father that she is not a dependent. And I have come home, this late autumn of 1943, because my mother wrote me, "Your grandmother has had to give up the house in Memphis because she is not strong enough to take care of it and your grandfather, too."

Between the lines of the letter, I read that my mother is expecting the imminent death of her mother and I ought to stop in Saint Louis on my bus trip between the West and East coasts, so I have stopped there.

I arrive there late one night in November and as I go up the front walk I see, through the curtains of the front room windows, my grandmother stalking across the living room like a skeleton in clothes. It shocks me so that I have to set down my luggage on the front walk and wait about five minutes before I can enter the house.

Only my grandmother has stayed up to receive me at this midnight hour, the others thinking that I had probably driven on through to New York, as I had so often before after promising to come home.

She makes light of her illness, and actually she manages to seem almost well for my benefit. She has kept a dinner plate on the stove for me over a double boiler and a low flame, and the living room fire is alive, and no reference is made to my failure in Hollywood, the humiliating termination of my six-months option as a screenwriter at MGM studios.

"Grand" says she's come here to help Edwina, my mother, who is suffering from nervous exhaustion and is very disturbed over Cornelius's behavior. Cornelius has been drinking heavily. Mother found five empty bottles under his bed and several more under the bathtub, and his position as sales manager of a branch of The International Shoe Company is in jeopardy due to a scandalous poker fight in which half of his left ear was bitten off, yes, actually bitten off, so that he had to go to a hospital and have a plastic-surgery operation, taking cartilage from a rib to be grafted onto the ear, and in spite of elaborate precautions to keep it under wraps, the story has come out. Mr. J., the head executive and my father's immediate superior, has at last lost all patience with my father, who may have to retire in order to avoid being dismissed. But otherwise everything is fine, she is telling me about these things because Edwina may be inclined to exaggerate the seriousness of the family situation when we talk in the morning. And now I ought to go up to bed after a long, hard trip. Yes, I ought to, indeed. I will have to sleep in brother Dakin's old room rather than in my usual retreat in the attic, since the bed in the attic has been dismantled so that I won't insist on sleeping up there and getting pneumonia.

I don't like the idea of taking Dakin's room since it adjoins my father's doorless appendage to it.

I enter the bedroom and undress in the dark.

Strange sounds come from my father's sunroom, great sighs and groans and inebriate exclamations of sorrow such as, "Oh, God, oh, God!" He is unaware of my sleepless presence in the room adjoining. From time to time, at half-hour intervals, he lurches and stumbles out of bed to fetch a bottle of whiskey from some place of naive concealment, remarking to himself, "How terrible!"

At last I take a sleeping pill so that my exhaustion can prevail over my tension and my curiously mixed feelings of disgust and pity for my father, Cornelius Coffin Williams, the Mississippi drummer who was removed from the wild and free road and put behind a desk like a jungle animal put in a cage in a zoo.

At supper the following evening an awful domestic scene takes place.

My father is one of those drinkers who never stagger or stumble but turn savage with liquor, and this next evening after my home-coming he comes home late and drunk for supper. He sits at one end of the table, my mother at the other, and she fixes on him her look of silent suffering like a bird dog drawing a bead on a covey of quail in the bushes.

All at once he explodes into maniacal fury.

His shouting goes something like this: "What the hell, why the hell do you feel so sorry for yourself? I'm keeping your parents here, they're not paying board!"

The shout penetrates my grandfather's deafness and he says, "Rose, let's go to our room." But my grandmother Rose remains at the table as Edwina and Grandfather retire upstairs. I stay as if rooted or frozen to the dining-room chair, the food turning sick in my stomach.

Silence.

My father crouches over his plate, eating like a wild beast eats his kill in the jungle.

Then my grandmother's voice, quiet and gentle: "Cornelius, do you want us to pay board here?"

Silence again.

My father stops eating, though. He doesn't look up as he says in a hoarse, shaky voice: "No, I don't, Mrs. Dakin."

His inflamed blue eyes are suddenly filled with tears. He lurches up from the table and goes to the overstuffed chair in the living room.

This overstuffed chair, I don't remember just when we got it. I suspect it was in the furnished apartment that we took when we first came to Saint Louis. To take the apartment we had to buy the fur-niture that was in it, and through this circumstance we acquired a number of pieces of furniture that would be intriguing to set designers of films about lower-middle-class life. Some of these pieces have been gradually weeded out through successive changes of address, but my father was never willing to part with the overstuffed chair. It really doesn't look like it could be removed. It seems too fat to get through a doorway. Its color was originally blue, plain blue, but time has altered the blue to something sadder than blue, as if it had absorbed in its fabric and stuffing all the sorrows and anxieties of our family life and these emotions had become its stuffing and its pigmentation (if chairs can be said to have a pigmentation). It doesn't really seem like a chair, though. It seems more like a fat, silent person, not silent by choice but simply unable to speak because if it spoke it would not get through a sentence without bursting into a self-pitying wail.

Over this chair still stands another veteran piece of furniture, a floor lamp that must have come with it. It rises from its round metal base on the floor to half a foot higher than a tall man sitting. Then it curves over his head one of the most ludicrous things a man has ever sat under, a sort of Chinesey-looking silk lamp shade with a fringe about it, so that it suggests a weeping willow. Which is presumably weeping for the occupant of the chair.

I have never known whether Mother was afraid to deprive my father of his overstuffed chair and weeping-willow floor lamp or if it simply amused her to see him with them. There was a time, in her younger years, when she looked like a fairy-tale princess and had a sense of style that exceeded by far her power to indulge it. But now she's tired, she's about sixty now, and she lets things go. And the house is now filled not only with its original furnishings but with the things inherited from my grandparents' house in Memphis. In fact, the living room is so full of furniture that you have to be quite sober to move through it without a collision . . . and still there is the overstuffed chair.

A few days after the awful scene at the dinner table, my dearly loved grandmother, Rose Otte Dakin, bled to death in the house of my parents.

She had washed the dinner dishes, had played Chopin on the piano, which she'd brought with her from Memphis, and had started upstairs when she was overtaken by a fit of coughing and a lung hemorrhage that wouldn't stop.

She fought death for several hours, with almost no blood left in her body to fight with.

Being a coward, I wouldn't enter the room where this agony was occurring. I stood in the hall upstairs. My grandmother Rose was trying to deliver a message to my mother. She kept flinging out a wasted arm to point at a bureau.

It was not till several days after this death in the house that my mother found out the meaning of that gesture.

My grandmother was trying to tell my mother that all her savings were sewn up in a corset in a drawer of the bureau.

Late that night, when my grandmother had been removed to a mortuary, my father came home.

"Cornelius," said Mother, "I have lost my mother."

I saw him receive this announcement, and a look came over his face that was even more deeply stricken than that of my mother when she closed the eyelids of "Grand" after her last fight for breath.

He went to his overstuffed chair, under the weeping-willow floor lamp, like a man who has suddenly discovered the reality in a nightmare, and he said, over and over again, "How awful, oh, God, oh, God, how awful!"

He was talking to himself.

At the time of my grandmother's death I had been for ten years more an irregular and reluctant visitor to the house than a member of the household. Sometimes my visits would last the better part of a year, sometimes, more usually, they would last no more than a week. But for three years after my years at college I was sentenced to confinement in this house and to hard labor in "The World's Largest Shoe Company" in which my father was also serving time, perhaps as unhappily as I was. We were serving time in quite different capacities. My father was the sales manager of that branch that manufactures, most notably, shoes and booties for kiddies, called "Red Goose Shoes," and never before and probably not to this day has "The World's Largest" had so gifted a manager of salesmen. As for me, I was officially a clerk-typist but what I actually did was everything that no one else wanted to do, and since the boss wanted me to quit, he and the straw boss made sure that I had these assignments. I was kept on my feet most of the time, charging back and forth between the office and the connecting warehouse of this world's largest wholesale shoe company, which gave me capable legs and a fast stride. The lowliest of my assigned duties was the one I liked most, dusting off the sample shoes in three brightly mirrored sample rooms each morning; dusting off the mirrors as well as the shoes in these rooms that were intended to dazzle the eyes of retailers from all over the States. I liked this job best because it was so private. It was performed before the retailers came in: I had the rooms and the mirrors to myself, dusting off the sample shoes with a chamois rag was something that I could do quickly and automatically, and the job kept me off the noisy floor of the office. I regretted that it took only about an hour, even when I was being most dreamily meticulous about it. That hour having been stretched to its fullest, I would have to take my desk in the office and type out great sheaves of factory orders. It was nearly all numerals, digits. I made many mistakes, but for an amusing reason

I couldn't be fired. The head of the department had gotten his job through the influence of my father, which was still high at that time. I could commit the most appalling goofs and boners and still I couldn't be fired, however much I might long to be fired from this sixty-five-dollar-a-month position. I left my desk more often than anyone else. My branch of "The World's Largest" was on the top floor but I had discovered a flight of stairs to the roof of the twelve-story building and every half hour or so I would go up those stairs to have a cigarette, rather than retiring to the smelly men's room. From this roof I could look across the Mississippi River to the golden wheat fields of Illinois, and the air, especially in autumn, was bracingly above the smog of Saint Louis, so I used to linger up there for longer than a cigarette to reflect upon a poem or short story that I would finish that weekend.

I had several enemies in the office, especially the one called "The Straw Boss," a tall, mincing creature who had acquired the valuable trick of doing nasty things nicely. He was not at all bright, though. He didn't realize that I liked dusting the shoes and running the errands that took me out of "The World's Largest." And he always saw to it that the sample cases that I had to carry about ten blocks from "The World's Largest" to its largest buyer, which was J.C. Penney Company, were almost too heavy for a small man to carry. So did I build up my chest and slightly damage my arterial system, a damage that was soon to release me from my period of bondage. This didn't bother me, though. (I've thought a good deal about death but doubt that I've feared it very much, then or now.)

The thing I most want to tell you about is none of this, however; it is something much stranger. It is the ride downtown that my father and I would take every morning in his Studebaker. This was a long ride, it took about half an hour, and seemed much longer for neither my father nor I had anything to say to each other during the ride. I remember that I would compose one sentence to deliver to my father, to break just once the intolerable silence that existed between us, as intolerable to him, I suspect, as it was to me. I would start composing this one sentence during breakfast and I would usually deliver it halfway downtown. It was a shockingly uninteresting remark. It was delivered in a shockingly strained voice, a voice that sounded choked. It would be a comment on the traffic or the smog that enveloped the streets. The interesting thing about it was his tone of answer. He would answer the remark as if he understood how hard it was for me to make it. His answer would always be sad and gentle. "Yes, it's awful," he'd say. And he didn't say it as if it was a response to my remark. He would say it as if it referred to much larger matters than traffic or smog. And looking back on it, now, I feel that he understood my fear of him and forgave me for it, and wished there was some way to break the wall between us.

It would be false to say that he was ever outwardly kind to his fantastic older son, myself. But I suspect, now, that he knew that I was more of a Williams than a Dakin, and that I would be more and more like him as I grew older, and that he pitied me for it.

I often wonder many things about my father now, and understand things about him, such as his anger at life, so much like my own, now that I'm old as he was.

I wonder for instance, if he didn't hate and despise "The World's Largest Shoe Company" as much as I did. I wonder if he wouldn't have liked, as much as I did, to climb the stairs to the roof.

I understand that he knew that my mother had made me a sissy, but that I had a chance, bred in his blood and bone, to some day rise above it, as I had to and did.

His branch of "The World's Largest" was three floors down from the branch I worked for, and sometimes an errand would take me down to his branch.

He was always dictating letters in a voice you could hear from the elevator before the door of it opened.

It was a booming voice, delivered on his feet as he paced about his stenographer at the desk. Occupants of the elevator, hearing his voice, would smile at each other as they heard it booming out so fiercely.

Usually he would be dictating a letter to one of his salesmen, and not the kind of letter that would flatter or please them.

Somehow he dominated the office with his loud dictation. The letters would not be indulgent.

"Maybe you're eating fried chicken now," he'd boom out, "but I reckon you remember the days when we'd go around the corner for a cigarette for breakfast. Don't forget it. I don't. Those days can come back again . . ."

His boss, Mr. J., approved of C.C.'s letters, but had a soundproof glass enclosure built about his corner in "The World's Largest." . . .

A psychiatrist once said to me, You will begin to forgive the world when you've forgiven your father.

I'm afraid it is true that my father taught me to hate, but I know that he didn't plan to, and, terrible as it is to know how to hate, and to hate, I have forgiven him for it and for a great deal else.

Sometimes I wonder if I have forgiven my mother for teaching me to expect more love from the world, more softness in it, than I could ever offer?

The best of my work, as well as the impulse to work, was a gift from the man in the overstuffed chair, and now I feel a very deep kinship to him, I almost feel as if I am sitting in the overstuffed chair where he sat, exiled from those I should love and those that ought to love me. For love I make characters in plays. To the world I give suspicion and resentment, mostly. I am not cold. I am never deliberately cruel. But after my morning's work, I have little to give but indifference to people. I try to excuse myself with the pretense that my work justifies this lack of caring much for almost everything else. Sometimes I crack through the emotional block. I touch, I embrace, I hold tight to a necessary companion. But the breakthrough is not long lasting. Morning returns, and only work matters again.

Now a bit more about my father whom I have come to know and understand so much better.

My mother couldn't forgive him. A few years after the years that I have annotated a little in this piece of writing, my mother became financially able to cut him out of her life, and cut him out she did. He had been in a hospital for recovery from a drunken spree. When he returned to the house, she refused to see him. My brother had returned from the latest war, and he would go back and forth between them, arranging a legal separation. I suspect it was not at all a thing that my father wanted. But once more he exhibited a gallantry in his nature that I had not then expected. He gave my mother the house and half of his stock in the International Shoe Company, although she was already well set up by my gift to her of half of my earnings from *The Glass Menagerie*. He acquiesced without protest to the terms of the separation, and then he went back to his native town of Knoxville, Tennessee, to live with his spinster sister, our Aunt Ella. Aunt Ella wasn't able to live with him, either, so after a while he moved into a hotel at a resort called Whittle Springs, close to Knoxville, and somehow or other he became involved with a widow from Toledo, Ohio, who became his late autumn love which lasted till the end of his life.

I've never seen this lady but I am grateful to her because she stuck with Dad through those last years.

Now and then, during those years, my brother would be called down to Knoxville to see Dad through an illness brought on by his drinking, and I think it was the Toledo Widow who would summon my brother.

My brother, Dakin, is more of a Puritan than I am, and so I think the fact that he never spoke harshly of the Toledo Widow is a remarkable compliment to her. All I gathered from his guarded references to this attachment between Dad and the Toledo Widow was that she made him a faithful drinking companion. Now and then they would fly down to Biloxi and Gulfport, Mississippi, where Dad and Mother had spent their honeymoon, and it was just after one of these returns to where he had been happy with Mother, and she with him, that he had his final illness. I don't know what caused his death, if anything caused it but one last spree. The Toledo Widow was with him at the end, in a Knoxville hospital. The situation was delicate for Aunt Ella. She didn't approve of the widow and would only go to my father's deathbed when assured there would be no encounter between the widow and herself in the hospital room. She did pass by her once in the hospital corridor, but she made no disparaging comment on her when I flew down to Knoxville for the funeral of my father.

The funeral was an exceptionally beautiful service. My brother, Aunt Ella, and I sat in a small room set apart for the nearest of kin and listened and looked on while the service was performed.

Then we went out to "Old Gray," as they called the Knoxville Cemetery, and there we sat in a sort of tent with the front of it open, to witness the interment of the man of the overstuffed chair.

Behind us, on chairs in the open, was a very large congregation of more distant kinfolk and surviving friends of his youth, and somewhere among them was the Toledo Widow, I've heard.

After the interment, the kinfolk all came up to our little tent to offer condolences that were unmistakably meant.

The widow drove off in his car which he had bequeathed to her, her only bequest, and I've heard of her nothing more.

He left his modest remainder of stock in the International Shoe Company in three parts to his sister, and to his daughter and to my brother, a bequest which brought them each a monthly income of a hundred dollars. He left me nothing because, as he had told Aunt Ella, it didn't seem likely that I would ever have need of inherited money.

I wonder if he knew, and I suspect that he did, that he had left me something far more important, which was his blood in my veins? And of course I wonder, too, if there wasn't more love than hate in his blood, however tortured it was.

Aunt Ella is gone now, too, but while I was in Knoxville for Dad's funeral, she showed me a newspaper photograph of him outside a movie house where a film of mine, *Baby Doll*, was being shown. Along with the photograph of my father was his comment on the picture.

What he said was: "I think it's a very fine picture and I'm proud of my son."

James Wright as Two Citizens   *John Sokol* © *1981*

James Wright

Ohio

I was born on December 13, 1927, at 613 Union Street. I don't know
why I should cling to that particular useless detail. It may have something to do with the frequency of my family's moving. By the time I was
ten years old we had lived in at least half a dozen houses, which were
scattered apart from one another about as widely as possible in a small
town of 16,000 inhabitants. All this restless moving around didn't
bother me especially at the time. On the contrary. I love the variety of
neighborhoods in Martins Ferry, a skinny place stretched out along the
river between the railroad and the abrupt hills. By the time I was in the
fifth grade, I had attended three different grade schools. It was mildly
disconcerting to make new friends, whole worlds of friends, so often.
But, in a small town as in any town or city, a single grade school is an
entire human society, with its own heroes, beauties, snotty sons of
bitches, cruelties, lonelinesses, and basketball teams. By the time I
entered high school, where all the local nations gathered together like
all the bewildered Buddhists, Taoists, Mongolians, and Hindus wandering puzzled along the streets of Ch'ang-an during the high days of
the T'ang Dynasty, I sometimes rejoiced in the gifts of my wandering
and my restless dwellings for I cherished the friends I had made in distant places all the way from Kuckkuck Lane in the north of town, just
above Wheeling Steel and the Blaw-Knox factories, all the way down
south along the river, always the river, below the La Belle Lumber
Company and its yards of sawdust, fragrant as rancid pollen, down to
the old empty mill fields, the cherry lanes and hobo jungles lost in the
wilderness of Aetnaville, the junction where the traveling carnivals
camped during the summer and besieged the citizenry of Martins
Ferry and Bridgeport. I had lived in all of the neighborhoods except the
wealthy ones up on the hills away from the factories and the river, and I
knew most of the languages, and carry with me today the affections of
those words.

My father worked as a die-setter at the Hazel-Atlas Glass Company in Wheeling, West Virginia. He was a handsome man of great physical strength and the greatest human strength of all, an enduring gentleness in the presence of the hardship that the Great Depression brought to everyone.

My mother's family came from West Virginia, and they were honest-to-God hillbillies to a fare-thee-well. All her life my mother was moved by a longing to return to the kind of farming life she had had as a child, and by the time I had finished high school and gone to the Army, my parents did succeed in buying a small farm in the tiny community of Warnock, Ohio, a bleak little crossroads about twenty-five miles back in the hills from the Ohio River. The hills I have in mind were cornfields, some of them, but many others were smoldering slag heaps, crazily shaped piles of bluish-gray waste from the mines. After the Army I was away from the Warnock farm at college except for parts of the summers, so I never became as well acquainted with the local inhabitants as my younger brother Jack did. There was something darkly West Virginian about the country store in its perpetual fog, and Jack has told me of a place nearby called Blood Hollow, whose citizens frequently provided business for my father in his capacity as Justice of the Peace.

During the last couple of years before his retirement from the factory my father rose at four o'clock in the morning and rode a rickety bus down through the dank hills to Bellaire, Ohio, where he would take another bus across the river to Wheeling, where he worked. The difficulty of this arrangement finally persuaded him to rent a small furnished room near the factory. Until my parents were married around the time of World War I, my mother, too, had worked in the towns. She had slaved — it is the true word — in a laundry. I have visited such places more than once, and I can still understand my mother's dream of green quiet places and her struggle to reach them.

And there were green places. As I think now of my own childhood, I can still feel an abrupt pang that rises not only from the shape of my parents' lives but also from the very disruption of the earth in southeastern Ohio. Take the river. In form and body it remains itself one of the magnificent rivers of the world. It could gather into itself the Seine, the Arno, and the Adige, and still have room for a whole mile of drifting lost lives.

Many lives were lost to the river, and a few were saved. My friend Harry Schultz, who was in the first-grade class with me at the old Central School, got caught in a suck-hole one afternoon just above the Terminal Bridge (long since condemned), and maybe he would have drowned; but a strong and courageous boy named Joe Bumbio saved him. At the same time and place, little Patsy di Franco was lost. Even Joe Bumbio couldn't find him, and turned the search over to the hands of a man named John Shunk, a professional diver skilled in the use of those awesome hooks that James Dickey described toward the end of his novel *Deliverance*. I still do not know what Mr. Shunk did for a living during those days and nights when the river ran on quietly minding its own strange business. But whenever somebody drowned, sure enough Mr. Shunk would appear from somewhere and, sooner or later, perform his ghastly labor. For many years he seemed to me to carry a kind of solitary holiness about him. His very name in the local newspaper hinted at the abiding presence of some hopeless and everlasting grief that waited for us all as we looked at one another and wondered about ourselves. This summer, after all these years, as August approached me far away from the Ohio River, I thought about Mr. Shunk again, and I mourned for him, for he carried the visible terror of good and frightened people in his arms, and he was brave as even the river never knew how to be brave. I wrote something in his memory.

A FLOWER PASSAGE

(IN MEMORY OF JOE SHUNK, THE DIVER)

Even if you were above the ground this year,
You would not know my face.
One of the small boys, one of the briefly green,
I prowled with the others along the Ohio,
Raised hell in the B & O boxcars after dark,
And sometimes in the evening
Chawed the knots out of my trousers
On the river bank, while the other
Children of blast furnace and mine
Fought and sang in the channel-current,
Daring the Ohio.

Shepherd of the dead, one of the tall men,
I did not know your face.
One summer dog-day after another,
You rose and gathered your gear
And slogged down hill of the river ditch to dive
Into the blind channel. You dragged your hooks
All over the rubble sludge and lifted
The twelve-year bones.

Now you are dead and turned over
To the appropriate authorities, Christ
Have mercy on me, I would come to the funeral home
If I were home
In Martins Ferry, Ohio.
I would bring to your still face a dozen
Modest and gaudy carnations.

But I am not home in my place
Where I was born and my friends drowned.
So I dream of you, mourning.
I walk down the B & O track
Near the sewer main.
And there I gather, and here I gather
The flowers I only know best.
The spring leaves of the sumac
Stink only a little less worse
Than the sewer main, and up above that gouged hill
Where somebody half-crazy tossed a cigarette
Straight down into a pile of sawdust
In the heart of the LaBelle Lumber Company,
There, on the blank mill field, it is the blind and tough
Fireweeds I gather and bring home.
To you, for my drowned friends, I offer
The true sumac, and the foul trillium
Whose varicose bloom swells the soil with its bruise;
And a little later, I bring
The still totally unbelievable spring beauty
That for some hidden reason nobody raped
To death in Ohio.

For all its dangers, the river still had the power to make the banks green, and some of us children of the blast furnaces and factories and mines kept faith with the river. Even after the workers of the WPA had built a modern swimming pool next to the Martins Ferry City Park, where the citizenry repaired on weekend afternoons, my father would take my older brother Ted and me to swim in the river. Later I often joined my friends from Aetnaville and southern Martins Ferry to swim naked from the bare-ass beach to the northern tip of Wheeling Island. The water there was beautiful in its rawness and wildness, though something was forever drifting past to remind us of the factories that lined the banks to the north. They were always there, just as the Martins Ferry Cemetery that overlooked the entire town seemed, wherever one stood, to hang in the sky above the Laughlin Steel Mill.

I am afraid that I must have seemed often solitary and morose in my childhood, and it is true that I did a good deal of wandering around all by myself, daydreaming along the river bank or plundering certain apple trees in the hills behind home. But I think also of the vividness in the lives of my brothers and my most beloved cousin. My brother Ted is only two years older than I, and two years seems little enough to me now. But he still seems to me an admirable man, and his authority rises from his character, not his age. He is a photographer in Zanesville, Ohio. My younger brother, Jack, has long since left Ohio for southern California. I suppose I spent more time in the close company of my cousin David Lyons than anyone else. His parents were divorced when he was a small boy, and he was raised by my aunt Grace and by our grandmother, Elizabeth Lyons. I will leave my grandmother as she is, for she blessed my childhood with such a glory of intelligence and anarchic humor that I have had to find other ways of writing about her. She appears in every one of my books in one form or another.

It seems to me that José Ortega y Gasset was speaking the plain bone truth when he said that, at the start, life is a chaos in which one is lost, and I have certainly spent most of my own life in confusion. But some people when I was young brought me the sense, the vista, the realization of a deep world in the Ohio Valley itself and the huge world of time and space beyond the place. I am thinking of my teachers, and now that I am middle-aged I look back and marvel at the vitality and devotion of all those young men and women in the public schools of my home. I think of them all with affection and there are two I want to name. Miss Elizabeth Willerton (now Mrs. Henry Esterly of Cupertino, California) introduced her high-school students to literature with a clarity and intelligence, a kind of summons to enter whatever nobility there is in the human race, with something very like genius. As for Miss Helen McNeely Sheriff, an authentic aristocrat of mind and character, her teaching of Latin embodied a vision of uncompromising excellence. She is now in her nineties in Cadiz, Ohio; and, no matter what life has flung down on me during the past thirty years, I have never lost touch with her, thank God. Her hair is white now and she needs a cane. But she has the same classic and exalted face, the same eyes, so witty and so deep, the most beautiful intelligent eyes. It will come as no revelation to many critics that my own writings are not always distinguished by clarity and grace; but I have never written anything without wondering, sooner or later, whether or not Miss Sheriff would find it worthy.

I want to return sometime. If I do, I imagine I will feel what George Orwell felt when he thought of returning to the place of a particularly vivid childhood: How small everything has grown, and how terrible is the deterioration in myself.

The friend I loved best, as radiant a spirit as any I have ever known, was Harley Lannum. Dear Pete, where are you? Once, among the shadows of the years, I heard that you were working on a newspaper in Sandusky, or some such place. I wonder if you have ever read anything I have written. I wonder if you will read these words. Salvatore Quasimodo said that every man stands alone at the heart of the earth, transfixed by a ray of sunlight, and suddenly it is evening. Pete, why don't we go home? Why don't we find each other, and go home, while we are still alive?

THE SUMAC IN OHIO

Toward the end of May, the air in southern Ohio is filling with fragrances, and I am a long way from home. A great place lies open in the earth there in Martins Ferry near the river, and to this day I don't know how it came to be. Maybe the old fathers of my town, their white hair lost long since into the coal smoke and the snow, gathered in their hundreds along the hither side of the B & O railroad track, presented whatever blades and bull tongues they could spare, and tore the earth open. Or maybe the gulley appeared there on its own, long before the white-haired fathers came, and the Ohio changed its direction, and the glacier went away.

But now toward the end of May, the sumac trees on the slopes of the gulley are opening their brindle buds, and suddenly, right before my eyes, the tough leaf branches turn a bewildering scarlet just at the place where they join the bough. You can strip the long leaves away already, but the leaf branch is more thoroughly rooted into the tree than the trunk itself is into the ground.

Before June begins, the sap and coal smoke and soot from Wheeling Steel, wafted down the Ohio by some curious gentleness in the Appalachians, will gather all over the trunk. The skin will turn aside hatchets and knife-blades. You cannot even carve a girl's name on the sumac. It is viciously determined to live and die alone, and you can go straight to hell.